T0329473

KILLING THE ARAB SPRING

KILLING THE ARAB SPRING

Hasan Afif El-Hasan

Algora Publishing
New York

© 2019 by Algora Publishing.
All Rights Reserved
www.algora.com

No portion of this book (beyond what is permitted by
Sections 107 or 108 of the United States Copyright Act of 1976)
may be reproduced by any process, stored in a retrieval system,
or transmitted in any form, or by any means, without the
express written permission of the publisher.

Library of Congress Cataloging in Publication Control Number: —

Names: El-Hasan, Hasan Afif, 1932- author.
Title: Killing the Arab Spring / Hasan El-Hasan.
Description: New York: Algora Publishing, 2019. | Includes bibliographical
    references and index.
Identifiers: LCCN 2018061577 (print) | LCCN 2019006472 (ebook) | ISBN
    9781628943498 (pdf) | ISBN 9781628943481 (soft cover:¬alk. paper)
Subjects: LCSH: Arab Spring, 2010- | Middle East—Politics and
    government—21st century. | Islam and politics—Middle East.
Classification: LCC DS63.123 (ebook) | LCC DS63.123 .E54 2019 (print) | DDC
    909/.097492708312—dc23
LC record available at https://lccn.loc.gov/2018061577

Printed in the United States

Acknowledgement

The author is particularly beholden to Professor Wayne Martin for his wise counsel and encouragement to write the book.

Appreciation is also due to my son Firas for reading the manuscript and correcting many grammar errors.

I dedicate the book to the memory of my parents.

Table of Contents

INTRODUCTION

Killing the Arab Spring was written with one thing always in mind, the flagrant abuse of human rights in the Arab countries by their own governments. Arab regimes have undermined the prospects for democratic governance by severely restricting freedom of expression and the press, freedom of association, freedom of peaceful assembly, and due process. The unprecedented scale of human rights abuses including the killings of political activists has amounted to crimes against humanity.

I have been perplexed by what I perceive to be the hypocrisy implied by the West. The United States and European governments have been overlooking the ongoing human rights abuses and lack of accountability of the Arab regimes, especially in their close allies Saudi Arabia, the UAE, and Egypt. The US and the European Union have failed to find a principled response to the Arab regimes' crackdown on dissent and the imprisonment of critical journalists, activists and political opposition.

In political, social, economic and strategic terms, the Arab Middle East (ME) is a diverse area that has been tied together and culturally unified over time by shared cultural developments and by historical and political events. For most people in the region, Arabic is the formal spoken and written language, and all have felt the influence of Islam, the Ottoman rule, Western colonialism, the discovery of oil, the establishment of Israel, and political life under authoritarian regimes.

For the purposes of this book, the Arab ME includes the Eastern Mediterranean, Iraq, the Arabian Peninsula, the countries of North Africa, Sudan and the Gulf States. These countries share much of the same history, culture, and politics, and they have been facing many of the same issues. Of course, in some contexts, the ME region is considered to include non-Arabic Persia, Turkey, Pakistan and even Afghanistan.

Before World War II, Europeans called the ME "the Near East." Britain colonized most of the area, as well as territories all over the world, and in that epoch it was said that "the sun never set on the British Empire." But the British Empire faded after World War II and the US emerged as a world super-power, and it became more common to refer to the area as "the Middle East."

ME people, like everyone else in the world, are shaped by their history. No attempt to study the conflicts and the prospects for peace or war in the ME can be complete without understanding the impact of the peoples' history of tribalism, Islamic culture, sectarianism, foreign involvement, Israel, and oil.

The ME is often referred to as "the Cradle of Civilization." People on the banks of the Tigris, the Euphrates and the Nile Rivers made the first transition from the nomadic to the agricultural life style. They were the first to write words and produce literature and the first to issue codes of law and create systems of justice.

Four or five thousand years ago, people of the ME built world's first known towns it was the birth place of the three monotheistic world religions, Judaism, Christianity and Islam and it has been the source and the possession of great empires, the seabed where the dynamics of various world cultures ebbed and flowed over time and space. The ME is at the strategic crossroads of Eurasia and Africa, and its people controlled the trade routes by land and sea long before the discovery of oil. With or without petroleum, the historic significance of the ME would remain important. But too much history brought too many issues.

The ME is not only "the cradle of civilization," it is also "the cradle of warfare and bloody conflicts" where the oldest recorded battles among nations took place for control of the fertile regions. Here, ancient armies were the first to use horses, chariots, and swords.

Almost a thousand years ago, European Christians of several "holy" military orders, knights, took up arms and marched to Jerusalem in eight Crusade expeditions, over two centuries, to recapture the Holy Land from Muslim control. In the 18th century, during Europe's industrial revolution, the Portuguese, French and British navies engaged in wars competing over colonizing ME countries, prized for their strategic locations and commercial and agricultural potential. America's first foreign war, the 1801-05 'Barbary War', was fought at the shores of Tripoli, Algiers, Tunis, and the Sultanate of Morocco. The US commemorated that war in its Marines' Hymn, the oldest official song in the US Armed Forces, whose lyrics start with "From the Halls of Montezuma to the shores of Tripoli."

In the 20th century, there was the threat of nuclear war in the ME by Russia when Britain, France and Israel invaded Egypt in 1956 and seventeen years later, Israel assembled a nuclear weapon, ready to detonate to stop the Egyptian army from advancing toward its population centers in the 1973 October War [Yom Kippur War]. The current view of the ME is that it is the land of oil and sheikhs, a sphere of supremacy for one foreign power or another, an arena for conflict between civilizations, the land of global jihadists, land of bloody civil wars and refugees, and the Palestinian–Israeli issue. Conflicts of today include the new, the century-old and the thousand-years old.

Decades after emancipation from direct colonial rule, the quest for real independence still figures highly on the Arabs' agenda. The oil-rich Arab states remain virtual colonies of the West due to the value of their main product to the world economy, and the non-oil states for their strategic locations. Poverty, regional disparity, ethnic and religious cleavages, corruption, and clientelism under authoritarian regimes have prevented the Arab countries from joining the newly developed nations and have left their economies firmly based on oil and natural gas, and hardly self-sustained agriculture. The Arab states provide strong evidence that corruption and growth simply cannot coexist.

While the newly developed states of East Asia, East Europe and Latin America are creating products, providing high-tech services and competing for a greater share of world production output, Arab regimes have created an environment that further stands in the way of human potential and economic growth. They divert billions of dollars from their local economies and return it to foreign investors in military armament. Under their discredited economic policies, farmers have left the countryside, swelling the ranks of the urban poor and accentuating food shortages. Citizens are forced into poverty with little prospect of rising from it. Many recognize that they may need to move to foreign countries to escape poverty and conflicts, and invest in their God-given potential.

The failure of the ME states to evolve into inclusive democracies, with state and civil institutions where people can address their grievances and seek justice peacefully, has created a deep political, social and cultural crisis that had been simmering beneath the surface for some time. The spread of the news media and the effect of the twitter and the internet highlighted the division between rich and poor, the repression, the corruption, and the interference of foreign powers. The mounting grievances among the young and the working class brought people together social unrest intensified and erupted in urban rebellions which threatened regimes' legitimacy.

The people in the 2011 "Arab Spring" popular uprising demanded inclusive and equitable democracy, social justice and economic development. They were looking more critically at their own system of governing and societies and no longer willing to accept that their problems are caused by colonialism, Zionism or imperialism.

Different Arab countries face different local and international pressures and not all of them race from the same starting line or live under similar conditions. They differ in base of their economies and how colonialism and the external environment at independence affected them. But certain common grievances and concerns characterize people experience in all the ME countries ranging from traditional monarchies of Jordan and Morocco to the single party regimes of Tunisia, Algeria and Syria, to the military regimes in Egypt and Libya to the Gulf States where the ultimate power rests upon family clans.

The Arab Spring rebels failed to bring democracy the uprisings even created unpleasant realities that will make the transition in the ME more difficult to achieve. Sectarianism rose within the domestic political sphere in the region Iran and the rich Arab states have expanded their spheres of influence. That may play even more destabilizing role in the future. The "Arab Spring" final outcome is yet to be seen, but its lasting legacy was ending the myth of Arab-people's political passivity and the perceived invincibility of their arrogant ruling class. Due to weak states and civil society institutions, democratic transition failed and religion replaced other characteristics as the national identity. After they failed to make the transition, most Arabs emphasized their sectarian identity as Sunnis, Shi'as, Wahhabis, fundamentalists, mainstream Muslims, and Muslim Brotherhood. Professor John Esposito of Georgetown University made the point that "the most effective opposition to authoritarian regimes in the ME is expressed through a reaffirmation of the Islamic identity and heritage." (WRITENET Paper No. 10/2000 at https://www.refworld.org/pdfid/3ae6a6ca4.pdf)

Of all the factors that have spurred violence which fractured Iraq, Syria and Yemen, and widened fissures in the Gulf States after the Iraqi-Iran war, the US invasion of Iraq, and the "Arab Spring," none is fundamental as the fourteen centuries old Islamic faith schism. It has become the prism through which to understand the underlying tensions in many countries and it has divided Muslims of the world including the Arab Muslims into two hostile political groups, Sunni and Shi'a fighting each other intellectually, politically and in bloody proxy wars.

Saudi Arabia and Iran, the two countries that compete for the leadership of Islam, have used the sectarian divide to further their regional ambitions. What is happening in Iraq, Syria, Lebanon, Yemen, Bahrain, Saudi Arabia, and Egypt today suggest that the ME societies have made the transition from a collection of ethnic tribes to sectarian tribes within the nation-states rather than one nation as active nationalists wish them to be. For some actors, the problem is very much one of unbridgeable differences. Preachers of sectarian-hate see the "other" as enemy and threat to the faith. For them and for their followers, the "other" is considered heresy. Saudi Arabia and Lebanon have opted for a religion-centric identity that coincided with their states formation, and in Iraq, Syria, Yemen, Bahrain, and Egypt, religion gradually replaced others as the pre-eminent national identity especially after the Iraqi-Iran war and even more after the civil war in Syria.

The ME people today are searching for identity, but there is struggle between the people seeking change and the well-financed and more powerful rulers who are threatened by the change. A century after the disintegration of the Ottoman Empire from whom most of the ME countries emerged none has been able to recognize, integrate and reflect its ethno-cultural diversity. States were carved out with little concern over people, geography or history. At the end of First World War, British policy makers dominating the Arab lands played a major role in organizing the new governments in the region. They supported profoundly undemocratic monarchies over republicanism with no democratic features whatsoever. In Iraq and Jordan, the states were tailored to suit colonial interests and commitments, and the leaders of the states were brought in from outside. In Palestine, people were brought from outside to colonize the country, the indigenous population was written out, and the region was destabilized. Most states of the Gulf were handed over only to those who could protect and safeguard imperial interests in the post-withdrawal phase. The region as a whole that includes the Arab states, Turkey, Iran and Israel refuses to address, let alone resolve, the core issue of national identity that reflect their heterogeneity which include numerous ethnic, religious, cultural, and linguistic communities. The internal tensions in many ME countries are in part due to their inability to accommodate the religious or the ethnic "others."

Absolute monarchy that rests on dynastical succession continues to be the dominant form of governance in the ME where as many as ten countries are ruled by royalties. Ruling families dominate the economic and political systems and have become both symbol and representative of their states. The Gulf sheikhdoms are still quasi-feudal principalities, vulnerable to military assault and nationalism there does not yet have roots. Their system of government excludes the entire population from ruling the country, and the regimes tolerate only the loyal minorities.

Al-Khalifah family which rules Bahrain is Sunni while the majority of the population is Shi'a treated by the government as second class citizens. In the oil rich Gulf States, Arab and non-Arab expatriates make up more than three quarters of the country's population they work as long as their service is needed but have no rights. The national identities merely mean only the dynasty that rules the state rather than it being a reflection of their wider population. In Saudi Arabia (SA), the orthodox Wahhabi-Islam that provides legitimacy and religious sanctity to its ruling dynasty rejects heterodox Islamic sects including Shi'a, who make up more than 10% of the population, as non-Muslims. They are marginalized from the Saudi national identity.

In Iran, according to the constitution, "Twelver Ja'fari School of thought" is the official religion of the Islamic republic. This narrow Shi'a-Islamic identity excludes a large portion of its population, including Arabs, Turkmen, Assyrians, and Kurds who are not Shi'a, and non-Muslims like Baha'is and Christian Armenians.

In Jordan, the majority of the population is of Palestinian origin. However, the parliamentary districts have been gerrymandered so that the voting power clearly favors the Bedouins, who form the backbone of the ruling monarchy. This reduces the representation of areas populated by Palestinian-Jordanians.

In Egypt, Article 2 of the constitution declares: "Islam is the official state religion and the principles of Sharia are the primary sources of legislation." The Christian Copts, who had been the Egyptians before the arrival of the Arab people and Islam in the 7th century, have been systematically marginalized, almost erased from the national identity.

Arab regimes of North Africa force the Arabic language and Islamic culture on the Berber population that have their own heritage and liberal culture. The Berber, North Africa's original indigenous inhabitants, feel neglected by Arab-dominated governments and denied of their civil rights. While most Berbers have converted to Islam, they pride themselves on secular traditions that are at odds with some of the Islamic movements which are gaining grounds in the region.

Israel has not reconciled its inherent contradiction between its Jewish identity and its claim of being a democracy. It has refused to come to terms with the indigenous Palestinians who were evicted and became refugees. The Arab-Israeli citizens who constitute 20% of the population have religious and political rights, but they are unable to identify with the explicitly Jewish symbols of the state, such as the flag, national anthem, holidays and other cultural motifs. The Palestinian–Israeli conflict is a major issue that has been going since the early 1900s when Arab Palestine was part of the Ottoman Empire and the colonialist Britain granted it as homeland for the world-wide Jews.

Violence, unrest and forced migration today have become the only news from the Arab ME. The ME makes only 5% of the world population they receive 50% of all worlds' arms shipments and produce 90% of the world conflicts' refugees. Saudi Arabia alone has the world's fourth-largest defense budget. One can argue that most of the internal tension in many countries and regional conflicts in the ME are due to their inability to accommodate the religious and ethnic others. The Sunni-Shi'a sectarianism, the ancient Islamic-religion divide is behind much of the recent conflicts and violence in the ME. The sectarian divide and the discrimination against the religious "other" has been routinely argued with passion and anger in terms that reach back more than a millennium into the past. The sectarian clashes have sparked transnational jihadi networks that pose violence even beyond the ME.

There are always advocates of religions or more precisely sects as the defining frame of reference in the same way as racial or ethnic extremists exist, but throughout the 20th century, the Arab world struggle was far more related to competing nationals than to competing religions. Muslim-Arabs allied themselves with the Christian-West against the Muslim-Turks in First World War. Sectarian mobilization was more concerned with access to political and economic rights within the framework of the nation-state, rather than with the validation of religious truth. But all of this has been changing by the rising relevance of the sectarian dogma since the 1980 Iraq–Iran war that eventually led to more wars and the 2003 US invasion of Iraq and more so since the Syrian civil war.

Muslims tried unity under the Ottoman Empire, then after its fall, Muslims of the ME broke down into ethnic tribes of Turks, Persians, Kurds, Berber, and Arab. The Hashemite clan allied themselves with the colonialist Britain against the Ottomans the Saudis clan allied themselves with the British against the Hashemite the Lebanese tribes allied themselves with the French for protection and the wanted-to-be in the ME, European Zionists, allied themselves with the British against the Palestinian-Arabs. The Arabs who had been for so long united but oppressed by the Turks became divided and colonized by Great Britain and France. They gained independence only after the Second World War, while Palestine was effectively handed over to the European Jews. The area has been racked by constant conflicts since then, but the frontier demarcation of most of the nation-states that make up the modern ME remained fixed exactly as drawn by their former imperial masters, well before the outcome of the First World War had become clear.

The post First World War boundaries of Iraq, Syria, Lebanon, Jordan, Palestine and the Gulf states served the interests of the colonial powers and the Arab regimes directly affected by the carve-up have been prepared to defend them. The means of the colonialists' policy changed with the passage of time, but the objective of stable Middle East, willing to cooperate or subject to control, remained the same. The West strategic motives for holding on to the area had been dictated by their "vital interests" such as maintaining safety communications, keeping up commerce and first of all, controlling the oil resources and oil flow.

The post-World-War-One mandate system was outdated, but Britain and the West showed adaptability in controlling the region by having its client states leading the League of Arab States. Arab regimes became part of comfortable strategic arrangement that secured Western interests in the region, including a forward military posture and access to energy resources. Their leaders were installed then bequeathed by the departing Western imperialists without establishing Western style parties, parliaments, the promise of human rights, and representative governments.

After the Second World War, the most significant change in the spirit and temper of the people in the Middle East was the rise of nationalism. Pan-Arab movement sought legitimacy by appealing to a broader Arab culture unity in the context of a nationalist, secular, socialist, modernist ideology. The more powerful challenge of a vigorous Jewish nationalism (Zionism) in Palestine added new explosive elements. Arab nationalism presented potential challenge to Western powers and the Zionist project. But after the humiliating Arab defeats in 1948 and the establishment of Israel, Arab regimes found reasons to justify military coups and authoritarian rule. Their leaders championed the fight against corruption, the continued dominance of the Western powers and Israel's threat to the region.

Once in power, Arab leaders' ideology failed to improve the livelihood of the average citizen and they became pre-occupied with their own survival at any cost. The military-led governments became increasingly corrupt, brutal and dictatorial. They often adopted the religious symbolism, exaggerated the threat of their political opposition and the need to challenge Israel's existence to justify their authoritarian rule. The rhetoric to restore the Palestinians' rights by force became the strategic means to enlist the political support of the middle class to the Arab repressive regimes. The need of large segment of the middle class for the protection of its socio-economic status against the perceived threat overlapped with the regime's strategy to stay in power. After the failure of 1955 Baghdad Pact and Egypt's claimed victory in the 1956 Suez Crisis, the idea of Arab nationalism was popular.

The line was far from clear between loyalty to the leader in a "nation" such as Egypt or Iraq, or Syria, or even Libya and wider loyalty to the pan-Arab or pan-Islamic ideas. But the Arabs failed to achieve unity in all and opted to defend their nation-states under autocratic and repressive regimes. Arab nationalism was not at the same stage in all countries whereas narrow tribal loyalty was paramount in all of them. The Pan-Arab nationalists failed to transcend the borders drawn by the colonialists and establish United Arab Republic in 1958, from which Syria seceded in 1961. The Arab nationalist Baath Party failed even to unite its own wings in Syria and Iraq the Syrian Social Nationalist Party failed to unite Syria and Lebanon the Arab Nationalists shriveled of their ambitions after the Arab devastating defeat by Israel in 1967 and the death of Egypt's President, Nasser and transnational Muslim fundamentalists were doomed to fail because they could not transcend tribalism and local national identities. They failed because each of the Arab regimes attempted to impose the national identity from above, whether ideological, religious or dynastical. This was problematic because the regimes lack legitimacy and their imposed identity does not reflect the diversity of the population, and that created schism and sectarian tensions.

The Arab countries were ruled by absolute monarchs, military generals and colonels, autocrats and tyrants who ensured that no opposition party or civil society institution was strong enough to challenge them. The ruling classes in the so called Arab world either belong to a blood-tribe or created their own powerful tribal institution to override reason and morality and anything that could dim their chances of survival. There was no hope for political competition based on ideas among them because their tribalism was built on zero-sum idea and no compromise.

Public criticism of the government was forbidden, but people and the press was free to vent their frustration on Israel. Authoritarian Arab regimes failed to deal with the Israeli-Palestinian issue, but they found it useful to emphasize it in rhetoric as a means of distracting attention from their own domestic and foreign policy failures. The Palestinian issue was the only grievance that can be safely expressed in the Arab countries where the media is wholly owned or strictly overseen by the government. It serves as a useful stand-in for complaints about economic privation and political repression. The Palestinian issue was the Arab ruling class excuse for their authoritarian rule before Egypt signed the peace treaty with Israel. They claimed that they could not democratize as long as they were still in a state of war with Israel.

After the peace treaty, Egypt's military continued to rule under state of emergency to protect the country from "the other threat," the Islamists and the Arab countries were going wherever Egypt goes. Many Arab governments have pursued a dual policy of continuing to denounce Israel and the US' support for Israel while at the same time pursuing cooperation with both.

Saddam Hussein, supported by the US, Saudi Arabia and the Gulf States, re-ignited the centuries-old Sunni versus Shi'a conflict when he attacked his neighboring Iran in 1980. The war on Iran was the spark that started a chain of bloody wars and events which eventually led to the US invasion of Iraq and the Arab Spring uprisings. Kuwait, Saudi Arabia, the UAE and Bahrain supported the 2003 US invasion of Iraq by providing bases and logistics facilities for the invading military. The invasion created deep humanitarian crisis in Iraq and fostered a sectarian Iraq that has helped Iran to manipulate the religious sentiments and extend its primacy in the region.

The wars highlighted the crisis of citizenship and exclusion that existed in Iraq before and after the US invasion. They destroyed any semblance of Iraq's fragile unity, alienated large segments of Sunni population and allowed ISIS (Islamic State in Iraq and Syria) to rise out of the ashes of al-Qaeda which presented itself as the defender of Iraqi Sunni against the Iranian-backed Shi'a-dominated regime. ISIS is a more radical refinement of al-Qaeda. The movement is currently fragmented, with ISIS copy-cat groups emerging in Syria, Sinai, North Africa, and even in Afghanistan. The US invasion was the start of a historical pivot for the restoration of Persian hegemony in the region and the "Arab Spring" uprisings. The undignified capture of Saddam Hussein, the most ruthless and feared Arab dictator, to the US military, showed the Arab masses the hollowness and vulnerability of the Arab regimes.

The "Arab Spring" was unavoidable because the autocratic model of governance in the region from Morocco to Bahrain was neither accountable nor effective. Citizens have no influence on the state and in rare cases they do it through patronage, clientelism and informal relations all of which undermine the notion of citizenship. Arab ruling class saw themselves above the law, demanded obedience and destroyed the fabric of their diverse societies. And when adding poor economic conditions to the mix, an opportunity to rebel for change presented itself, something that has been badly needed for decades across the region of 300 million people. In the first year of the "Arab Spring," in which brave, enlightened protesters stood up to the dictators, Tunisia got rid of Bin Ali, Egypt put an end to Hosni Mubarak regime, Colonel Muammar Gaddafi of Libya was killed, and President Ali

Abdullah Saleh was forced to resign. None of the post Arab Spring regimes, except in Tunisia, ended with anything remotely resembling success.

After their counter-insurgency actions killed the Arab Spring, the despotic regimes which survived the uprising continue to feel insecure and threatened by even modest calls for reform. Seven years after the start of the Arab Spring, the Saudi government has been cracking down on reform advocates, journalists, bloggers and anyone who dared criticize the regime and call for reform. Actors with excessive power will tend to abuse it. Saudi government officials took that to the extreme. They killed and dismembered, mobster style, Jamal Khashoggi, a moderate progressive Arab Springer journalist. The brutal killing that took place inside the Saudi Arabia's Consulate in Istanbul, Turkey, suggests that its government which has spent billions of petro-dollars in killing the Arab Spring across the region still considers the aspiration for democracy and social justice as an existential threat to their absolute monarchy regime.

The aftermath of the "Arab Spring" has disappointed the world's hopes for better outcome, but the popular uprisings and their failures gave a text book lesson on revolutions and their failures. Arab states had been ruled by brittle dictatorships and weak or non-existing political and civil institutions. Getting rid of dictatorial and corrupt rulers is not enough if there are no such institutions to pick up the pieces, restore confidence in the inherited flawed state, and make the transition to democracy. The spontaneous Arab Spring movements of 2011 were unsuited to take on the roles of political parties with inclusive ideology. It was not only the advocates of nonviolent civil resistance who missed this point. The US policy makers who spend billions of dollars on think-tanks research failed to anticipate that the US military adventures in the ME which toppled authoritarian regimes would lead to anarchy and sectarian war in Iraq, and the war in Afghanistan would be the longest ever with no end in sight.

To understand the Arab Spring and its aftermath, the following chapters will provide narrative about the Middle East common culture that includes the Islamic religion and Arab tribalism, and a short review of each country's own history

1. The Religion of Islam

Islam is one of the most formidable spiritual and political forces in the world, the power of which is evident for all to see. It has a personal and social significance that most contemporary Middle Eastern regimes must take seriously when they set policies. Even those leaders who wish to minimize the role of religion in politics must pursue their programs with acute consciousness of the Islamic environment. The social thought of Islam has had a decisive influence on state politics throughout the region since the death of the Prophet Muhammad.

The idea of the Islamic state based on Sharia laws has stimulated diverse political ideologies in many Muslim-majority countries since the collapse of the Ottoman Empire in the early decades of the last century. The recent fervor in many Arab countries for creating Islamic states had always existed. The role Islam plays in the Arab world politics has always been a hotly contested issue. Debate has even intensified since the "Arab Spring" when majority of people freed of dictatorial rule openly chose moderate political Islam.

The 2012 Egyptian presidential elections seemed to confirm the acceptance of the MB motto "Islam is the Solution." The MB is an organization that had been banned in Egypt until the Arab Spring. A century of thought and activism since the establishment of the MB culminated in the election of its candidate, President Morsi. It was followed by default resetting and throwing out the MB regime by the military.

The first free elections held in Tunisia in October 2011 saw a landslide victory for Ennahda Islamic Party. This was a shock for many because for the past 60 years, all Tunisian regimes had championed the idea that Tunisia was a secular country, perhaps the most secular country in the Arab World. Tunisia is credited with being the birthplace of the "Arab Spring" and has earned the reputation as the only country where "Arab Spring" brought a relatively successful regime change.

Different models of Islamic states and Islamic movements were fashioned by a host of local, political, historical and economic factors. This has been demonstrated by the establishment of the Wahhabi-Islamic state in Arabia under the Saudi dynasty since 1921, the rise of the MB in Egypt since 1928, the creation of the Islamic Republic of Pakistan in 1947, the 1978-9 Iranian uprising that ended the Pahlavi monarchy and established the Islamic Republic of Iran, and the Islamic Salvation Front triumph in the 1992 Algerian elections. Turkey's 1995 parliamentary elections brought the Islamic AKP party to power after 73 years of Mustafa Ataturk's secular nationalist revolution that stripped the Ottoman Empire from its Islamic history and in 1994, the Taliban Islamic fundamentalist movement took over the government in Afghanistan after a failed experiment with communism. The Islamists won the 2006 elections in Palestine, and in Tunisia, Libya and Egypt after the 2011 Arab Spring uprising.

Immigrants from Algeria, India, Pakistan and Turkey have expanded the reach of Islamic culture in many European countries and their population will continue to grow. Most of the Middle East countries have constructed their modern institutions on a base of traditional social arrangements, values, philosophical assumptions, and every-day practices that are deeply rooted in their Islamic cultural heritage. The Arab world is religiously conservative and the people generally like to see "certain version of Islam" playing an important role in their lives. When secular parties have failed on all accounts, the Islamists have assumed the role once played by national liberation movements and leftist parties. Mainstream Islamic parties have distilled a complicated philosophical tradition into simple slogans that have supplanted the Pan-Arabism and socialism that dominated the region until 1967. The organized political Islamic parties have established themselves as major political players in the ME. Politics, not violence, is what gave them their influence. They have crafted messages with widespread popular appeal and created organizations with genuine social bases and political strategies. They had a powerful impact on social customs by halting secular trends and changing the way Arabs dress and behave, especially women.

Foreign powers military interventions that destabilized Middle East countries, the rule of the autocratic regimes and poverty led to the surge of Islamic extremism. Islamism has taken root in poverty-stricken areas especially the shanty towns at the outskirts of major industrial cities. The authoritarian secular regimes failed to solve the social and economic problems of the masses. Their reliance on the security and intelligence services as main instruments to deal with the opposition gave birth to Islamic radicalism and violence which swept through the Middle East and elsewhere over the past few decades. The growth of ISIS since 2014 shows that extreme Islamists' movement can emerge in places where government has broken down.

The aftermath of "Arab Spring" uncovered the weakness of civil institutions and nationalism never was fully supplanted narrow tribalism in the Arab countries. It was not a matter of coincidence that the "Arab Spring" and much of the turmoil that is consuming the Middle East today came after the US invasion of Iraq. The invasion was not the cause of the "Arab Spring," but it was a phase of the wars that came in the wake of Saddam Hussein's 1980 war on Iran.

The US invasion was the trigger that unleashed the uprisings. Saddam Hussein's Iraq-Iran war awakened the ancient sectarian conflicts between the followers of the major denominations of Islam, and the US invasion has laid bare the hollowness of the Arab regimes.

The Islamic-faith's claim to combine spiritual and earthy authority with no separation between the mosque and the state has been a factor in politicizing the religion and creating divisions among its followers. Some militants sought legitimacy through fanatical interpretation of al-Quran. Others, threatened by violence and civil war, have sought refuge in their sect.

Different ideas of an Islamic state are based on the diverse interpretations of injunctions in al-Quran, the account of the Prophet Muhammad's life (570–632) and the recorded history of the state under his successors. Some Muslims call for a strict adherence to the practices of the first Islamic state in al-Madina, and others who claim that Islam does not even have the concept of a state, derive their opinions from Muslims' history and Islamic doctrines. The authoritative source on Islamic religion that the believers must not question is al-Quran.

The revelation of al-Quran began in 610 when the Prophet Muhammad claimed that the Angel Gabriel appeared to him in Hira cave near Mecca reciting to him the first verses that started with the word "Iqra" (read). Even Muslim scholars do not agree on the real meaning of "Iqra" within the context of its delivery. Some suggest the Prophet was illiterate and only with the heavenly miracle, he was able to read. Others do not agree. Non-Muslim historians and even the Muslim historian Ibn Ishaq (704–768) in his biography of the Prophet tell us that Muhammad had interest in religions at an early age and he was not illiterate. When he took trips to Syria with camel caravans, he met Jews and Christians who told him there was one God. He travelled with his uncle Abu-Talib since he was a teenager, and on his way he met and spent time with a monk named Bahira living in Busra,

Syria, who had been well-versed in Christianity and theology. The two must have talked religion.

People then matured early and life expectancy was short although some could have lived into their sixties. When Muhammad was fifteen, he had gained a life experience that must have enhanced his natural talents and prepared him to play his unique role in the history of the world. His father had died few weeks before he was born and his mother had died when he was only six. He was raised by his paternal grandfather Abdel-Muttaleb until the age of eight when his grandfather died. He then had to live with his paternal uncle, Abu-Talib, a tribe leader and a caravan trader.

When the young Muhammad lived in his grandfather's household, his grandfather was the leader of the Quraish Tribe and he took care of the holy sanctuary of "al-Ka'ba" that was then filled with three hundred sixty idols worshiped by Arabia's tribes. Muslims believe al-Ka'ba was the first house built by the Prophet Ibrahim (Abraham) and his son Ismail (Ishmael) for the worship of Allah, but the original message of Ibrahim was lost and it became mixed with paganism and superstition. Under the guardianship of his uncle, Muhammad began to earn living as a businessman and a trader when he was a teen-ager. Because of his reputation as a reliable and trustworthy man, Muhammad was hired as a travelling trader and business manager by his future wife, Khadijah, a rich merchant widow. According to the Muslims, Khadijah was the first to believe in his prophecy when he described to her his first encounter with the Angel Gabriel in the Hira cave.

The Prophet continued to have revelations through the rest of his life he died in 632. Over a period of twenty-two years, it is said, the Prophet would repeatedly go into the wilderness and each time received a few more verses of "God's final revelation," which he would memorize. Returning home, he would dictate these verses to family and friends, who wrote them down for posterity. According to Sunni Islam, the Prophet was illiterate and so there was no other way for the word of God but to be memorialized. Long after the Prophet's death, these verses were collected in the work we know as al-Quran.

Al-Quran scripture is a unique in that it has remained completely unchanged over the past fourteen centuries, a fact which is attested to by Muslim and non-Muslim scholars alike. There are no "versions" of al-Quran and every copy in the world remains identical, word for word in its original Arabic language. Practicing Muslims emphasize the importance of memorizing and reciting parts of al-Quran while praying five times a day, recognizing that it is the speech of God.

Al-Quran book form was established two decades after the death of the Prophet, during the time of the third pious Caliph Othman Ibn-Affan who reigned as a political leader from 644 to 656. During the time of the early caliphs, al-Quran had been memorized and passed in oral tradition by the Prophet's close followers. With the spread of Islam, non-Arabs who converted to Islam began writing al-Quran in various different scripts and languages. Ibn-Affan decided that there must be only one official version of the "Holy Book" written in the style used in al-Madina. He felt it was important to compile the text of al-Quran in a standardized Arabic dialect of Quraish tribe form. He took possession of the original Quran that had been written on stones, bones and leather and kept with the Prophet's wife Hafsah, who was also the daughter of Caliph Omar ibn al-Khattab. Ibn-Affan ordered all other unofficial copies to be destroyed. According to the historian Muhammad al-Tabari (839–923), Ibn-Affan ordered Zaid bin Thabit, Abdullah bin Az-Zubair, Saed bin Al-Aas, and Abdul-Rahman bin-Hisham to rewrite the original manuscripts of al-Quran that had been with Hafsa. Five official copies were sent to the greatest cities of the Muslim Caliphate.

Muslims believe that al-Quran is a "Message from God (Allah) to humanity," revealed to the Prophet over a period of twenty-two years in 114 chapters (soras) that are not arranged in chronological order and each chapter consists of a number of verses (aayat) composed in a rhythmic style resembling modern blank verse. Al-Quran stresses most often the majesty and sovereignty of Allah, the 'Generous Forgiver' and the 'Wrathful Punisher'. It includes Commandments similar to Moses 'Ten Commandments' that incumbent on every Muslim to obey, and it makes liberal usage of symbolic imagery, many cryptic narratives, allusions and indirect explanations. Al-Quran is filled with comments on social matters including orders for a humane stand on behalf of the weak. The rest of the subjects in al-Quran cover the Prophet Muhammad and his divine message, social legislation, stories with moral inferences, commentary on contemporaneous events, accounts of past civilizations, the nature of different phenomena, rewards and punishment for individual and collective conduct, the evil role of Satan, prophecies about future events, Doomsday, life after death and many remarks on knowledge and intellectual reflection. There are instructions on how to provide justice, protect the rights of orphans and women, show kindness to slaves and the poor, negotiate treaties and conduct wars on enemies.

Al-Quran appeals repeatedly to the conscience of the individual to accept and comply with the Islamic tenets. There are five articles of Islamic faith belief:

1. Belief in God (Allah) the Supreme and Eternal, the Merciful and Compassionate. A Muslim believes God is Just and Loving, and whatever He does must have good motives.

2. Belief in His angels as purely spiritual and splendid beings that have no free will and require no food or drink or sleep.

3. Belief in His holy Books, the Psalm (Zabour), the Torah (Taurat), the Gospel (Injeel) and al-Quran as they were complete and in their original versions.

4. Belief in all God's messengers and prophets as human beings, endowed with Divine revelations to teach mankind. The message brought by the prophets is the belief in one God, staying away from sins and devote life to earning God's pleasure. Al-Quran mentions names of twenty-five prophets including Adam, Noah, Abraham, Ishmael, Isaac, Moses, Jesus and Muhammad as the last Prophet.

5. Belief in the Day of Judgment when this world comes to an end and the dead will be resurrected from the state of death to stand for their final and fair trial.

Living according to his religion, a Muslim has to put the faith into action and practice by fulfilling five obligations that every Muslim individual must perform

1. Reciting the Muslim profession of faith, that there is no god but "Allah" and that Muhammad is the messenger of Allah (Shahadah).

2. Praying five times daily (Salat), facing Mecca when praying. The call for prayer does not demand attendance in a mosque. Prayers could be made in the privacy of a home, in the field or at places of work. The Prophet Muhammad and his followers prayed facing Al-Aqsa Mosque in Jerusalem for more than ten years before the Prophet was "commanded by Alla (God)" to pray toward Al-Ka'ba in Mecca.

3. Fasting every day during the lunar month of Ramadan (Siyam).

4. Giving alms tax annually on the person's wealth that includes property and income (Zakat). The beneficiaries of zakat are all categories of the poor including the non-Muslims.

5. Pilgrimage to Mecca once in a life time, if one can afford it (Hajj).

Al-Quran asks people, not only Muslims, to do good things and to shun evil. It provides forgiveness for those who repent, but it sets a number of punishments for crimes and sins such as murder, theft, sexual promiscuity and false accusation of adultery. Islam stresses superiority of the individuals due to their good deeds and faith rather than rank and nobility, and it disapproves racial pride and tribalism. Unlike Christianity, the Sunni Muslims do not have priests as intermediaries between man and God, and there is no separation between the church (mosque) and state. The Shi'a Muslims too do not have intermediaries with God but they attribute divine authoritative status on their Imam's decrees. Christians and Jews, custodians of the scripture 'People of the Book' are given higher status than idolaters by Islam.

Islam is a religion that preaches the same principles of earlier religions while claiming it corrects their accumulated defects. Al-Quran includes narratives about the Jewish and Christian prophets and messengers. It recounts details of Moses' life story and the Exodus from Ancient Egypt in a number of chapters. Mary (Mariam), the mother of Jesus (Issa) received the most attention of any woman mentioned in al-Quran. She is among eight people who have a chapter named after them. And the third chapter in al-Quran is named after her family, Aali-Imran. Marriage between Muslim men and Christian or Jewish women is allowed in Islam, but Muslim women are not permitted to marry non-Muslim men.

The leading role of men in the family is upheld, polygamy is allowed up to four wives but husbands are ordered to treat their wives with love and care and be fair, and wives are asked to respect their husbands. According to Muslim historians, number of the Prophet's wives exceeded thirteen women. Only his first marriage with Khadijah was monogamous until she died. They had two sons, Kassim and Abdullah (both died young), and four daughters, Zainab, Ruqaiya, Um Kulthum and Fatima, and they adopted a slave, Zaid ibn Haritha, as a son. Slavery was not banned in Islam, but humane treatment of slaves was emphasized.

The second most important source of ascertaining the will of Allah in Islam is what the Prophet did, said and instructed. These, the "Prophet traditions," called the Sunna of the Prophet, are recorded in various books of Hadith. The subject of Hadith attained importance and was collected by scholars more than a century after the death of the Prophet. It has been understood that the authors of Hadith devised stringent methods for cross-checking the validity of every hadith. The chain of five generations of Muslim transmitters had to go back to the Prophet or one of his companions. The total number of collected "Prophet's sayings" (quotations) runs into several thousands. Six collections are recognized by Sunnis and twenty are accepted by the Shi'as as authentic. Each of the Shi'as and Sunnis have their own collections that sometimes tell different and contradictory stories about the Prophet, which suggest that the collections of Hadith contain spurious narrations, distortion and myth about the Prophet's life. Some modern scholars argue that Hadith is not a valid source for deriving any authoritative ordinances of Islam.

In economy, Islam recognizes the right to own and dispose of private property, sets laws of inheritance, approves mercantile activity, but property is deemed a trusteeship, with ultimate ownership vested in 'God'. Al-Quran bans usury and condemns greed. Paying annual zakat is one of the obligations on Muslims, but al-Quran did not set the rate at which it is to be charged. The zakat tax is viewed as an egalitarian measure to facilitate redistribution of wealth. Because property and income should be taxed, elaborate system was devised by Muslim jurists over the years.

The Islamic advance through military invasion was incredibly swift. It got all the way to the Atlantic and to Spain within 100 years of the death of Muhammad, and it also went in the other direction, where it conquered one of the great powers of the day, in Persia, and went further, to India. Islam was introduced to the East Indies by Arab and Persian Muslim traders. The nearest approximation to a world-wide order of politics, trade and science was achieved by the Muslim empire in Asia at about AD 1250 and in Spain in the middle of the 16th century. Their position was slowly challenged and their vitality sapped by the Mongol invasions from Asia in the 13th and 14th centuries, the Ottoman Turks' leadership of the Muslims, and later by European naval expeditions.

Muslim scholars (ulama) specialized in interpreting al-Quran and the Hadith created many schools of exegesis, some sectarians with ritualistic variations and others even deviate considerably from the conventional understanding of Islam and interpreting it in light of rational and today scientific values. In the Islamic tradition, there can be no imitation of the political system under the Prophet-in-Authority.

The first Islamic state that the Prophet established in al-Madina provided what Muslims consider the ideal leadership in spiritual and worldly matters. The confluence of religion and politics under his leadership gave birth to Muslims that there should be no separation between religion and governing. The Prophet in his authority as the ruler of al-Madina was the source of legislation, Muslims were enjoined to obey him, but al-Quran instructed him to seek advice on matters of government. The first four Rightly-Guided Caliphs governed as the temporal rulers of the population under their control without invoking the property of divine revelation. Only the Shi'a Muslims attribute divine authoritative status on their Imam's decrees including the fourth Caliph Ali Ibn-Abu-Talib. But all Muslims including the Shi'a agree that only the text of al-Quran is the direct revelation from God.

Muslims believe Sharia, the established Canon Law of Islam stemmed from God's revelation. It is therefore beyond human review the believers must not question the revealed instructions and the Muslim state is expected to enforce it in its entirety as the body of laws for the Islamic community. Sharia recognized sources are al-Quran, the Sunna, al-qiyas, and al-Ijtihad. Muslim scholars discovered over time that al-Quran and the Sunni did not suffice for providing answers for all situations. They developed al-qiyas method by which a rule contained in al-Quran or Sunni could be extended to a similar but not identical situation and they validated al-Ijtihad which is the use of one's own independent judgment to reach a decision conforming to the needs of society in matters beyond the scope of the revelation and al-Sunna as long as the decision does not traverse Quranic principles.

Four schools of orthodox Islamic schools of law were established by Sunni theologians (imams) after the death of the Prophet Muhammad (AD 570–632). They were named after their founders, Abu-Hanifa (699–767), Malik (711–795), Al-Shafi (767–820] and Ahmad bin-Hanbal (778–855). These doctrines have been accepted by the Sunni Muslims in different parts of the world. The Wahhabi traditions in Saudi Arabia, for example, are rooted in the strictly traditional bin-Hanbal jurisprudence. The Abu-Hanifa school predominates in Pakistan and India. Majority of Shi'a have their own separate school associated with their sixth Imam Jafar al-Sadiq (702–765). He was the fifth generation of the descendants of the first Imam, Ali Ibn-Abu-Taleb, the Prophet's nephew and son-in-law. Thus Islam is not a monolithic religion it comes in many forms.

Tasawwuf

Before the 12th century, the Islamic culture had focused solely on Sharia and Fiqh, including the rituals, then some adherents of the faith turned inwards and focused more on its spiritual than on its physical sciences. The transformation came with Abu Hamid Al Gazzali (1058–1111) writings. Al-Gazali believed that the traditional Islamic beliefs were threatened by the rising nihilistic philosophy and extreme political Shi'aism. He was against ideas and arguments pertaining to Islam based on the philosophical models of Aristotle and he rejected Shi'aism. In his book, "The Incoherence of the Philosophers," Al Gazzali took on the challenge of showing the problems in the philosophers' arguments that would come to the conclusion of God-non-existence.

Critics of Al-Gazzali accused him for refuting the philosophy that led to the achievements of the leading scientific scholars of their time, Ibn Sina, al-Farabi and others who wrote great mathematical and scientific treatises. But Al-Gazzali warned that 'students must be careful to accept the scientific ideas of scholars without blindly accepting everything they say regarding philosophy and other problematic subjects.' Al-Gazzali also had to refute the rising tide of Muslims who accepted the Shi'a belief in the infallible Hidden Imam. Al Gazzali gave birth to Tasawwuf which emerged as a force in Islamic teachings in many regions of the Islamic world.

The Sufis called for less materialism and more on purification of their souls and development of consciousness of God through submission to the Sharia and Sunnah. Tasawwuf is described as the spiritual dimension of Islam. The Muslim historian and sociologist, Ibn Khaldun (1332–1406) defined Tasawwuf as , "total dedication to Allah." The Afghani born Sufi-Islamic poet and mystic Jalal-al-Din Rumi (1207–1273) communicated his spiritual experience in a collection of poetry as joy and love songs to the Prophet and God. He wrote: "I used to recite prayers. Now I recite rhymes and poems and song." He described his masterwork as "the roots of the roots of the roots of the (Islamic) Religion," and the text has come to be regarded by some Sufis as the Persian-language Quran.

During the twelfth century, Arab and Persian Muslim traders introduced Islam to the East Indies, mostly as a spiritual religion that focused on the soul than on the ritual practices. Commerce stimulated cultural and religious interaction in these countries. Islam spread in East Asia mostly as Tasawwuf during the period between 1100 and 1500. John Shah, the ruler of Sumatra, converted to Islam in 1204, and by 1500, Islam was a major religion in the region and the Sufi order spread the faith throughout the area. The 14th century traveler and explorer Muhammad Ibn Battuta (1304–1368) visited Pasai city in the island of Sumatra. He described its ruler as a pious man, a patron of scholars and an enthusiastic propagator of the Islamic faith.

Today, this region that includes Indonesia, Malaysia, Brunei and the Philippine has one quarter of the Muslim population of the world. Indonesia alone is the country of the largest Muslim population in the world. Because of their remoteness, Muslims in these countries were not affected by the military and political events in the rest of the Muslim world landmass extending from Morocco to Bengal. They had to forge their Islamic belief and practices based on its spiritual, intellectual and religious content.

There are many Islamic-Sufi Orders today in Muslim countries and in the West they claim to follow the Islamic Sharia as interpreted by each founder leader (shaykh) of the order. Some of these orders are: the Shadhili, the Naqshbandi, the Chishti, the Qadiria, the Tijani, the Jerrahi, and the Muridiyah. There are Quasi-Islamic Sufi Orders where members adhere to the Sharia but do not have to practice Islam. And there are Non-Islamic Sufi Organizations in the West who teach various Sufi doctrines and practices. They claim that Sufism pre-dates Islam and thus in principle it is universal and independent of Islam. Some in the West refer to Sufism as 'the Islamic mysticism" a way of life detached from politics and world matters and focused on direct personal experience of God. But unlike Islamism which is concerned with permeating external areas of life, Sufism teaches that the material world is all illusions.

Belief is a personal matter, but the potential problem with Sufism is that, it reminds its followers of having a benevolent shepherd who looks out for their welfare and they may not need to recognize their personal responsibilities to perfect their own lives.

Ahmadiyya

The Ahmadiyya Islamic sect was founded in 1889 in the British controlled north India by Mirza Ghulam Ahmad (1835–1908), a self-described divinely messenger to fulfill promises found in 'the scripture of the Islamic faith'. Some refer to the sect as Qadiani after his birthplace, the town of Qadian. The name 'Ahmad' that he took was the alternative name of the Prophet Muhammad. He based his conviction on the belief that "Muslim religion and society had deteriorated to the point where divinely inspired reforms were needed." His objective was to propagate Islam through peaceful means and to establish peace in the world through the teachings of Islam. Based on this principle, he was against fighting the British in the name of Islam when India was a British colony. He actually preached support for the British because they protected the Muslim minority from the Hindu majority.

The followers of the Ahmadiyya sect subscribe to the same beliefs as the Sunni-Muslims, but with a different opinion on the meaning of al-Quran reference to the Prophet Muhammad as the last prophet to guide mankind, as Orthodox Muslims believe. They share the same articles of faith that the Sunni Muslims believe in. But they also believe that their apostil, Ahmad, was divinely commissioned as a true reflection of the Prophet Muhammad prophecy to remind mankind of their duties toward God and His creation. They regard him the "Promised Mahdi" to fulfill the promises of all Abrahamic religions prophecies. The followers of Ahmadiyya are considered non-Muslims by many mainstream Muslims and they have been victims of religious persecution and discrimination by other Muslims. Many have been killed and their mosques burnt in the 1974 riots in Pakistan and even Quranic verses were removed by Pakistani police in 2012 from Ahmadi graves. Saudi Arabia and Indonesia have laws that restrict the religious freedom of the Ahmadi Muslims.

Shi'a Islam

The Shi'a or Shi'ats form one of the two great branches of Islam. There are about 150 million Shi'ats or thirteen percent of the total worldwide Muslim population. They live everywhere in the Middle East and constitute the majority of population in Iran, Iraq, Yemen and Bahrain, and they are large minorities in Lebanon, Pakistan and Afghanistan. Regarding their religious belief, the Shi'a and the Sunnis share many fundamental beliefs and practices, but they differ in rituals, laws, theology and religious organization. After all, even main stream Sunni-Muslims can't keep themselves from splitting into different denominations. The big issue between the Shi'a and Sunni has been the unforgotten centuries old competition over the Muslims' political leadership that emphasizes the sectarian divide and tears the communities apart today.

The division between the Shi'a and Sunni started fourteen centuries ago over the succession of leadership after the death of the Prophet Muhammad in 632. Followers of the Shi'a doctrine maintain that the rightful successor of the Prophet was his cousin and son in law, Ali Ibn-Abu-Talib. When the Prophet died and disputes cropped up among Muslims over the question of succession. There were three tribal contenders, and a small non-tribal group of Muslims that took a position that any Muslim even if not from Quraish tribe or even Arab could lead the Muslims if he was morally irreproachable. The supporters of the tribal contenders were the Prophet's clan of Bani Hashim, his tribe of Quraish, and the tribes of al-Madina town where the Prophet was forced to immigrate and establish the first Islamic state. The opinion of the majority was in favor of having Abu Bakr the caliph as a temporal leader from the tribe of Quraish. He was a respected member of the tribe, a father-in-law and a senior companion of the Prophet. The supporters of this choice later became the followers of the Sunni orthodox doctrine. The group of Muslims that considered the leadership belongs to Ali Ibn Abu-Talib as a divine right because he was the Prophet's nephew, a son-in-law, and the first child to accept Islam when the Prophet declared his prophecy. Those became known as the Shi'a Muslims, some refer to them as Ahlul Beit (household of the Prophet, Ali, Fatima, Hasan, Hussein and their descendants).

Abu Bakr became the first caliph to succeed the Prophet, but Arab tribal tradition and belief in nobility and class system based on birth among the early Muslims was strong. Muslims who called for choosing the leader based on his personal qualifications regardless of his race or tribe were considered radicals, ostracized and called 'al-Khawarij' which literally means 'outsiders'. Some Khawarij developed extreme doctrines and violence against both Sunni and Shi'a when the fourth Caliph, Ali who ruled from 656-661 accepted arbitration to deal with the rebellious Mu'awiyah ibn-Abu Sufian to bring about peace. They believed that arbitration was sin based on al-Quran text. They adopted the concept of declaring some mainstream self-described Muslims as non-Muslims, 'Takfeer'. A member of this group assassinated Caliph Ali ibn Abu-Taleb, and for hundreds of years, 'al-Khawarij' members were the source of insurrections against the Caliphate. This Khawarij group was the first to use violence against Muslims in the name of Islam. They can be the fore-runners of today's ISIS.

The Shi'a and Sunni Muslims follow the five articles of Islamic faith belief and both embrace the same five obligations and rituals that Muslim individuals are obliged to perform.

The Shi'as give great reverence to the descendants of Ali (Imams) and to their succession of scholars and regard them as spiritual and political leaders. Some of these figures are memorialized by elaborate tombs and objects of devotion and pilgrimage. They still mourn the event of the assassination of Ali that took place in 661 in the City of Najaf and the murder of Hussein, son of Ali and grandson of the Prophet that took place in 680 in Karbala, Iraq. They commemorate this event each year on Ashura, a day of mourning and pilgrimage recognized throughout the worldwide Shi'a communities. When the Shi'a pilgrims go to Mecca, they visit the graves of Fatima and other Ahl al-Bayt who are buried in the cemetery of Jannat al-Baqi' but they do not visit other Sahabas (companions of the Prophet).

Shi'a sects worldwide believe that Ali Ibn-Abu-Talib and his descendants are the only legitimate custodians of the Islamic faith based on the notion of their closeness to the Prophet and some sects believe in their infallibility. The largest group is the Ithna-Ashar (the twelver) or the Ja'faris. Its members believe that the spiritual authority and divine guidance and the right to the Muslims leadership (Imams) had passed on from the Prophet to his twelve descendants beginning with Ali. Ali is the first Imam, his sons as the second and third up to Muhammad al-Mahdi, his twelfth descendant, must be free from error or sin according to the sect doctrine. Followers of the Ithna-Ashar believe that the twelfth Imam al-Mahdi who had disappeared from a mosque in 878 will return at the end of time to restore justice on earth. The Ithna-

Ashar Shi'a followers are majorities among Muslims in Iran, Iraq, Bahrain Lebanon and Azerbaijan. They also make significant minorities in Yemen, Kuwait, Qatar, UAE, Saudi Arabia, India, and Pakistan.

The denial of the legitimate right of accession to the caliph for Ali and his descendants and their tragic history gave rise to the Shi'a concept of martyrdom and the ritual of grieving. Ali was assassinated in 661 after he served as a caliph for five years. Supporters of Ali's eldest son, Hasan, believe that he had been poisoned by the Umayyad caliph Mu'awiyah Ibn Abu-Sufian in 680. Ali's second son, Hussein, was killed on the battlefield by the Umayyads in 681. Zaid, the respected son of Imam Zain al-Aabidin was killed by the Umayyads and his body was hung on the gates of Kufa for years. One year after Zaid death, his son Yahya received the same fate as his father. Many descendants of Imam Hasan were killed and some were allegedly buried alive while rising against the Abbasids caliphs.

Shi'a Muslims worldwide consider the tenth day of the lunar month of Muharram, Aashura, a holy day to commemorate and mourn the death of Imam Hussein Ibn-Ali at the Battle of Karbala in AD 681. Thousands of people listen to the accounts of his death under the golden dome of his mausoleum in Karbala, Iraq. They interpret his death as a symbol of the struggle against injustice, tyranny and oppression. Mourning rituals in Iraq, Bangladesh and India sometimes include self-flagellation with chains and knives.

The Zaidi Shi'a Sect

Zaidi is another Shi'a sect who got its name from Imam Zaid Ibn-Ali Zain-al-Abideen (698–740), the fourth Imam after Ali. His followers view him as a luminary scholar, a fighter for the Shi'a, and Imam, but not the last Imam nor being infallible. Unlike most Sunni-Muslims, Zaidis believed Muslims can revolt against an oppressive ruler, even if he is a Muslim. There are differences between the Ithna-Ashar and the Zaidis sect. The Ithna-Ashar limits the number of imams to twelve, but there is no limit for the Zaidis and there can be two imams in different geographic locations at the same time. They even believe anyone in the house of Ali is eligible for the Imamate. The Zaidis reject the doctrine of Hidden Imam and the return of the Mahdi, and they do not believe that the Imam is capable of performing miracles. But he was expected to be knowledgeable in religious scholarship and he must prove himself a worthy leader in peaceful time and in war. They are considered the closest Shi'a sect to the Sunni tradition. Number of Zaidi faith followers is estimated at seven million of the 150 million Shi'a population of the world. The Yemeni state of Zaidis was founded in 890 by

Yahya ibn al-Husain his son al-Hadi proclaimed himself the first Zaidi Imam the state has lasted until the 20th century. Yemen's Shi'a today, the Huthis, are the largest followers of the Zaidis' belief.

The Ismaili Shi'a Sect

The Ismaili sect of the Shi'a acknowledged the claim to the imamate of Ismail, the eldest son of the sixth imam, Ja'far As-Sadiq, even when his father denied him the imamate because he had been guilty of drinking wine. Muslims are not permitted to drink alcohol. The Ismailis say that as the imam could do no wrong, his action showed that wine-drinking was not sinful. They are the only Shi'a Muslims to have living hereditary Imam. It is the presence of the living Imam that makes the Ismailis unique. Number of Ismailis is estimated at 10-15 million of mostly prosperous people in twenty-five countries under the 49th Imam, Aga Khan IV. The Ismailis accept the interpretation of Islam according to the guidance of the Imam of the time. Under Imam-leadership, they have evolved into a progressive institution dedicated to the common good of all citizens in their communities regardless of their race or religion. They provided a variety of social and economic services like building schools, hospitals, and health centers.

The adherents of this sect are initiated by degrees into the secrets of its doctrines and are divided into seven classes. It starts with the interpretation of Islam and in the sixth and seventh classes the believer is induced to give up the practices of Islam (prayer, fasting, and pilgrimage) all together. The doctrine was taken up by the 'Hashashin' in Persia in the 11th century. Followers of the Ismaili doctrine today are very highly sophisticated. They may be found as tightly connected groups in small numbers in Persia, India, Syria and Zanzibar. There are Ismaili-Shi'a centers of religious education in Iranian City of Qom, the Iraqi City of Najaf, and in Pakistan City of Karachi.

The Alawite Sect

Alawite doctrine is a Shi'a-Muslim sect they are followers of Imam Ali Ibn-Abu-Talib and portray themselves as close to the Twelver-Shi'a Islamic sect. They believe in the prophecy of Muhammad, the Day of Judgment, and the holy leadership of the twelve imams. But some observers familiar with the sect's practices argue that some of the Alawites beliefs are neither shared with the Twelver-Shi'a nor with Sunnis. They refer to the Alawites as a third sect of Islam with different interpretation of al-Quran. Faith and salvation, according to them are not linked to a sect. They believe in goodness among all religions and sects and reject the belief of some sectarians that only they will receive salvation.

The Alawites Islamic group was founded by the 9th century theologian Ibn-Nusayr as an Islamic religion. That is why sometimes its members are called 'Nusayris'. The sect originated in Iraq, then, an apostle of the founder, Hussein al-Khusaibi (874–961), an Islamic scholar who helped in establishing the practices of the group, moved with many of his followers to the Emirate of Aleppo in Syria that was under the rule of Sayf al-Dawla al-Hamadani (890–1004). Al-Hamadani embraced the Alawites' doctrine and helped spread the faith in his emirate and neighboring area. All Islamic regimes that ruled the Levant considered the Alawites as apostates rejecting the Islamic faith. Members of the group were persecuted based on fatwas ruling issued by Sunni theologians in the thirteen and fourteen centuries issued against the Alawites, Druze and Ismaeli sects. When they were persecuted by the Mamluks and the Ottomans, the Alawites fled to Latakia's mountains after a large massacre in Aleppo in which thousands of them died.

The Alawites are primarily centered in Syria where they make more than twelve percent of the population. They are the majority religious group on the Syrian coast towns that are inhabited also by Sunnis, Christians and Ismailis. During the French Mandate of Syria, the Alawite tribes enjoyed good relations with the French, a considerable number of their youth chose military career in the French armed-forces, and some of them were promoted to high rank officers. France created an Alawite state that was later dismantled when Syria took its independence, but many Alawites continued to serve in the Syrian military in leadership positions. Hafez Al-Assad (1930-2000) the father of Bashar Al-Assad, who ruled Syria for three decades, was an air force officer. He came from a prominent Alawite family in Latakia. Hafez Al-Assad staged a military coup and took power in 1970, established 'the Corrective Movement of the Ba'th Party" that was dominated by the Alawite Al-Assad clan. After Hafez' death, the party elites brought his son Bashar, a medical student in Britain at the time, and appointed him the president of Syria.

Hashashin Shi'a Sect

A violent rebellious branch of Ismaeli sect of the Shi'a-Islam known as 'Hashashin' was founded by Hasan Sabbah in the 11th century. Its leaders established an independent network of strongholds in the mountains of Persia and Syria to challenge the new-converted Turkish-Sunni Muslim rulers. Outnumbered by the Turks, the 'Hashashin' could not defeat them in a traditional war. The sect decided to weaken them by assassinating their leaders and supporters. They did not defeat the Seljuk Turks, but they were able to kill many of them and strike fear among the region's political and religious leaders.

Like today's mafia, the followers of Sabbah sect were trained to murder their political enemies. They infiltrated the inner circle of their intended victims, sometimes disguised as professionals serving for a while in any capacity, then, they mercilessly assassin the victim with their preferred weapon, a sharp dagger. Their victims were mostly Sunni Muslims accused of mistreating the Shi'a. The name 'Hashashin' is a derogatory Arabic nickname for people under the influence of 'hashish,' a drug related to what is called today 'marijuana'. It is interesting to know that the English word "assassin" came from the name of this group, according to many linguistic sources.

The Islamic Monarchy

Othman ibn-Affan was chosen in 644 to be the third caliph by the committee that was appointed by Caliph Omar ibn al-Khattab to name his successor. Once Caliph ibn-Affan started running the Islamic state from al-Madina and appointing the governors of the provinces, he became the subject of criticism by fellow Muslims. He was accused of nepotism for appointing his relatives from Bani Omayya clan in high position and for his profligate life style. According to his critics, Ibn-Affan could not live up to the standards set by his predecessors who were known for their modesty and frugality in their personal lives and followed the principles of guaranteed equality for all Muslims regardless of their lineage or race.

While Muslims recognized ibn-Affan contributions to the faith especially for preserving al-Quran text in its present form, his critics charged him of violating the principle of Sharia by not appointing the most pious Muslims to positions of authority. According to the Indian Islamic theologian Abdul Ala Maududi (1903–1079), "ibn-Affan sowed the seeds of hereditary rule in Islam. The divine republic was thus corrupted and supplanted by hereditary succession." Ibn Affan belonged to Bani Omayya clan known in the pre-Islam period as the most powerful and the wealthiest of Quraish tribe that accumulated its opulence through trade. The aristocratic Bani Omayya was known for its traditional enmity with the Prophet's clan of Bani Hashim. Ibn Affan's reign was marred by widespread protests and unrest that eventually led to his assassination at the hands of a Muslim dissenter.

Ali bin Abu-Taleb, the Prophet Cousin and son-in-law, was chosen as the fourth Caliph by an open assembly of al-Madina Muslim elders. Bani-Umayya clan led by the governor of Syria, Mu'awiya ibn Abu Sufyan, opposed Ali's Caliphate choice accusing him of supporting the killing of Ibn Affan. A tribal civil war between supporters of the two competing Quraish clans, Bani-Umayya and Bani-Hashim ensued. Caliph Ali was assassinated by a member of al-Khawarij Muslims in 601 after six years of his rule and Mu'awiya Captured the leadership of the Muslims by force and the threat to use force. He established the first Islamic royalty, the Umayyad's hereditary monarchy rule that lasted ninety years with its capital in Damascus.

The Omayyads (661–750) retained the title of Caliph, but they were kings demanding the oath of allegiance from tribe leaders and secure by force the allegation of the reluctant. They introduced the alien concept of hereditary succession and created the first Muslim dynasty to rule the empire. During his lifetime, Mu'awiya secured an oath of allegiance to his son Yazid, disregarding the traditional election (bay'ah) where the caliph to be chosen by his peers as "the first among equals." Most Muslims consider the first four successors of the Prophet as the 'Rightly-Guided Caliphs' or the 'pious Caliphs' of the Prophet. The bloody big strife and tribulation that divided the Muslims for ever took place after Mu'awiya's death and the ascendance of his son Yazid to the caliphate.

Al-Hussein Ibn Ali rejection to the legitimacy of Yazid as Caliph led to the war between the supporters of the two clans, Bani Omayya and Bani Hashim. Al-Hussein was killed in the infamous Battle of Karbala, October 10, AD 680, and his death gave rise to the Shi'a movement that developed into a powerful opposition sect rejecting Sunni doctrine. They believe that Ali and his descendants must have been chosen as caliphs of the Prophet because of his close relations with the Prophet. Many Muslim leaders including companions of the Prophet refused to swear allegiance to Caliph Yazid and launched an insurgency in al-Madina. Yazid's army invaded the cities of al-Madina and Mecca, crushed the rebellion in the 683 Battle of Harrah. His army killed prominent Muslim leaders of the opposition and destroyed and damaged holy Islamic symbols including al-Kaa'ba. Only when Yazid died suddenly in 683, the Umayyad army was called off the siege of the holy cities.

The loyal Syrian people and the powerful Syrian army were the basis of Umayyad strength. Their army kept the empire united by defeating rebellion Arab tribes that opposed the Umayyads, and it conquered foreign lands. Under their rule, Muslims expanded into central Asia, northwestern India and northwestern Africa, and their navy was dominating the Mediterranean and even threatened Constantinople. But Bani Hashim clan and their non-Arab Muslim allies opposed Umayyad's rulers in Damascus and kept accusing them of corruption and usurping the right of the Prophet's family to lead the Muslim nation.

Leading members of the Hashimites succeeded in ending the Umayyads' rule by carrying out a bloody crude palace coup. They proposed a reconciliation banquet with all the Umayyad leaders to end the two clans' feud, and once the Umayyads arrived, they were massacred. Their rule ended tragically and a new era of Abbasids leadership started. One of the Umayyads managed to escape, went to Spain and established Islamic state there that survived hundreds of years. Supporters of the Umayyads tried to fight back, but they were defeated by an army led by Abdullah Abu al-Abbas in the 750 Battle of the Zab. Abu al-Abbas proclaimed himself the caliph and moved the capital from Syria to Iraq to be close to his constituents in Persia. Many Arabs but mostly the non-Arab Persians supported the caliphate of Abu al-Abbas, a descendant of Abbas, the youngest uncle of the Prophet.

By 762, Baghdad city was built on the Tigris River and was declared the capital of the Abbasids. The management style of the Abbasids' empire was decentralized, giving total authority to local emirs and less interference in managing their provinces. After a while, the real power became in the hands of the viziers and emirs, who were mostly non-Arab Persians and the caliphate's official role, became a mere ceremonial. In the three hundred years of the Abbasids rule, Muslims produced great intellectual, science and art heritage that was influenced and enriched by the cultures of different nations that embraced Islam. During the last century of the Abbasids era, power passed into the hands of princes and sultans, who established their own mini states, some Arab head of these states claimed they descended from the Prophet through his daughter Fatima. An independent Shi'a Fatimid dynasty was established in North Africa by Ubaid Allah al-Mahdi who gave himself the title of caliph and claimed to be a descendant of Fatima.

For more than two centuries the lines of division between Islam and Christianity were stabilized. Then in the late 11th century, Christians conquered Sicily and in 1095, Christendom launched the Crusades. For a century and a half, Christian potentates attempted to establish Christian rule in the Holy Land, even going so far as to plunder Christian Constantinople in the interests of their campaign against the Levant, but they failed. They lost their last foothold in 1291. One hundred and fifty years later, the Muslim Ottoman Turks appeared on the scene. They swept across the ME, conquering much of the Balkans as well as North Africa. The Ottomans captured Constantinople, the badly weakened capital of Orthodox Christianity in the East, in 1453, and established a new caliphate in 1517.

The Ottoman Empire was created by Turkish tribes in Anatolia, after embracing the Sunni-Islam at the turn of the 14th century it spanned more than 600 years and grew to be militarily the most powerful state of the world during the 15ᵗʰ and 16ᵗʰ centuries. Their empire covered the area from Central Europe to the Indian Ocean. About the same time other Turkish armies invaded India and founded the Mughal (or Mogul) Empire. The Ottomans besieged Vienna in 1529, but they could not take it over. They made one last push to conquer Vienna in 1683 and failed again, marking the beginning of a long retreat from their campaign against Christendum. In the course of a century, the Ottomans were transformed into "the sick man of Europe."

The rise of the West undermined both the Ottoman and Mughal empires.

After First World War, the territory of the Ottomans was, in considerable measure, divided among Western powers, and the Ottoman Empire left Islam without a core state. Since then, there has been no Islamic state that has the economic resources, the military power and the organizational competence to provide the political and religious leadership. Egypt was the mostly mentioned to take the role of Islamic leader state because it was the most populous Arab country with the leading Islamic learning institution, Al-Azhar University. Egypt's Muslim intellectuals called for reforms in the 19ᵗʰ century long before the Ottoman Empire was dismantled.

Arabia: The Birthplace of Islam and Wahhabism

Before oil was discovered in the Middle East, Arabia was viewed by the environmental specialists as one of the most forbidding regions in the world. And very few heard about Bahrain, the UAE, Kuwait, Qatar or Saudi Arabia. Saudi Arabia did not even exist then, but Muslims all over the world knew Mecca and al-Medina because they are the holiest cities of Islam.

The Prophet Muhammad of Islam was born in about A.D. 570 in the City of Mecca in Hejaz province, the mountainous region of Arabia's Red Sea coast. At the time of his birth, Arab speaking people, mostly Bedouin nomads occupied the Arabian Peninsula. Mecca's residents were settled descendants of Bedouin ancestors who occupied themselves with trade and agriculture. Agriculture in that region was not as good as in the more fertile regions of the Tigris-Euphrates (Iraq today) that was controlled by the Persians, and the Mediterranean coast to the north (Syria) which was part of the Byzantine Empire, or the Yemen to the southeast which was under the threat of domination by the African Abyssinian Empire.

The Prophet Muhammad belonged to the Arab tribe of Quraish that had founded Mecca as a trade settlement at the center of major trade routes which crossed the region and established a viable urban-mercantile economy for their city. When the Prophet was growing up, the Meccan society was structured according to the Bedouin traditions with some modification, although they were several generations separated from the nomadic pastoralist Bedouin's life. The leadership of Quraish tribe was vested in its elders who managed to avoid blood feuds by emphasizing tribal loyalties over more divisive issues. Quraish had to enter into alliances with surrounding desert tribes to ensure needed security of regions through which their trade caravans passed. Mecca was a commercial and religious center.

The Meccans won influence and respect for controlling the venerated shrines of al-Kaaba, which housed hundreds of idols including a meteorite called al-Hajar al-Aswad (the Black Stone), and drew pagan pilgrims from all around the Arabian Peninsula once a year. The pilgrims who came to Mecca to worship at al-Ka'aba, together with the merchants of the camel caravans, brought great wealth to the city. According to Islamic tradition, Mecca's history goes back to Abraham's (Ibrahim) time "when he and his son Ismael built al-Ka'aba House of Allah" around 2000 BC. When the Prophet Muhammad conquered Mecca in AD 630, he cleansed al-Ka'aba of all its idols and all the cult images, and for some unknown reasons he kept al-Hajar al-Aswad.

Since the revelation, Al-Ka'aba has been a building toward which practicing Muslims face in prayer, five times a day, and it is incumbent on every Muslim to make the pilgrimage (al-Haj) to Mecca once in their lifetime if they can afford it. These are the two spiritual components of the fundamental practices known as the "Five Pillars of Islam." Quite literally, nothing in the history of mankind has even begun to encroach upon the number of people who bow down and pray five times a day to Al-Ka'aba shrine in the mosque that lies in Mecca, if roughly half of the 1.6 billion Muslims in the world pray.

Yemen in Southern Arabia had good weather where several indigenous prosperous kingdoms and civilizations existed through millenniums, but the north of Arabia has the vast sand desert, known as the Rub' al-Khali (Empty Quarter).By the 18th century, the north was mostly home for warring Bedouin tribes roaming the desert with their camels and other live stock searching for fresh grazing fields and water for their families close to the scattered oasis. An austere form of Islamic faith that insisted on literal interpretation of al-Quran was preached by Muhammad Bin-Abdel Wahhab (1703–1792) a theologian from Najd area of Arabia. It was an austere and intolerant creed of medieval theologian Ibn Taymiyya, who was a controversially puritanical figure even in his own lifetime. Bin-Abdel Wahhab advocated a return to the original form of Islam as incorporated in the Qura'n and Hadith (traditions of the Prophet), for which he was persecuted by local religious leaders who viewed him as a threat to their power. Bin-Abdel Wahhab believed that his strict interpretation of Islam adhered to the original practice of the faith and that anyone who does not practice it is a heathen and enemy of Islam. He called for following literalist interpretations of Al-Quran and maintains that all spheres of society must be ruled according to strict Sharia law. His movement labeled all other Muslims as polytheists. What made his movement out of the mainstream was his belief that his faith is not an option it must be mandated by force.

The Wahhabi cause was embraced by Emir Muhammad bin-Saud, the rulers of Diriyah, a town located in the center of Arabia northwestern outskirts of Riyadh. Bin Saud and Abdel-Wahhab agreed to work together as a team to restore "the original teachings of Islam." From then on, the political fortunes of the Wahhabis have been closely identified with those of the Saudi dynasty. Diriyah served as the seat of the first Saudi dynasty Emirate from 1744 to 1818. It was marked by the Saudi clan alliance with the Wahhabis. The latter preached and tried to enforce their version of Islam in the region under the protection of the Saudis.

Bin Saud expanded his rule and the Wahhabi doctrine through conquests. By 1788, the Saudis succeeded in establishing the First Saudi State and enforcing the Wahhab version of Islam over Najd and much of the Peninsula including Mecca and al-Madina. The patchwork of fanatic Bedouin tribesmen called "Ikhwan" under Al-Saud protection, imbued with Wahhabi religion zeal, became too aggressive destroying early Islamic relics including the graves of the Prophet's companions in Mecca. They also invaded Iraq and destroyed Shi'a religious symbols. The rise of Wahhabi doctrine in Arabia was in significant measure a response to changing circumstances of the time. The long, slow retreat of the Ottomans and the advance of Christianity in the Balkans and the rise of Sufism in India under the British were felt in Arabia through the pilgrims who came to Arabia from all over the world every year.

The coercive actions of the Wahhabis under their Al-Saud allies aroused the wrath of the Ottomans when their armed tribesmen raided the Iraqi city of Karbala, a holy city of the Shi'a branch of Islam, and demolished shrines and tombs of early Islamic figures because Wahhabism prohibits the veneration of dead people. The Ottomans, the dominant power in the ME dispatched a large Egyptian expeditionary force under Ibrahim Pasha, armed with heavy artillery, to Arabia in 1818. It besieged Diriyah, the Saudi center of power and leveled the city with field guns and made it permanently uninhabitable. The Egyptian army defeated the Wahhabi armed bands and their Saudi tribal allies, and put an end to the Saudi Emirate of Diriyah.

It took the Saudi dynasty six years to recover from its defeat and restore its power over tribes in Najd. Turki bin Abdullah Al-Saud and his son Faysal established the Second Saudi State with its capital in Riyadh in 1824. Under their leadership, the Saudis and their tribal allies recovered most of the land lost to the Ottomans in Najd, but not al-Hejaz area that included the Islamic holy shrines of Mecca and Madina which were under the guardianship of the Hashemite family under the protection of the Ottomans.

After two decades of their Second State rule in Riyadh, the Saudis were challenged by another Najd clan, Al-Rashid, rulers of the Emirate of Jabal Shammar. For years, Al-Rashid tribe, a formidable enemy of the House of Saud, supported by the Ottomans fought the Saudis over the control of Najd, and finally Al-Rashid won the tribal wars they overthrew the second Saudi Emirate, and Abdul-Rahman Al-Saud and his family were forced to flee to Kuwait in 1891. For twenty-one years, al-Saud family was a refugee in Kuwait under the protection of al-Sabbah family. Najd region in center Arabian Peninsula was ruled by al-Rashid family of Hail from the City of Riyadh and in West Arabia, Hejaz region had local autonomy from the Ottomans under the Hashemite family in Mecca.

In 1902, the young Abdul-Aziz al-Saud came from Kuwait with forty of his tribesmen and staged a daring attack at night into the town of Riyadh. He executed the ruling members of al-Rashid clan in their compound and declared himself Sultan Abdul-Aziz al-Saud, the ruler of Najd. It took Abdul-Aziz two decades to consolidate his control over Najd using many strategies including marriage diplomacy in hostile tribes to have their loyalties as in-laws.

After World War I, When the senior Hashemite and the guardians of the Islamic holy shrines of Mecca, Sharif Hussein Ben-Ali who was declared "King of Hejaz," refused to accept the British Balfour Declaration commitment to support the establishment of a national home for the Jewish people in Palestine, the British abandoned him. They supported his rival, Sultan Abdul-Aziz al-Saud of Najd, in his war to conquer Sharif Hussein's kingdom in 1924. Abdul-Aziz united Najd and Hejaz under his family rule, declared himself a king and on September 23, 1932, the country was named the Kingdom of Saudi Arabia. He established the kingdom as an Islamic state with Arabic as its official language and al-Quran as its constitution. Al-Quran and the Sunni of the 7th century remain subject to different interpretations but the Kingdom follows 18th century al-Wahhabi doctrine.

King Abdul-Aziz presided over the discovery of petroleum in his country in 1938 and the beginning of large scale production after World War II. Britain was the first country to recognize Saudi Arabia as independent state and provided protection of the Saudi territory from any foreign power. And when oil was discovered and Ibn-Saud granted a concession to the US

Standard Oil of California to explore for oil in his country, the US extended full diplomatic recognition of Saudi Arabia. The February 14, 1945 meeting between King Abdul-Aziz and President Franklin D. Roosevelt onboard the US Navy cruiser Quincy in the Great Bitter Lake of the Suez Canal was the foundation of the close relationship between the two countries. The two countries have been allies since then despite stark clash of values between the two countries, the ultra-conservative Islamic absolute monarchy, and the US secular constitutional republic. The cooperation between the US and the Saudis peaked in the 1991 first Gulf War when more than half a million US troops flooded the region to expel Iraqi forces from Kuwait, with majority based in Saudi Arabia. The US has increased sales of military arms significantly and provided training and advisors to the Saudis after the Gulf wars. Common economic, security, and geopolitical interests are likely to maintain strong ties between the two countries for the foreseeable future.

Abdul-Aziz headed a polygamous household comprising more than twenty-two wives from different tribes. He also arranged for his sons to enter into marriages from noble clans of different tribes. Abdul-Aziz had 45 sons of whom 36 survived to adulthood and had children of their own, and he had more than 40 daughters. Many of his sons served in prominent leadership positions in Saudi Arabia including six of the nation's monarchs since his death. The Saudi royal family today is perhaps the largest in the world and its net worth according to June 2015 Forbs was estimated at well over $1.4 trillion. Their vast numbers allow them to control most of the kingdom's important posts and be involved at all levels of government.

The alliance and the power sharing between Abdul-Aziz and the descendants of ibn-Abdel-Wahhab (the Sheikh family) remained strong. The Wahhabis legitimize the political power of the House of Saud by approving succession and endorsing the king's decisions and the Sheikh family enjoys a privileged position by controlling the Ministry of Islamic Affairs, the Ministry of Education and the "Committee for Promotion of Virtue and Prevention of Vice." The Wahhabis tried to demolish the historic sites of shrines, homes and graves of the Prophet's companions in Mecca and Medina because they reject the practice of venerating saints. Only the outcry of Muslims around the world prevented them.

The Saudis established a tribal aristocracy of the royal family and their allies in the ultraconservative Wahhabi religious leadership. It has been conferring status and wealth on members of their clan and limited the political participation outside the royal family. Citizens can petition the king directly while he holds traditional public meetings known as the "majlis."

The Saudi regime does not accommodate religious diversity or religious expression other than its Wahhabi version of Islam.

Saudi Arabia today thrives on its links to Islam under the House of Saud which does not have a pedigree to the Prophet's tribe like the Hashemite of Jordan or the royal family of Morocco who claim to be descendants of the Prophet. The Saudis claim to Islamic leadership due to their control of the two holiest towns in Islam, Mecca and Medina since they threw out the Hashemite from Hejaz Province in 1932. Following criticism from some Islamic groups, the Saudi king changed his official title to "Custodian of the Two Holy Places."

Saudi Arabia openly discriminates against a sizable minority of its citizens who follow the Islamic-Shi'a tradition, because of their religious belief. The Saudis limit their political participation and civil liberties, and deprive them of economic prosperity. Shi'a religious public expressions are often forbidden or allowed only within the Wahhabi-Sunni interpretation of Islam. The government even restricts the names that Shi'a can use for their children, and public school textbooks often characterize the Shi'a faith as a form of heresy.

More than one million Christians of all denominations from many countries work in Saudi Arabia for the government and private companies, but they are not allowed to build churches and practice their faith openly. Items belonging to religions other than Islam such as crucifixes, status, carvings, bibles and other publications are prohibited in Saudi Arabia. Christians and other non-Muslims are not allowed to enter the city of Mecca and the central district of Medina. In the pursuit of the Wahhabis' strict interpretation of Islam, conversion to other religions is punishable by death. But no such a punishment has been reported in the Kingdom.

The Saudis created a true theocratic Islamic state as laid down in their interpretation of "Wahhabi-Sunni traditions." It is against other interpretation of Islam and against secularism and democracy. Islam never established clergy, and yet senior religious figures "ulama" can issue edicts or "fatwas" that have legal power in Saudi Arabia. They insist that the Islamic state does not need codified laws because the laws and punishments are found in al-Quran and the oral tenets of Islam. This allows the Islamic court judges to be free to improvise charges such as "breaking allegiances with the ruler" or in the case of the 2017 executed Shi'a cleric, "seeking foreign meddling." Issued "fatwas" decide individual cases, and with the absence of democratic institutions, the Saudi government has been using them to legitimize its policies.

Saudi Arabia is still governed as an absolute tribal monarchy that King Abdul-Aziz established in 1932, but with more regional and international power due to the oil rental wealth. With the discovery of oil, Saudi Arabia and the rest of the Gulf States underwent fast social and consumption economic restructuring. These countries were once the poorest in the world, but quickly became one of the wealthiest in the Arab world after the discovery of massive oil reserves.

Despite imposing rigid adherence to a strict version of Islam on their subjects, some Saudi princes became fixtures at high-rolling pleasure capitals like Monte Carlo and Paris. Princes and princesses, of whom there are thousands, are known for the stories of their lavish lifestyles and tendency to squander wealth. Saudi royals use many ways to accumulate wealth the most common is the formal government budgeted system of monthly stipends that every Saudi royal receives. The share of Saudi budget that ultimately makes its way into royal coffers has never been disclosed by the government. There are other money-making schemes including cozy government contracts and siphoning off money from sponsoring expatriate workers who then pay a monthly fee to their royal patron. Princes and princesses have privileges like royal special hospital wings decorated like palaces, free first class travel on Saudi airlines, and royal airport terminals with chandeliers, intricate tile-work and rich carpet.

Willie Morris, who served as the British ambassador to Saudi Arabia from 1968 to 1972 wrote: "The Saudi family regards Saudi Arabia as a family business and the rest of the world as existing for their convenience." The Saudi royal family is viewed internationally as the most corrupt in the world and ironically, it is the most influential government in all Islam primarily because it is the custodian of the holiest places of Islam. It is the host of the annual pilgrimage which brings millions of Muslims from all parts of the world to share in its rituals.

The outward flow of oil and the inward flow of money brought immense changes to the Saudi Kingdom, its internal structure and way of life. It increased its external role and influence, both in the oil consuming countries and in the Muslim world. The most significant change was in the impact of Wahhabi-Islam and the role of its protagonists. Saudi Arabia has been spending much on spreading the 18th century Islamic tribal doctrine as an ideology by building and maintaining thousands of large, fancy and expensive mosques around the world. Scholars educated in Saudi Arabia's Sharia schools spread their Wahhabi ideology in their sermons and contributed over time to more conservative and more intolerant atmosphere. This has been fuelled by growing Saudi hegemony in the Islamic world due to its oil riches and boosted by the supposed "threat of Shi'a Islam." The Salafi movement, as the Wahhabis prefer to be called, is gaining ground in many countries with Islamic majority. According to the US State Department, beginning in the 1970s, Saudi Arabia has invested more than $10 billion into charitable foundations in an attempt to replace mainstream Sunni Islam with the harsh intolerant Wahhabism, and as a result, the movement underwent worldwide "explosive growth."

Since the days of its modern-day founder, the ultimate power in Saudi Arabia rests upon House of Saud family members. The king has absolute powers as head of the state and head of the government he appoints the ministers who manage their respective ministries in his name ministers of defense, the interior, foreign affairs, most of the thirteen regional governorships and high ranking military officers are always held by members of the royal family. Decisions are made after consultation among a group of senior Saudi family princes. Tribes' leaders in the country swear allegiance to the Saudi clan, and there is no citizens' participation through the ballot box. Saudi Arabia is the only Arab country that its government rejects Western democracy openly. The preeminence of the religious establishment made Saudi Arabia the most conservative state in the region. It has a large religious police force enforcing the strict Wahhabi codes of public behavior including observance of Islamic rituals and gender segregation. Justice, education, and family matters are handled by "the religious establishment" under the control of "al-Sheikh" family, the decedents of the founder of the Wahhabi doctrine, one of the most influential religious leaders and theologians in modern history.

Early Reformers

For centuries, the Arab world under the Ottomans suffered from isolation and lack of intellectual progress and scientific innovation while the Europeans were disengaging themselves from the spiritual hold of Rome and embarking upon the challenging road of freedom. The isolation came to an end with Napoleon invasion of Egypt in 1798 when the young general and his expeditionary force were able to conquer, occupy and rule the country. There had been, before this, attacks, retreats, and losses of territory on the remote frontiers. But for a small Western force to invade one of the heartlands of majority-Muslim countries was a profound shock. The departure of the French was, in a sense, an even greater shock. They were forced to leave Egypt not by the Egyptians, nor by their suzerains the Turks, but by a small squadron of British Royal Navy, commanded by a young admiral named

Horatio Nelson. Not only could a Western power arrive, invade, and rule at will but only another Western power could get it out. Egyptian Muslims were alarmed when the resistance against the French invaders was crushed, their country was exploited, their political freedom was in peril and their culture including their faith was threatened.

At the height of the debate on the impact of adopting Western beliefs and ideas on Islamic culture, some intellectual Egyptians felt disturbed by the effects of Westernization, the rise of secularism and the devaluation of traditional Islamic morals. The advent of Christian missionary at the same time strengthened this belief and Islam became a rallying call for existence and an instrument of protest against foreign invasion. Arab intellectuals blamed the Ottomans for the decline of the Muslims.

The Ottoman Empire that was created by Turkish tribes in Anatolia after embracing the Sunni-Islam at the turn of the 14th century spanned more than 600 years and grew to be militarily the most powerful state of the world during the 15th and 16th centuries. Their Empire covered the area from Central Europe to the Indian Ocean. It came to an end after its defeat in World War One by France and Great Britain and signing the 1920 Treaty of Sèvres and the 1923 Treaty of Lausanne. Turkey renounced all rights over Arab Asia and North Africa and provided for an independent Armenia, for a Greek presence in eastern Thrace and on the Anatolian west coast, as well as Greek control over the Aegean Islands, and for a possibility of a Kurdish state. Modern Arab states, Israel, and the Republic of Turkey have been created after the overthrow of the Turkish monarchy by **Kemal Ataturk**. Arab states' borders, their rulers and their form of governments were decided by the British and the French colonialists after the collapse of the Ottoman Empire. Arab reformers, especially in Egypt, home of al-Azhar University, the center of the Islamic education, have been debating the future of political Islam in their countries even before the collapse of the Ottoman regime when it was described as "the sick man of Europe."

Muslims were awakened from their medieval slumber and demanded the modernization of the Islamic institutions, and the role Islam plays in politics has become a hotly contested issue in the Arab World. Reformers started discussing how Islam can accommodate science and philosophy and how Muslims could live in a modern socio-political environment without losing their identity. They questioned whether Islam accepts replacing the traditional institutions of "Shura" and the authority of the elite "Ulama" with modern political institutions such as democracy, elections and parliaments.

The Persian-born Muslim activist and journalist Jamal ud-Deen Al-Afghani (1838–1897) was considered the founder of the first movement to modernize Islam. His belief in the power of the Islamic civilization in the face of European domination had influenced the development of the Muslim thought in the nineteenth and early 20th centuries. He called for an end to all traditional religious theories and interpretations that might stand in the way of Muslim unity and for a modern understanding of Islam that would inculcate the virtues of modern science and technology. He sought to unite the Muslim world under the banner of the Faith capable of withstanding Western encroachments. He was less interested in theology than in organizing a Muslim response to Western pressure. He sought to revive Islamic civilization in the face of European domination by founding a pan-Islamic movement in the late 19th century. Al-Afghani blamed Islam devastating state when its adherents lost their philosophical spirit and yielded to the European accord with science. He blamed the Abbasid Caliphs and the Ottomans after them who ceased to encourage scholars and those trained in religious matter to exercise free thinking (ijtihad). Al-Afghani believed that science is the reason for the success of nations and that science has no religious boundaries. When al-Afghani started spreading his philosophical and political ideas through classes and public lectures, the Khedive Tawfiq and the British considered him a political agitator propagating republicanism in Egypt. They ordered his expulsion from the country.

Al-Afghani mentored the Egyptian scholar and liberal reformer, Muhammad Abdo (1849–1905). Abdo is considered one of the first and most liberal reformers of the Arab world. His status as a Grand Mufti was the primary factor in his success to influence the reform of the nation's exclusive al-Azhar University. His famous intellectual work was "the Theology of University" including the chapter on "Islam, Reason and Civilization" that summarized his reforms. He incorporated secular subjects, such as philosophy, science including Darwin work and literature into the university curriculum. Abdo considered the study of logic and similar disciplines essential to life in this age against foreign aggression and for the defense of Islam. He also established on-site hospital devoted to research. Abdo believed the form of the Western parliamentary system was suitable to the needs of Egypt.

Ahmad Lutfi as-Sayyid (1872–1963), a journalist, a lawyer and the first director of Cairo University, was a leading spokesman for Egyptian secularism and liberalism in the first half of the 20th century. He was against pan-Arabism, pan-Islamic, and pan-Ottoman ideologies, and he insisted that the Egyptians were not Arabs. He believed in equality and rights for all people regardless of their religion, ethnicity and gender. During his presidency of

Cairo University, he encouraged women to enroll in all academic majors. He translated and introduced to the Egyptians the works of his favorite philosophers, Aristotle, John Stuart Mill, Herbert Spencer, and Jean Jacques Rousseau.

Muhammad Rashid Rida (1865–1935), a Syrian disciple of Muhammad Abdo and a journalist, was concerned with preserving Muslim identity and culture while disseminating reformist ideas. He called for reform based on the right interpretation of al-Quran, the Sunni and consensus. Rida promoted the idea of Western type democracy by calling for establishing organized civil political institutions that restrict the power of the government.

The Muslim Brotherhood (MB)

The Egyptian scholar and a pan-Islamic advocate Hasan Al-Banna (1906–1949) was worried about where the Islamic beliefs were headed under the expected culture changes especially after reading the writings of the Islamic reformers Muhammad Abdo, Ahmad as-Sayyid and the Syrian journalist Rashid Rida (1865–1935). He was deeply concerned about the Islamic traditions In Egypt by what he saw in Ismailliyya, a city heavily influenced by the British presence, when he took a school teaching job in the city in 1927. Ismailliyya was home for the headquarters of the British military in Egypt since First World War and of the Suez Canal Company since the waterway was under construction in 1859. Western beliefs and traditions began to enter Egypt under the call for modernity and Al-Banna did not like it. He felt that reviving the waning Islamic culture and civilization was the means to secure its survival throughout the Muslim world. In 1928, Al-Banna and a small group of supporters pledged to live and die for Islam and established the "MB" organization. His charisma and conviction inspired others to listen to him, and by 1936, his organization became a movement and expand to most Egyptian provinces. Al-Banna was assassinated by an alleged Egyptian government agent in Cairo, but his organization has survived and played a major role in the politics of Egypt and other Arab countries.

Both Lutfi as-Sayyid, the architect of modern Egyptian secular liberal nationalism, as well as the militant Islamic fundamentalist Hasan al-Banna of the MB were inspired by Islam but they differed in their conclusions. Hasan al-Banna argued that Islam possessed a complete system of social life that includes equality, freedom, social security and justice. But Lutfi as-Sayyid was against religion as a base for nationhood and advocated the assimilation of Western civilization.

A radical wing of the Brotherhood led by Sayyid Qutb (1906–1966) broke away and followed a violent path in dealing with its political opponents. Qutb was an author, Islamic theorist and a teacher by profession the big event in his life that impacted his views about Western culture and the future of Muslims was a 1949 three-year scholarship in Colorado State Teachers College in the US. He observed in his book, The America I Have Seen, how he viewed Western culture: materialistic and greedy, lacking morality and spirituality. He rejected Western democracy and secularism and he leveled criticism at the condition of the Muslim world. When Qutb returned to Egypt in 1951, he joined the MB and in a short time he became the head of the Brotherhood's public relations department.

Following the assassination attempts on President Jamal Abdel Nasser's life by Brotherhood members, the organization was banned and Qutb was arrested. He was convicted and executed for plotting to kill the Egyptian president. His followers believe he died a martyr. While in jail, Qutb wrote and smuggled his most famous book "Maalim-Fi-al-Tariq (Milestones) outlines his plan for political jihad (war) that would lead to Islam's global power. He advocated the establishment of believers to lead a war against Jahilyya, a state of ignorance similar to the conditions that existed in Arabia before the Prophet Muhammad's message which introduced the religion of Islam to the world. Qutb's ideas might have constituted the inspiration for the formation of the 1980s radical Islamist groups, such as, Jihad, Jamaat al-Muslimun and al-Qaeda.

By the early 1990s, the MB in Egypt had developed an extensive network of organizations that filled a vacuum left by the government, provided health, welfare, educational, and other services to a large number of Egypt's poor. After the 1992 earthquake in Cairo, members of the MB were on the streets within hours, handing out food and blankets while the government's relief effort lagged. The political manifestations of the MB have been less pervasive than its social and cultural manifestation, but it was the single most important political development in Egypt.

2. Arab Tribalism

Tribalism is "the loyalty to a tribe or other social or political group combined with strong negative feelings for people outside the group." A tribe is a form of limited social organization with its own culture, ethics, system of justice and politics whose interests are primarily focused on its own members and territory. Its members are united by blood, or religion, or political ideology, or other common interests they may fear other tribes and often fight them.

Tribalism based on ethnic differences, common language and culture is the pernicious ideology that afflicts all human societies in every time. When a group feels threatened or mistreated, they retreat into tribalism by closing ranks and become more defensive, more insular and more us-versus-them.

Nationalism is a universal form of tribalism, but the danger of tribalism is when members of the tribe accept the notion that they as individuals are helpless, intellectually and morally, and their only moral significance lies in selfless service to the tribe. Tribalism, then, controls behavior and overrides reason. It lets people feel their tribe is better than the others, closes minds to views that conflict with the beliefs of the group with which they identify. The more the tribe's views are challenged, the more its members defend them and the more they become closed-minded. If there is no change then the group is locked into a kin-based system for all time there can be no modernity, no progress and no future. Tribalism and sectarianism are roots of racism and human rights violations.

Arab nomadic Bedouin tribesmen had no home to fight for, no country to defend, and no central government to look after them, but they had to survive. Arab desert tribes' livelihood was based on camel herding. People and their animals existed in a symbiotic relationship where the camels supplied much of the food and other needs of the tribe while the tribes-people assured the animal's survival by leading them to adequate pasturage. This required knowledge of the land and the environment and a flexible social structure. Arab tribal social structure was based on the ramification of patrilineal ties among men. Arab desert nomad and semi-nomad tribes, who learnt the hard way to live with nature and the harsh conditions of the environment, find themselves sometimes in conflict with other tribes over the scarce resources.

Before the emergence of nation-states, Arab tribes used to raid other tribes, caravans of merchants or even pilgrims. One of the core mechanisms of Bedouin socio-economic-culture systems was institutionalized raiding practice (ghazu'), as a major factor in the persistence of their society regardless of its deplorable immoral piracy and pillaging traits. According to the Bedouin culture, non-lethal raids were necessary practices prosecuted mutually among tribes and against settled communities and trading caravans. They were supposed to be predatory mainly for camels and must avoid destruction of human life and did not seize territory permanently.

The minimal camping unit of the tribe, often called clan (Ashirah), is comprised of a group of same paternal-lineage. One lineage of the same clan ranks above others as the chiefly lineage, and the chief is chosen from its men. Members of the group are closely concerned with mutual aid and defense of the camel herds they regularly mark their camels with a common brand of the clan and regularly organize and prosecute raids (ghazu') on other tribes' herds.

What sets the camel breeding Bedouin tribes from other societies is the structure of rank lineages of tribes, some are noble (aseel)-and-dominant and others are not-noble-and-subordinate, based on exclusive descent ranks. And within the tribe, there is total control by the chief. The Aseel Bedouin of North Arabia are not supported by the productive labor of subordinate tribes in the sense of stratified agrarian societies. Both are independent camel breeding societies, but the power and prestige acquired by the Aseel tribes depend upon their "wealth," their great camel herds and means of maintaining them at full strength. The tribes who have been fluctuating between cultivating and desert pastoral are not acknowledged to be Aseel. So as the shepherd tribes like the Shararat, Hutaym and Awazim, whose animals are primarily sheep and goats and whose camel wealth is small, are among the desert people who are subservient to the camel Bedouin, pay tribute or provide services in return for security.

Arabia's desert-dwelling, nomadic pastoralist Bedouin tribes infused the Middle East region with a deeply tribal culture, impacting everything from family relations to governance and conflicts. During the six hundred years of

Ottoman rule, only big towns in the Levant, Arabia and even in north Africa were under direct Ottoman control and the rest of the territories were under the nomadic tribes' rule. Nomadic pastoral Bedouin tribes specializing in camel breeding have been living in the Arabian Peninsula desert for centuries, probably over millennia, as autonomous segmented societies of kinsmen. They controlled primarily desert pasturages and wells, routes crossing their territories, the small oases and some major oases. Most prominent among them have been the Anazah group of tribes of the Hamad in northern Arabia, south Iraq and Syrian Desert, the Shammar tribes of Northern Najd, the Mutair and Ajman of the east near Kuwait and al-Hasa, and Beni Sakhr in Jordan. These were known as the aseel (noble) Arabs, that is, they have positions in the great traditional scheme of Arabian tribal genealogies which distinguish them from non-aseel Arab. The ruling family of Saudi Arabia belongs to Anazah tribe.

During the 7th century, the Islamic religious and political culture was reinforced in the military conquest. The armies of Islam marched out from the Arabian Peninsula and moved on to conquer the homelands of the Middle East nations. Within forty years, they conquered the Byzantine states of Syria, Palestine and Lebanon, the Sassanid Empire in Iraq they took over Egypt and reached the shores of the Atlantic. They brought with them their Arabic language, Islamic religion, their calendar and the culture of tribalism. The recruits of the invading Muslim armies were members of federations of Arabia's tribal groups. Their soldiers were not paid like modern armies. Their only material rewards came from the spoils of war, exactly like the spoils of the tribal raids (ghazu') that were practiced in the Arabian Peninsula. Their armies achieved astonishing military success, but the real victor in the conquest was Islam and the Arab cultures, not the war-lords. The power of Islam and the Arab culture was separate from and more permanent than those of the armies with which they came. Its administration by the first generation of simple and honest men like Caliph Omar ibn al-Khattab was preferable to the corruption that was the norm in the aging Byzantine and Sassanid empires. After the death of al-Khattab, the young Muslim federation came under the strain of tribalism that became a major component of their political identity.

Tribalism is evident in all the Arab states whose history is largely a chronicle of tribal conflicts, invasions and dynastic replacements. The pervasive and continuous conflicts in the Arab world between clans, tribes and "religious groups" today are manifestation of a tribal culture that does not seem to accept modern organizing principles such as constitutionalism and rule of law. Tribalism was justified as a culture of survival in the desert when families banded together to find water and grazing lands for their flocks. Once they established the resources through collective effort, they set up boundaries to protect them from outsiders and restrict membership. But the role of tribalism today in local political order has become an integral element of Arab countries conflicts. It is a powerful player in the civil wars and insurgencies and it is a key part of the counter-insurgency. In failing Arab states such as Iraq, Libya and Yemen, tribalism threatens the rebuilding of nations by contributing to rapid decline of nationalism once the sates are collapsing. But in non-failed states such as Jordan and the Gulf states, tribalism has sustained both the social power of the tribes and the political stability of the regimes.

Arabs' response to their increasingly chaotic world is to think of their tribe upon which they depend. The Arabs today are doing what they have been doing since time immemorial, living in a state of perpetual tribal conflicts. The only difference now is that the Arabs are feuding in big cities and across borders, not only in the deserts. State-building elites took the traditional tribalism, adapted it to the new realities especially in oil rich renter states, and clocked it in national sovereignty.

The Syrian tribes are interlinked in a web of tribal relations from Syria to Iraq to the Gulf States. They originated in the Arabian Peninsula and moved north centuries ago in search of water and grazing areas. The largest is the Egaidat tribal confederation with more than 1.75 million people across 40% of Syria's territory that has links to the tribes in Saudi Arabia, Kuwait and Qatar.

When the Arab Spring uprising erupted in Syria, different countries in the region established close relations with individuals or groups in the opposition. Turkey for one, hosted the Sunni Free Syrian Army France played host for defected Sunni-Muslims military officers including General Manaf Tlass the Syrian tribes in Dera'a appealed to their "cousins" in the Gulf to help them. The Gulf States stance against Assad regime has been driven by the tribes' ties and the competition with Iran. Syria's Alawite tribe is trying hard to sustain its control over the country. Shi'a Revolutionary Guards and Shi'a volunteers from Iran, Iraq, Afghanistan and Lebanese Hezbollah-Shi'a have been fighting and dying in support of the Syrian Alawite-Shi'a tribe regime.

The Palestinians were not immune from internal cleavage along tribal and familial demarcation even while struggling against colonialism. After World War I and the Balfour Declaration to establish "national home" for the Jewish people in Palestine, the indigenous Palestinians were led by competing prominent families rather than unified national movement. The influential Jerusalem families of Husseinis and Nashashibis that had achieved prominence during the Ottoman era maintained their leadership role under the British mandate. The two clans with their political power bases in towns and villages created their own tribes fighting each other during the Mandate period. The lasting split caused by their rivalry was among the factors which contributed to the failure of the 1936 rebellion and the stalling of the national movement. It was the internal fight between these two clans that prevented the Palestinians from creating national institutions in anticipation of their future state when the British mandate ended. The Palestinians in the occupied lands today have not learnt their lessons. They are divided into two political groups, the Islamists and the seculars. Relations between the two rivals are tense and at times erupted into deadly conflict. And under Abbas leadership, Fatah faction of the PLO is divided into two hostile groups based on personal conflicts, one headed by Abbas and the other by Dahlan.

3. The US and the Arab Spring in Tunisia

The US intervened on the side of the rebels in oil-rich Libya against Gaddafi's regime, supported the counter-Arab-Spring military coup in Egypt against the democratically elected MB government, and sided with the oil-rich Saudi Arabia and the Gulf States regimes in the war against the rebels in Yemen.

The 2011 anti-Gaddafi coalition that established a provisional government in Benghazi with the ultimate goal of overthrowing Gaddafi's must have been a CIA creation. The US policy makers never liked Gaddafi, and as a member of the multi-state NATO led coalition air-force targeting Libyan government security units, the US sided with the rebels and helped them capture al-Gaddafi and execute him. But once Gaddafi fell, chaos and conflicts plagued Libya, the terrorist organizations in the ME raided the country's abundant supply of different conventional weapons. They became more violent, killing more people and staging more low intensity guerrilla warfare.

When the Arab Spring uprisings broke up in Syria, the US decided to do as little as possible. It displayed passivity when Iran, then Russia, filled the void in support of the regime. The US has expanded its illegal military presence in the north and south of Syria supporting the Kurds and some secular rebel groups and foreign mercenaries sent by Syria's rivals against the elected government of Bashar al-Assad. The US and its allies have been bonbing Syria since 2014, targeting what it has called ISIS and other Jihadist groups. The US under President Trump staged a one-time missile attack on a Syrian military air-base in retaliation for using nerve gas against the rebel areas. The missile attack was "not a harbinger of some change in the US military campaign" according to Defense Secretary Jim Mattis. The war and the chaos that weakened the Syrian state was acceptable to the US and

Israel, even at the expense of giving Russia a foothold in the region. Syria officially requested that Russia intervene to help it defend its sovereignty in the face of these attacks, and it refused to have a peace treaty with Israel.

The Gulf mini-states and Saudi Arabia are virtual US colonies, and Egypt and Jordan are US satellites invested in the protection of Israel for billions of dollars annually. The US Navy's Fifth Fleet is headquartered in Bahrain and it has al-Udeid Airbase in Qatar and Camp Arifjan in Kuwait. The US would prefer stability over uprisings, turmoil and chaos in these countries to make sure the oil production is not interrupted and the peace treaties with Israel are not revoked. As allies, it would support them with intelligence about the protesters and foreign interference and provide them with military advisors. Armed US military are stationed in north Jordan on the borders with Syria and Iraq to protect Jordan from the infiltration of rebels. US military monitors the situation in Syria on the ground and advises Jordan's military. The US provided Jordan's government with hundreds of millions of dollars in financial aid during the Arab Spring, maintained the military aid to Egypt and supported its military coup.

In Yemen, the US had been exploiting the power vacuum in the country to wage a covert war against terror organizations linked to al-Qaeda using drones and fighter jets long before the Arab Spring started. These military operations were among the Obama administration's most closely held secrets to protect Yemen's President Saleh's standing among his people. It was all coordinated with the CIA teams in Sana'a, the capital of Yemen. At the approval of President Obama in 2011, American drone aircraft fired missiles and killed the radical American-born fugitive Anwar al-Awlaki who was on the run in Yemen's tribal area. The US would not support an uprising against Saleh. After the Arab Spring, and the fall of Ali Abdullah Saleh's regime, the US has been in bed with the Saudi coalition, supporting its war on Yemen.

The military coup against the MB elected government must have been planned by the CIA and Israel's Mossad, and executed by Abdel-Fattah Sisi. The first action by the Egyptian military after the coup was closing the tunnels that were supplying Gaza with smuggled civilian needs and military weapons. The tunnels had been Israel's main grievances against Egypt's Husni Mubarak regime.

Hypocrisy and double standards are the principles of the US policy-makers, before and after the Arab Spring. Democracy is promoted but not if it brings Islamic fundamentalists to power in Egypt or the Palestinian Authority. Nonproliferation is preached for Iran but not for Israel. Human rights are an issue with China, but not with Saudi Arabia, the Gulf States, and Israel. Aggression against oil-owning Kuwaitis is repulsed but not against non-oil owning Bosnians. That is why the US is likely to continue having difficulties defending its interests against those of the ME societies. This is an observation, not in defense of any undemocratic regime or abuser of human rights.

The Arab Spring in Tunisia:

In Tunisia, the government was overthrown on Jan 14, 2011 President Zin al-Abidine Bin Ali went into exile and free elections for a Constituent Assembly were held on October 23 of the same year. A new constitution and a compromise politics between Islamist and secular parties helped Tunisia avoid the turmoil seen in other Arab nations. Compared to the other Arab states, only Tunisia's revolution achieved a consensual democracy with competing parties, free elections and the losing parties conceded. Three rounds of free elections took place and democratically elected assembly passed a progressive constitution and sweeping bills on economic liberalization.

The transition was smooth, where regime change was civil and without the military involvement the old armed forces survived and provided a bridge between the new and the old. Its refusal to fire on protesters ensured that the old order was co-opted rather than purged. The Constitutional Democratic Rally (RCD) Party, which had ruled Tunisia since independence in 1956, was dissolved, but only a few of its senior members were put on trial for alleged corruption. Others, including Bin Ali himself, were allowed to flee into exile, and revenge killings were remarkably rare.

Tunisia made the transition to a functioning democracy in which citizens have political rights and civil liberties. To end alleged torture and ill-treatment in police custody, the parliament elected a sixteen-member "High Authority Commission" in 2016 with the mandate to conduct inspections of detention centers and recommend reforms. Post-Arab Spring Tunisia-Constitution liberalized the press code, eliminated most of the penalties these laws impose on speech offenses. The media can now scrutinize the behavior of government officials and bring government corruption to light, but some Tunisian activists claimed that the media was only "partly freed" because some provisions of the Constitution have been presented in vague language and broad terms.

The dictatorship has disappeared and the transition has been good, but not perfect. The new Constitution left unchanged the articles in the penal Code of the Military Justice that impose up to three years in prison as punishment for some speech offenses. Penal code articles that criminalize "insulting a public official" allow the police to prosecute and prison individuals for arguing with law enforcement police. Five years after the transition, many journalists including the online journalist Moez Jemai and the blogger Lina Ben Mhenni were prosecuted for alleged "insulting the police" charges. There were isolated violent clashes and social unrest in Tunisia after the uprising and two opposition leaders were assassinated in 2013, but the confrontations did not lead to a civil war as in other Arab countries.

When Ben Ali left after the uprising, his regime did not fall just because of his departure. That was the beginning of a long process. There was systematic effort to replace the corrupt regime and devise a new constitutional order which succeeded because there was a measure of trust between the different parties involved. Factors that made it possible for Tunisia to make the transition to a multiparty democracy included the passive role of its military, the involvement of civil society institutions and the influence of the French culture on middle class Tunisians. Tunisia does not have oil that draws foreign interference, the army is known for its traditional apolitical ethos, and its middle class has great affinity and understanding of the French democracy.

The other important factor was the role of the political parties. The two major parties, the secular al-Nida Tounes and the mainstream Islamist Ennahda movement established close relationship based on cooperation rather than confrontation after Ennahda separated its politics from its religious ideology. Its leadership tried to distinguish their party from other Islamic organizations by dropping the Islamic ideology from its platform and focus exclusively on politics, economic and technocratic issues. Ennahda won the first post-Arab-Spring elections by appealing to majority of Tunisians who recognized its Islamic identity even without the Islamic ideology as an antidote to decades of repression and corruption under the region's most secular regime. Since its independence from France in 1956, Tunisia dominated by two long-standing autocratic rulers, Habib Bourguiba and Zain a-Abidin Bin Ali. It went through a process of state-led secular social reform and became socially-progressive country, but politically authoritarian and repressive toward the Islamists.

Long before the 2011 Arab Spring, unlike other fundamental Islamic groups, Ennahda Party had been developing in a democratic direction in concert with other political parties and civil societies. In the 2014 elections, Ennahda lost and immediately conceded. Once Ghannouchi, accepted the voters' verdict, he provided the political model that the Arab world had not seen in generations.

The Labor Union (UGTT), the Tunisian Trade, Industry and Handicrafts Union (UTICA), the Tunisian Human Rights League (LADH) and Tunisian Order of Lawyers launched the National Dialogue (ND) and signed the Social Pact for peaceful transformation in the country. The ND was recognized by the international community as a major factor in the peaceful transition and was awarded the Nobel Peace Prize for playing a significant role in drafting the Tunisian National Constitution and adopting in 2013 the Law on Establishing and Organizing Transitional Justice that was a crucial part in the democratic transition of the country.

The law established the Truth and Dignity Commission (TDC) to investigate the state crimes and human rights abuses committed since the period before the revolution going back as far as the rule of Habib Bourguiba. A commission elected by the National Constitutional Assembly held public hearings and gave victims of the former regimes' atrocities a platform to share their stories and demand justice. It received 62,065 complaints from people alleging human rights abuses, and in November of 2014, the TDC held the first public hearings of victims of human rights violations, but justice has been too slow. After five years since the ex-President Ben Ali overthrow, authorities have failed to hold major former officials accountable for the politically motivated imprisonment and torture of thousands of victims during his tenure.

Despite its political success, the revolution fell short in creating stable conditions and solving the economic and security issues that impacted the daily life of the Tunisians. The country marked its first anniversary with many protests against inflation, unemployment and corruption instead of celebrations. And the 2014 attacks on two tourist destinations, Sousse and Bardo Museums led to less foreign investment and decline in tourism which constitutes important source of revenue for the state, causing a rise in unemployment. The economic reform lagged behind the political reform leading unemployed Tunisian youth to leave the country and join the ranks of jihadist groups in Iraq and Syria. The security forces clash sporadically with militant Islamists causing death and injury on both sides.

The Tunisian government is making big effort to cope with the returning fighters from Syria and Iraq including emergency law and increase in public funding devoted to security. To make things worse, the phosphate production, a major source of the country finance, has been falling dramatically due to less demand since 2011. Seven years after the downfall of Bin Ali, the daily protest and rioting by angry unemployed youth in impoverished suburbs of the capital and in the mineral rich south echoes the country's 2010 Arab Spring revolution. The state of emergency was declared in November 2016 after a suicide bomber killed twelve members of the presidential guards in the center of the country. Riot police deployment and overnight curfew has been imposed quite often in population centers.

In the eyes of many Tunisians, the revolution was a failure if the economic needs are not met and the transition is limited solely to the political aspect. According to the International Labor Organization, national joblessness in 2017 stands at 15%, and it is 32% among the youth. By raising and then frustrating expectations, the revolution created conditions for radicalization, but democracy gave many Tunisian youth the freedom to act on their anger by joining civic and political groups and express dissent. Some, mostly from poor suburbs, took advantage of the new openness and called for imposing Sharia laws in their neighborhoods. Tunisia, however, had been kept rigidly secular. It is remarkable that Tunisia's democracy has endured even when it has not produced prosperity while fellow Arab states have fallen into civil war or dictatorship.

The government of President Caid Essebsi proposed the "Law on Economic and Financial Reconciliation" in 2015 the parliament debated it and approved it in 2016. The law would halt the trial and prosecution of people accused of corruption and misuse of public funds if they negotiate a "reconciliation" agreement with the state and pay back unlawfully obtained money to the state treasury. The targets of this law were the family and friends of the ex-President Bin Ali who were accused of becoming rich by illegal means.

Amnesty International reported that there were few signs to show that things had improved for women since the Arab Spring. In 2018, the country passed a law that gave women the right to choose one's spouse even if he was non-Muslim. It was the first country in the ME and North Africa to remove the legal hurdles to marry outside the state's official religion. Until now, a non-Muslim man who wished to marry a Muslim woman had to convert to Islam. The new law has angered some Islamic countries which called to oust Tunisia from the Organization of Islamic Cooperation (OIC) because it contradicts Sharia laws. The organization that was founded in 1969 includes 57 member states. The Tunisian parliament also banned polygamy and gave women the same share of inheritance as the male.

4. YEMEN

Yemen is an ancient country, the southern part of the Arabian Peninsula where the Kahtani Arab tribes came from and much of the Arab culture originated. The relatively high rainfall of Yemen, easy access to the sea, and advanced irrigation systems created flourishing civilizations. Yemen was home for several indigenous prosperous kingdoms, dynasties, and legends that date back to the 14th century BC. They include Saba' (possibly the biblical Sheba), Himyar, Qataban, Minea (Ma'ien) and Hadramaut. The ancient walled Sana'a City is said to be one of the oldest in the world, built by the forefathers of Arab Kahtan tribe. It is near the ancient City of Ma'rib where Queen of Sheba that was mentioned in the Bible and Quran, ruled. The legendary Ma'rib Dam was built according to the archeologists around 1700 BC, but after centuries of providing irrigation water for thousands of acres of land, the dam finally collapsed in 570 BC. The breaching of the Dam was a historical event that was alluded to in al-Quran. The consequent failure of the irrigation system provoked the migration of tens of thousands of people from Yemen to other areas of the Arabian Peninsula and to the neighboring countries.

Ancient Yemenis prospered cultivating and exporting frankincense, myrrh and spices to the Mediterranean countries and dominated the trade of the aromatics of Asia. Coffee drinkers all over the world owe Yemen thanks for it was the place where coffee beans were first cultivated commercially and for some time Yemen was the sole source of the precious coffee green beans. When the demand for coffee increased especially in the 16th century, towns on the Red Sea like al-Mukha gained prominence as international center for exporting the beans. But the most important cultural and political event in Yemen's history that had most influence on its people's life and the

ME was the coming of Islam in the 7ᵗʰ century. Yemen people embraced Islam during the Prophet Muhammad lifetime Yemenis were on the front lines in the Islamic armies. They established Yemeni tribal culture in the conquered lands and Yemen became a province in the Islamic empire.

Yemen importance today is due to its strategic location at the southern entrance of the Red Sea, the waterway ancient traders with Asia navigated and modern commercial fleets carrying industrial products and crude oil have to navigate on their way to Europe through the Suez Canal and the Gulf of Aqaba. The country sits on Bab-al-Mandab strait, a narrow waterway linking the Red Sea with the Persian Gulf, through which much of the world's oil shipments pass. Yemen also has a long historic commercial and human association with sub-Sahara Africa, Ethiopia and Djibouti.

Like the rest of the Arabian Peninsula, the tribe is the primary unit of Yemen's social structure with its own ethics, system of justice and politics. Traditionally, the tribal leaders play a big role in the national politics. Yemeni tribal society is diverse in their social traditions and economy depending on locations. For centuries, every Yemeni town or village neighborhood has elders who administer local affairs, including justice based on tribal traditions. The Kahtan Tribe's descendants who established early agricultural civilization learnt navigation and joined the seafaring people, trading across the Gulf of Aden with East Africa. Kahtan tribes' counterparts in the north were mostly nomadic, then settled down in villages and engaged in agriculture and herding. The tribes in Yemen cite their traditions and know their own history and their roots.

Most members of the tribe are blood related and descendants of a common ancestor but they can switch allegiances if such request for backing another tribe is accepted. The tribes that the 10ᵗʰ century Yemeni historian Abu Muhammad al-Hamdani described in his chronicles still exist today in the same areas with some of the same traditions. Tribes in the region around Sana'a and further north are independent and militarily and politically active. The tribes in the middle, southern, coastal and in the east are urban or peasants focusing more on their economic situations and social issues and less on politics. With the collapse of the Yemeni government in recent years, tribalism has grown even more noticeable. The tribes of north Yemen today are the rebels, the Houthi insurgents. They are the main party that the central government and the Gulf States are fighting in the bloody war which is raging in Yemen especially since 2014.

Because of Yemen's society divisions based on sectarianism, tribalism, and geography, Yemen was rarely a united country under full control of a central government even when they tried to unite. There are two parts of

Yemen divided by sects and history, the mostly Zaidi-Shi'a North Yemen, and the mostly Sunni South Yemen. The two parts underwent different histories and sometimes their differences led to open conflicts. Unlike the south, the North never experienced any period of European colonialism because it has no economic or strategic value for the colonial powers.

Yemeni state of Zaidi-Shi'a was founded by Yahia ibn al-Hussein in 890 and eight years later, al-Hadi Yahia proclaimed himself the first Zaidi-Shi'a Imam (spiritual leader). He was able to attract followers from the tribes of North Yemen and established a Zaidi revivalist political dynasty headed by his descendants until the middle of the 20th century. Al-Hadi Yahia established a blend of religious and secular rule that survived varying circumstances and lasted until 1962.

The Zaidis belong to a Shi'a Islamic sect that emerged in the 8th century recognizing Zaid, the son of Imam Zain Al-Abedeen as the fifth imam after Ali. Zaid was a scholar and a fighter taking upon himself to fight the tyranny of the Umayyad Caliph Hisham ben-Abdel-Malk. He led his forces of many thousands of his supporters and gave a great fight, but he was killed in 740.

The Yemeni-Zaidi state retained its independence in the north until 1539 when it was conquered by the Ottoman Turks and became one of its provinces. Yemen Zaidis declared war on Turkey and won their independence in 1635. When the Ottomans tried repeatedly to annex Yemen to its empire, the Zaidi-Shi'a armed tribesmen defended their lands and defeated the invaders in 1568, 1613 and 1635. By 1872, the Ottomans succeeded in controlling cities in northern Yemen, but the Zaidi Imams contested them and the tribal areas stayed under their control. Following the Ottoman Empire dissolution in World War I, the Zaidi Imam Yahya was left in control of all North Yemen. There was opposition and sometimes violence against the Imams' rule. Yemen with its special Islamic culture and traditional society seemed to be frozen in time while the rest of the ME countries and other parts of the world were going through social and political modernization under imperial rule. A small number of Yemenis who became aware of the problems with their autocratic society formed "Free Yemeni Movement" in the mid-1940s. They rebelled against the regime in 1948, Imam Yahya was assassinated and his son Ahmad succeeded him and put down the uprising.

When Ahmad died in 1962, his son Muhammad al-Badr succeeded him and immediately after his inauguration, Colonel Abdullah Sallal staged a military coup, took control of the capital Sana'a and deposed Imam Badr. Sallal put an end to the Imams' rule that lasted more than a millennium, but the majority of North Yemen continues to embrace the Zaidi-Shi'a Islamic faith. Sallal established Yemen Arab Republic (YAR) in the north, and headed a ruling eight-member Revolutionary Command Council. The newly formed republic had to face a rebellion led by Yemeni royalists and supported by Saudi Arabia and Jordan. Egypt's military troops entered the fray in support of Sallal's regime until 1967 when they were withdrawn after the Six-Day-War. By 1970, the two sides of the conflict reconciled and Saudi Arabia recognized the YAR.

South Yemen was a British colony from 1839 to 1967, ruled as part of British India administration until 1937. Once the British dominated the South, they decided to classify the City of Aden as "Crown Colony" a status reserved for important strategic colonies administered directly from London. The British established a sizable military base and a Royal Air Force command in Aden. The remaining territory was designated a British Protectorate that its tribes enjoyed some self-rule autonomy.

By 1965, most of the tribes within the protectorate and Aden colony had joined the British sponsored "Federation of South Arabia." Two rival political groups in Yemen, a Marxist National Liberation Front (NFL) and the Front for the Liberation of Occupied South Yemen (FLOSY) fought for power over the control of South Yemen, and by 1967, the Marxist NLF was the winner. The Federation of South Arabia collapsed and the British left for good. South Yemen became known as the People's Democratic Republic of Yemen (PDRY) in December of 1970. It was hard to believe that the traditionally conservative tribal society in the South would embrace the radical Marxist philosophy of Communism, but this had happened in Africa during the Cold War and the Soviets tried it in Afghanistan.

By 1972, the Yemen Arab Republic (YAR) of the north and the People's Democratic Republic of Yemen (PDRY) of the south were engaged in open conflict over border demarcation. Saudi Arabia provided financial and military aid to the YAR and the PDRY received aid from the Soviet Union. For years, the Arab League tried to broker a cease-fire between the two combatants and finally succeeded to end the conflict and even form a unified Yemen. Ali Abdullah Saleh who had been previously President of the North Yemen from 1978 until 1990, was the first president of the shaky union. The marriage quickly soured with the Southern-tribes frustrated by what it saw as its economic marginalization at the hands of the Northern-tribes–dominated government.

The South seceded, war broke out between the two sectors, and the South was crushed militarily when its main and only patron, the Soviet Union, had collapsed. Saleh once again became Yemen strong man and the head of a seemingly unified country. Abdullah Saleh foreign policy created serious problems with the Gulf States that had serious consequences for Yemen's economy. He supported Saddam Hussein in his decision to invade Kuwait in the 1991 first Gulf War. Saudi Arabia retaliated by expelling Yemeni workers depriving Yemen of vital remittances.

Despite Yemen tribal structure and low ranking in the UN Human development Index, Yemen under Saleh was trying to show it as forward thinking society. Saleh had marketed himself particularly to the US as a modern leader who believed in civil liberties and fighting terrorism was one of his main concerns. To that end, he signed agreements allowing the US to use drones to target al-Qaeda in the Arabian Peninsula (AQAP) terrorists on Yemeni soil in return for $1.4 billion annually in military and economic assistance.

Prior to the Arab Spring, Yemen had a somewhat weak democratic system with regular elections, parliament, upper-house and a traditional political pluralism. Saleh had his own party, the General People's Congress (GPC), and the country had a political opposition block, the Joint Meeting Parties (JMP) that included Yemeni Socialist Party, the Nasserite Party, and the conservative Islah Party that was considered as a version of the MB. Saleh allowed political and civil organizations to exist and run out of steam by their own lack of capacity, stymie them through a series of legal or bureaucratic obstacles, co-opted their leaders or suppressed them from within by flooding their organizations with members of his party.

The Arab Spring in Yemen

Before the Arab Spring, Yemen was one of the first countries in which protesters took to the streets raising issues ranging from early marriage to government's corruption. The demonstrations were often led by Tawakkol Karman, who few years later would lead Yemen's version of the Arab Spring and win the Nobel Peace Prize. But incidents of harassment against journalists and political activists were rising and human rights situation continued to deteriorate by 2010, according to "World Report 2011." Yemen's problem stemmed from the poverty, corruption, nepotism, sectarianism and the secessionist Southern movement, known as Hirak which came to prominence during the 1994 civil war between the north and south.

The Yemeni Arab Spring anti-government protests began on Feb 3, 2011, shortly after the ouster of Tunisian president Bin Ali. It was initially against unemployment, economic conditions and corruption. Then the demands of the demonstrators escalated to calls for President Ali Abdullah Saleh to resign. Demonstrations spread into many Yemeni cities including the city of Taiz that emerged as an epicenter of the uprising then several high-ranking military officers deserted Saleh. After months of popular protests, Saleh was forced to step down and hand over power to his deputy Abed-Rabbuh Hadi, in February 2012. He and his family had amassed billions of dollars through corruption during his 33 years in power, according to 2015 UN report. The political transition that was supposed to bring stability after the downfall of Ali Abdullah Saleh failed and a civil war rocked the country. For more than six years, Yemen has been wracked by a bloody war between the Houthi rebels and the regional and international supporters of Yemen's government under Hadi.

Hadi presided over one of the poorest countries of the world and had to deal with too many problems, including Jihadist militant separatists in the south, al-Houthi insurgency, the continuing loyalty of the military to the deposed president, unemployment and food insecurity.

The deposed president was out of power but not out of the political scene. His cronies and relatives including his son and nephews, continued to exercise power by having their own military army and later on allying themselves with Ansar Allah militants against the Yemeni central government. Ansar Allah in Yemen is an Islamic-Shi'a organization affiliated with al-Houthi tribes that had been engaged in the bloody civil war that began in 2014.

Al-Houthis belong to the Zaidi-Shi'a mountainous tribes originally living in Yemen's impoverished province on the northern borders with Saudi Arabia. They have been accused of being proxies for Islamic Republic of Iran that had adopted the Shi'a Islam faith as the state religion since 1978-79. Al-Houthis were the first to support the uprising that called for the resignation of President Saleh, and as he prepared to leave office, they declared autonomy in northern Yemen. Yemen was ruled by Zaydi-Shi'a imams for millennium until 1962, and the Houthis had been founded as Zaydi's revivalist movement. But the Houthis in 2011 are not asking for restoring the imamate rule in Yemen. Their demands have been primarily for democratic participation and better economic opportunities.

In March of 2015, rebel al-Houthis surged out of their northern stronghold and declared general mobilization to overthrow the central government of Hadi. They seized control of Yemen's capital, Sana'a, with the help of rogue elements of the armed forces loyal to the country's deposed strongman, Ali Abdullah Saleh. They proceeded to push southwards toward the country's second-biggest city, Aden. In response to Houthi expansion, an alliance of tribes and militia fighters associated with the leading Sunni-Islamic party, al-Islah, had joined the fight alongside the Salafis group.

Saudi Arabia formed a military coalition of Arab states against the Houthis to restore power of the internationally recognized president Hadi who set up a parallel government in Yemen's southern port of Aden. The coalition included the United Arab Emirates, Bahrain, Egypt, Morocco, Jordan and Sudan. The Saudis and the Emirates sent troops to fight on the ground in Yemen, while the rest have only carried out air strikes against Houthi targets inside Yemen.

The US, that has been waging air-war against al-Qaeda in Yemen for many years, provided intelligence and the weapons in support of the Saudi-led coalition campaign. It has been reported that al-Qaeda in the Arabian Peninsula (AQAP) is controlling swathes of territory in the hinterlands and along the coast. Western intelligence agencies consider the AQAP the most dangerous branch of al-Qaeda worldwide because of its technical expertise and global reach. Its Jihadist militants took the advantage of the chaos following the ousting of Saleh in 2011, seized territory in the south and stepped up their attacks on the government-controlled Aden. And in 2015, the AQAP armed militants took over Mukalla, the fifth largest city in Yemen until they were driven out by Emirati troops and US air support. The emergence of ISIS affiliates in Yemen made the country even more unstable and of serious concern that it will exacerbate the regional tension and suffering of the Yemeni people. ISIS militants announced the formation of Yemen wilaya in 2014, and four months later, they took credit for bombing two Shi'a-mosques in Sana'a which killed 150 worshipers.

Al-Houthis allied with forces loyal to Abdullah Saleh controlled the capital Sana'a, and the government of Abed-Rabbuh Hadi controlled the business city of Aden. Each of the two opposing factions along with their supporters and allies claimed to be the legitimate Yemeni government. Hadi declared in March of 2015 that Aden would be the temporary capital of the country due to al-Houthi occupation of Sana'a. The US and the Saudi-led coalition accused the Shi'a Islamic Republic of Iran of intervening militarily and financially to sustain al-Houthi faction while Sunni Saudi Arabia and the Gulf states armed and financed the government of Hadi. The US military claimed that its navy had intercepted many arms shipments from Iran to Yemen. Three years since the people took to the streets demanding political emancipation, economic reform and the end of corruption, Yemen became ravaged by a bloody war Iran-vs-Gulf States by proxy. The Houthis' demands have been primarily economic and political in nature the war developed into Shi'a-vs-Sunni sectarian war.

While geo-sectarian rivalry between the Middle East Sunni dominated states and Shi'a-led Iran is played in Yemen, resources are wasted and innocent civilians caught in the cross-fire are dying. Yemen has always been a low-income country, the least developed in the region, and faces difficult long-term challenges to stabilize and grow its economy. The post-Arab-Spring conflict has exacerbated these issues and stalled any reform efforts. The ongoing war that started in 2014 has halted Yemen's export completely, pressured the currency's exchange rate, severely limited food and fuel imports and caused widespread damage to the infrastructure. More than 80% of the population is in need of humanitarian assistance.

The Saudi-led intervention, according to eye-witnesses, has caused massive damage to Yemen's Infrastructure and has resulted in the bombing of civilian targets including hospitals and even wedding parties and funeral processions. Saudi Arabia asked "aid groups" to leave the Houthi controlled area, claiming that the aid workers were at risk. Bombing by the Saudi Air force injured many people at a hospital run by Doctors Without Borders in October 2015, and a hospital operated by the same organization was hit by Saudi rockets in January 2016, killing many people. According to the UN, tens of thousands, mostly civilians, have been killed by the widespread bombing of civilian areas, and thousands died of starvation. A Saudi led airstrike killed 40 school children who were taken on a school trip in July 2018. The weapon used was a guided bomb made by the US sold to Saudi Arabia.

The UN refugee agency (UNHCR) reports that more than three million frightened, hungry and sick Yeminis have sought refuge in safe areas in Yemen and more than 200,000 have sought asylum in Africa including Somalia and Djibouti. The United Nations High Commissioner for Human Rights estimated that Saudi-led coalition air strikes caused most of the reported civilian deaths and al-Houthis caused mass civilian casualties due to their siege of Taiz, Yemen's third largest cities. A report presented to the Security Council in January of 2017 stated that ten coalition air strikes between March and October of 2016 killed at least 292 civilians, including some 100 women and children. "In eight of the 10 investigations, the panel found no evidence that the air strikes had targeted legitimate military objectives."

While the death of civilians has been mounting, millions have been displaced. An outbreak of cholera began in 2016 caused by the collapse of water and sanitation systems, the years of war and the blockade imposed by the coalition. 'Save-the-Children' charity organization reported that there are more than one million acutely malnourished children under the age of five living in areas with high levels of infection due to the food shortage and the widespread internal displacement. More than half a million cases of cholera had been reported by 2017, and nearly 2,000 people had died. In the meantime, al-Qaeda in the Arabian Peninsula and the so-called Islamic

State (ISIS) has taken advantage of the chaos by seizing territory in the South. The promise of the Arab Spring has become a distant memory for most of Yemenis, with years of conflict leaving the country in tatters and forcing many to lower their expectations of whichever ruling authority they happen to live under. Prior to the Arab Spring, Yemen had been struggling to build a unified state, but each attempt was faced with resistance from the traditional authority of sectarianism or tribalism. But after the Arab Spring, the civil war and the involvement of the Saudi-led-coalition, the Arab Spring became both sectarian and tribal conflict.

Abdullah Saleh, who was the most power man in Yemen for thirty-three years, was killed in December 2017 by the Houthi rebels, his former allies-turned enemies. He was trying to flee clashes with the rebels in the capital city of Sana'a when he was gunned down. Saleh's life story and tragic death are similar to those of Muammar Gaddafi of Libya and after their death, both left their countries in complete chaos.

5. EGYPT

Egypt is a country that spreads across more than 400,000 square miles in Northeast Africa and 7,500 square miles (Sinai) in Southwest Asia. Most of Egypt's land (97%) is a waste desert that is not inhabited or cultivated. Ethnic Egyptians constitute 91 per cent of the population, creating a generally homogeneous entity. Its eighty-five million people as of 2013 live along the banks of the Nile, the Nile delta that fans out north of Cairo, along both banks of the Suez Canal and on the Mediterranean. Very few communities live around oases and the recently irrigated land reclaimed from the desert. The inhabitable areas around the Nile are among the world's most densely populated.

Egypt has the Suez Canal that connects the Mediterranean and the Red Sea which controls international commerce between Asia and Europe. It is the artery for the tankers carrying the Gulf oil to the West. No single country in the Middle East and Africa affects Arab national interests in more ways than Egypt. Egypt's importance stems from its long history, its location and, and the potential of its human resources. Egypt's ancient and modern history supports the concept that "geography is a major determinant of history."

The centrality of Egypt in history was partly the product of its strategic location at the junction of the two continents of Africa and Asia, and within few nautical miles from Europe. It has a pivotal role in trade, conquest, communication and migration. Egypt has one of the longest histories of any modern state it has been continuously inhabited since the 10th millennium BC. Due to its long history and many invaders, Egypt's distinctive culture has been enriched by the ancient Pharanoiac, Nubian, Coptic, Byzantine, Arab and Muslim heritage.

In 639, Amr ibn al Aas, commanded the Arab Muslim troops that entered Egypt which was a tributary of the Byzantine Empire. The Copts did not resist the Arab invaders and in less than two years, Egypt was completely under the control of the Islamic state. Ibn al-Aas good will toward the Copts by virtue of Islam respect for Christianity and the traditional kinship between the Arabs and Ancient Egyptian Copts through Hagar, the Egyptian wife of Abraham and the mother of Ismail who is regarded as the ancestor of the Arabs including the Prophet Muhammad. The Prophet himself was married to an Egyptian Copt named Maria. Al-Quran verses mentioned Egypt thirty times in the context of the stories of Joseph, Moses and the Israelites.

An agreement was reached between Ibn al-Aas and the Roman garrison at el-Farma (Pelusiam) with the approval of the Christian Church. Alexandria City was granted a respite for nearly a year to allow the evacuation of those who wanted to leave including the Roman army and Rome loyalists. And on September 29, 642, Amr ibn al-Aas and his troops rode in Alexandria City. According to the terms of the treaty, ibn al-Aas granted the people of Egypt including Romans, Nubians and Jews, peace and freedom of worship provided they pay the Jizia (per capita poll-tax excluding women, children and aged men), a land-tax, and hospitality to the Muslim army. A clause stipulated that should the Nile flood be less than usual, the tax would be reduced in proportion. Before the Islamic invasion, only some Egyptian traders had been familiar with Arab tribes in East Egypt and in the Sinai Peninsula. But the transformation of Egypt into an Arab country began with the country being ruled by governors acting in the name of the Rashidin Caliphs in al-Madina, the building of Fustat City , part of modern Cairo, as the Islamic capital of Egypt, and when many Arab individuals and tribes settled in lower Egypt.

Vast majority of Egypt's population were Copts before Muslims conquered the country. Egypt remained majority Coptic for many centuries after the installation of Arab rule. There was well established relationship between South Arabia and ancient Egypt this was maintained and developed after the advent of Islam. It was only during Fatimid era of the 10th–12th centuries under Saladin that the population was Arabized in its majority through Arabic language and culture. Saladin and his heirs were ethnically Kurdish, not Arabs.

When Jawhar the Sicilian, commander of the troops sent by the Fatimid Caliph Al-Mu'izz to conquer Egypt, founded Cairo in 969 CE. He also built Al-Azhar, originally as a mosque and later on became a center of Islamic teaching and played a role in Islamic politics. The mosque was completed within two years and opened for its first prayers on 7 Ramadan 361 H / June

22, 972 CE. Historians differ as to how the mosque got its name. Some hold that it is called as such because it was surrounded by flourishing mansions at the time when Cairo was founded. Others believe that it was named after "Fatima Al-Zahra" the daughter of Prophet Muhammad to glorify her name. This last explanation sounds the most likely, as the Fatimids named themselves after her.

During the Fatimid times (972–1171), Al-Azhar was a minor educational institution whose objective was to spread the Shiite teachings in Egypt. The Ayyubids under Saladin put an end to the Fatimids rule and assumed power in 1171. They converted Al-Azhar to the Sunni (mainstream) Islamic teachings, but it was considered just another school among the many schools in Egypt, Baghdad, Syria and Andalusia. When the French invaded northern Egypt in 1798, Al-Azhar ulama led a rebellion against the occupying French in Cairo and gave the uprising a national and religious character. The Egyptians and the world wide Muslims began to regard Al-Azhar institution as a center of moral and political leadership.

Over time and with the intellectual and political prominence of Egypt in the 20th century, Al-Azhar became the major center of religious scholarly class of graduates (ulama) who played a role in Egyptian and wider Muslim politics. Egyptian ruling class sought legitimacy from the Ulama who sometimes granted it, and at other times served as supporters of public opinion against the governing elites. Nasser ended the independence of Al-Azhar by nationalizing its properties and assuming the right to appoint the University senior staff including the Grand Sheikh and forcing an integrated secular and religious curriculum. The regime used Al-Azhar institution as a counter balance against Islamic reformers, the MB and the Salafists. This facilitated more exchanges between Azharis and the Islamists, and created greater political role for Al-Azhar graduates in the 1980s. Once the institution lost its independence and the faculty became government bureaucrats under government oversight, the political judicial opinions issued by its senior scholars have been supportive of the regime.

During the early days of "Arab Spring," there was schism among Al-Azhar community. Both the Grand Sheikh of Al-Azhar, Ahmed al-Tayyeb, a Mubarak appointee, and the Grand Mufti of Egypt, Ali Goma'a affirmed the legitimacy of President Mubarak. But some Al-Azhar faculty and students sided with the anti-government protests. Sheikh Emad Effat, a senior Azhari and advocate of non-violent resistance, joined the protesters and was among those killed by the security forces during a sit-in in the early days of the uprising. He became a martyr and a symbolic support to the uprising by the highest Islamic authority in Egypt.

Sectarianism in Egypt

Egypt is a religiously polarized country where sectarian tribalism based on religion is alive, strong and divisive. There has been always tension between Egypt's Muslim majority and Coptic-Christians, who make up about 10% of the population. One of reason behind sectarian conflict in Egypt has been the inter-religious marriage, conversion issue, and religion-based family law. Copts complain that their religious freedom and constitutional rights have not been protected by the state institutions. Church construction or expansion, for example, requires the approval of the president. Copts and their religious symbols have been the targets of violence and vandalism committed by Islamic extremists.

The years after the start of the Arab Spring have marked a notable rise in violence between the two communities, mostly against the Christians. In the first hundred days after the resignation of Hosni Mubarak on February 11, there have been more than ten confirmed attacks on Christian places of worship or property, as well as other incidents of sectarian violence. Sectarian tension has become the most pressing danger in Egypt in the post-Mubarak era. This was evident especially in southern Egypt, where large communities of Copts live next door to Muslims. Violence erupts and bloodshed is ignited for any excuse even when a woman converts to the other religion.

Thousands of Muslims led by Islamic fundamentalists attempted to break into the Church of St. Mena recently looking for a woman who converted to Islam. Egyptian Christians are feeling under siege, in the City of Minya on the banks of the Nile where about 40% of the population is Christian or in the coastal City of Ismailia. There were series of attacks on Coptic Christians chapel in Ismailia by terrorists who describe themselves as Muslim fundamentalists. ISIS terrorists established a foothold in Sinai, massacred Coptic Christians and destroyed Christian churches in northern Sinai. On February 22, in the village of al-Shuraniyya in the Upper Egyptian province of Suhag, a number of homes were set afire and property inside destroyed when rumor spread that the Baha'is who had been expelled from the village in 2009 had returned. There have also been repeated attacks against Salafis especially on tombs belonging to their orders. Egypt needs to build democratic institutions from the ground up to end sectarianism. Its institutions should be structured to protect the minority from the tyranny of the majority, then its society's loyalty may be changed from sectarianism to citizenry.

Vast majority of the Bedouin tribes in the African-Egyptian area and Sinai today have abandoned the traditional nomadic or half nomadic life of the past and settled where there is water to be found in the desert or where there is work to make living. Members of the tribes in Sinai have farms, work as fishermen and run businesses. Poverty grows amongst the Bedouin tribes, but few of them became prosperous profiting from tourism they own land, hotels, shops and restaurants. The Bedouin tribes are conservative people with a rich culture and hospitality, but in their relations with other tribes, there is still the old tribal jealousy and blood feuds.

Egyptian Bedouin tribes were traditionally subordinate to the ruling regimes whereby families vote for whomever is in power in exchange for some services provided by the latter. But a change occurred after the 2011 as a result of Arab Spring. Because of poverty, illiteracy and neglect by the government, the angry youth who viewed themselves excluded from society focused their anger on people they saw as different. Poverty and injustice drove the youth into sectarian violence. Since the Egyptian Bedouin tribes are Muslims, the Jihadists had been able to infiltrate family and tribal ranks and sympathy in the name of religion. ISIS terrorists with the support of the Bedouins established a foothold in Sinai. They have been accused of committing crimes against Copts and destroying Christian churches in northern Sinai.

Egypt's Copts

Christian Copts, are the largest Christian community in the Middle East they constitute ten percent of Egypt's population they are everywhere in Egypt, practicing all professions and businesses, and contributing to the welfare and the development of the state, but most political analysts describe Egypt's identity today as Arab-Islamic. Until recently, Egypt's constitutions, with the exception of Nasser's 1958 constitution, stated that "Islam is the state religion." The Copts regard themselves as the true descendants of ancient Egyptians who inhabited the country thousands of years before the Muslims' invasion of Egypt.

It was St Mark the Evangelist who first brought Christianity to Egypt, following in steps of the Holy Family (Virgin Mary, Joseph el-Najjar and Jesus Christ) that many years before had fled into Egypt to avoid the vengeance of the Roman appointed King Herod the Great of Jerusalem. According to the 4th century AD historian Eusebius of Caesaria, St Mark arrived in Alexandria in the first or third year of the Roman Emperor Claudius reign which would be AD 41 or 43, ten years after the death of Christ. St Mark's first convert in Egypt to Christianity was a shoemaker named Hananiah or Anianus. St Mark was credited with having founded the diocese, or See, of Alexandria between AD 58 and 62 of which he became the first Patriarch. To this day, the Head of the Coptic Church in Egypt is called the "Patriarch of the See of St Mark and the Pope of Alexandria." He was one of the four evangelists and the one who wrote the oldest canonical gospel. Christianity spread throughout Egypt within half a century of **Saint Mark's** arrival in Alexandria as is clear from the New Testament writings found in **Bahnasa**, in Middle Egypt, which dated around the year AD 200. This is supported by a fragment of the Gospel of Saint John, written using the Coptic language found in Upper Egypt that can be dated to the first half of the second century. Because Rome officially classified Christianity as a sect of Judaism in the first century AD, the Church at Alexandria that was the chief expression of Christianity in Egypt, suffered greatly during the Roman persecution of the Jews.

Eusebius provided a list of Patriarchs of Alexandria who succeeded St Mark, but Julian (AD 188), the eleventh on the list seems to have been a special historical Patriarch according to Eusebius. He presided over several parishes in Alexandria, which suggests that the Church in Alexandria had become like that in Rome, divided into parishes where each perish had its own presbyter (elder). The Roman Emperor Septimus Severus (AD 145–211) issued an imperial edict in 202 forbidding proselytism to Judaism or Christianity. The punishment for transgression was banishment or forced labor in the imperial mines.

Patriarch Demetrius (AD 190–233) followed Julian, and according to contemporary historians, it is with him the history of the Church in Egypt began when Christianity was firmly established as an intellectual force. The Church established the Catechetical School of Alexandria where teachers whose task was to instruct, answer questions on Christianity to would be converts, and at the end of which they would present them for baptism. Several important treatises to appeal to intellectuals, the upper class and ordinary Egyptians were written by prolific scholars like Flavius Clemens and Origen. They included instructions for the schools, philosophical, theological and historical topics, Christian morals and manners in daily life, attack on paganism and advices to the heathen Greeks and native Egyptians to embrace Christianity. The Church of Alexandria had begun to enjoy a position of great importance throughout the Christian World. Origen was famous throughout the Christian world. He was even invited by leaders of Eastern Church to resolve their theological problems. In AD 249, Emperor Decius instituted an empire-wide persecution of Christians that was carried out with relentless cruelty from AD 249 to 251. The Roman soldiers roamed the streets demanding proof that suspects had made sacrifices to the state's gods. Origen as one of Christianity pillars at the time was arrested and tortured severely he died as a result of his sufferings in AD 254.

When the Egyptian military ousted President Morsi, many of his supporters blamed the Copts, and violent incidents against the Christian community have steadily increased even while President el-Sisi has made concerted effort to protect them. Many Copts reported more persecution since 2011, and since then, at least 150,000 have fled the country to Europe and the US. And in Egypt's northern Sinai region, where "ISIS" is taking direct aim against the Christians, the 5,000 Christian community population dwindled to less than 1,000 since 2011.

Nubia and the Egyptian Nubians

Nubia, located in South Egypt but there are no exact boundaries that are firmly marked on a map. Some historians believe the origin of the name "Nubia" came from the Ancient Egyptians word "Nub" which meant "gold" and Nubia meant "the land of gold." For thousands of years Nubia was an important region of Africa where wars had been waged for the control and supremacy of an important region of North Africa, the fertile parts of the land along the banks of the Nile. Ancient Egyptians pushed south through Nubia to exploit the gold mines and to trade in ivory, precious woods and other products of Sudan. And the people in Sudan were pushing north to the more fertile parts of the Nile valley and the Mediterranean coast. Nubia was the highway to battles between ancient contending armies of the north and south. During relative peace under the rule of one of the rival powers, Nubia had periods of prosperity, but it never attained an independent status of its own even though its inhabitants have been a distinct nation closely knit by a common culture and way of life. Nubia has been a divided territory between Egypt and Sudan since ancient times.

The British Egyptologist, Walter Emery wrote that the Nubians have their own language that belongs among special African tongues. It has been always a spoken language, but the Nubians today use the Arabic letters for writing it. The Nubian tribes were pagans until the early years of Theodosius Patriarchy when, around 540, a mission was established at the Temple of Isis just beyond Egypt's southern border, and many Nubians embraced the Christian faith. In the 550s, part of Isis Temple was converted into the Church of St. Stephen but the pagan tribes of Nubia were guaranteed access to the Temple. The native language of the church was Nubian, but Greek was used for worshiping. This remained the case until the Arab invasion of Egypt, the Nubian church was forced to turn to Alexandria bishops and the

Coptic Church exerted its influence over the Nubians. Centuries later, Islam was embraced by the majority of the Nubians.

The Nubians today consider themselves racially distinct from other Egyptians, although large proportion of their male population lives in Egypt's big cities employed mostly as domestic workers or as sailors on the Nile. Nubia became the center of world-wide attention when Egypt decided to build the Aswan High Dam in the 1960s to bring fertility to the desert and create new sources of power to future industrial projects. When the Aswan Dam was built, the middle valleys of the Nile have been turned into a vast lake "Lake Nasser." About seventeen percent of the lake is in Sudan. Large area of Nuba's villages and farm land, that was supporting its population, finally disappeared beneath the water of the big reservoir which has been formed behind the High Dam of Aswan to provide prosperity to the Northern Nile Valley and the Delta. More than 90,000 Nubians and artifacts of Ancient Egyptian temples and monuments had to be relocated.

The High Dam purpose was to utilize the Nile waters so that "no drop of the river will be lost in the sea." It is 225 ft. high and more than three miles in length. The dam created a reservoir behind it that has a surface of 1,150 square miles, holding at its maximum filling nearly 137 million acre-feet (130,000 million cubic meters) of water. Even with sacrificing Nubia fertile lands and the loss of many million cubic meters of water due to the intense heat in summer, the High Dam was designed to "increase the arable land surface in Egypt by nearly one third." In addition to this, the water collected by the dam during summer has been servicing turbines that have a total capacity of more than one million kilowatt hours a year.

The international concern focused on the threat posed by the dam to Abu Simbel Temple that was built in the 13th century BC by the Pharaoh Ramses II which was considered one of Egypt's great archaeological sites. A UN salvage operation systematically explored, recorded, relocated and assembled the whole Temple in a safe area, block by block, before the water of the reservoir could have destroyed the ancient site. Human rights organizations alleged that there was less concern for the fate of the area's indigenous Nubians who were forced to abandon villages and way of life they had inherited for millennia.

The Arab Spring in Egypt

After decades of political oppression and economic failure under the military rule that impacted people's life, the uprising in Egypt was overdue. Think about it: Egypt and South Korea in 1960 shared similar standards of living, GDP per head and life expectancy. While Egypt has more natural resources and controls World East-West commerce, the peoples of the two countries today inhabit different worlds economically and politically. More Egyptians now live in cities like in South Korea, but Egypt's GDP per capita today is less than one fifth of South Korea's the unemployment in Egypt is five times that in South Korea and poverty and malnutrition are widespread. Egypt's government budget is subsidized by the US and the Gulf States, and the only way the Egyptian citizen improves his/her standards of living is to leave the country and find a job in the Gulf States. The main cause of widespread poverty in Egypt that causes poor distribution of wealth and lack of employment opportunities is corruption. Immediate solution to poverty is unlikely to materialize under the existing government controlled economy where officials direct state funds towards sectors they and their cronies have strong ties with. And the lack of transparency under the authoritarian regime made it impossible to criticize and call for an end to corruption.

Eighteen days of overwhelming protest forced President Hosni Mubarak to resign in February 2011, after three decades in power. When he stepped down, he had already used his power systematically to weaken the liberal opposition parties and civil society organizations. He had tolerated the Islamist MB only enough to let him claim to that "It is his regime or the Islamists." He used electoral rules, corrupt judiciary and occasional police crackdowns to ensure that the MB or any other opposition party never gets governing experience. The military was the only institution that had become stronger during Mubarak's thirty years rule using patronage to buy the military loyalty. Only when he apparently planned to pass power to his son, Gamal, Mubarak lost the loyalty of the Egyptian military that holds all the levers of power.

Once Mubarak was deposed, the Supreme Council of the Armed Forces (SCAF) assumed the presidential powers and drafted an interim constitutional declaration that was approved by referendum on March 30, 2011. It incorporated provisions from the 1971 constitution and new measures to make presidential and legislative elections more open, imposed presidential term limits, and restructured the use of emergency laws. Mubarak was tried in Egypt's court and convicted of complicity in the deaths of 846 people killed during the uprising, but the verdict was overturned on appeal. The Islamists were the overwhelming winners in the parliament elections, and Muhammad Morsi, a university professor and a former member of the MB and once a political prisoner became Egypt's first democratically elected president in June, 2012. He revoked the decree that limited his power and the

Islamist majority in the parliament passed an Islamist-leaning constitution that gave him the powers to run the country unchecked.

President Morsi retained many of Mubarak's powers that he had previously castigated. He rushed the approval of a constitution by the Islamic majority parliament in one overnight session in December 2012 despite the boycott of the Copts and the liberals. He could've learned a lesson from Muslim majority countries outside the Arab world like Malaysia, Indonesia or Turkey that practice democracy, but he did not. Turkey today under Recep Tayyip Erdogan, even with all his faults, is more democratic than it was under the 1960s secular army generals.

Following Mubarak's departure and the second round of the first freely presidential election in Egypt, the MB candidate Muhammad Morsi beat the military candidate Ahmed Shafik by a narrow margin of 52% to 48%. Morsi had the only party machine and a base of public support, but his administration showed these are not sufficient qualification for governing. He was elected democratically but he flouted the norms of democracy during his short stint as president. Had he remained in power, he might have learned the pragmatism needed to run a country with a large non-Muslim minority and secular population. The Morsi government, in its one year of rule, did many things wrong. The Egyptians are religious people, but they rebelled to end tyranny and corruption and preserve their dignity and human rights, not to have a government dedicated to stamp out sin.

Even if Morsi had been better at governing, the hollowness of Egypt's state would have his regime doomed. When Morsi faltered, the latest constitution had no democratic rules of "Checks and Balances" to constrain the president and the majority from having too much power. The new constitution under Morsi created a presidential system, limited the freedom of the press and gave al-Azhar, the Islamic theological institution, the power to review and disapprove legislations. Morsi critics accused him of establishing himself as an autocrat by issuing executive orders preventing the courts from overturning his decisions. He tried to enshrine Islamic principles in the constitution and was unwilling to protect broad range of interests outside of his Islamic coalition, especially those of secularists, liberals, and the Christian minority. There were no political parties, organized citizens, free journalists and unwritten rules to defend the constitution and rein in the elected president peacefully. No less than the fate of Egypt's transition was at stake. His actions triggered the protest of spring 2013 that provided the pretext for Egypt's deep state (the military) to stage a coup paving the way for Abdel-Fattah el-Sisi to assume the presidency after the 2014 presidential elections.

The country's democratic transition collapsed and the military filled the void left by the rest of the state's institutions in a tragic way. The military that withdrew its support from Mubarak regime re-asserted its "patrimonial" authority and installed one of its own, a younger and more aggressive dictator copy of Mubarak, in his place, and the problems that brought Mubarak down have never been fixed. The military rulers of Egypt have perfected the route to authoritarianism by using the very institutions of democracy gradually, subtly, and even legally, to kill it. Egypt experienced the overthrow of two presidents and the return of the military rule after the start of their Arab Spring.

Actually, Morsi set the stage for his regime demise by defeating the presidential candidate of Egypt's most powerful institution, the military, and by alienating the liberal and the Christian minority. He tried to wrest control from a military institution that had been the mainstay of authoritarian power for decades. The military ruled Egypt since 1952, and it was not easy to surrender the government to civilian Islamists and give-up their privileges. It used its extensive network apparatus throughout the country to impede public service delivery, and undermine the nascent democratic order. The coup was supported by the rulers of Saudi Arabia and the United Arab Emirates with billions of dollars, who were worried the waves of change would knock at their doors.

The military launched a crackdown on the opponents of the coup sit-ins in Cairo killing more than 1000 people, and thousands including members and leaders of the MB were jailed. An interim government led by chief justice of the Supreme Constitutional Court was created to run the country. The 2012 constitution was amended and approved by the voters in 2014. It left out the controversial religious language featured in the previous document.

Abdel-Fattah el-Sisi ran for president and won 90% of the vote. Egypt's first post-revolution election was won by the inexperienced MB. One year later, its regime was not replaced by a more democratic alternative but by a resurgent and reinforced military dictatorship – General Abdel-Fattah el-Sisi, a younger Mubarak on steroids. The army had learned its lesson and was determined to increase its stranglehold on power and the Egyptian economy, even at the price of hundreds of deaths of protesters on the streets. El-Sisi is ruling the country with an iron fist, crushing any dissent, whether from the MB or the early secular revolutionaries of the 2011 protests.

How to explain why 52% of the Egyptian people preferred Morsi over the military candidate and two years later 90% of the same people voted for the General who removed the freely elected president from power and ordered the killing of hundreds of protesters? People who supported Sisi felt the MB lost control, the country had become chaotic, and only the military can provide security and stability. The vast majority of the Egyptians had lived their entire lives under military dictators, Nasser, Sadat, and Mubarak. They never had known a day of freedom of expression, but the regime had the resources and managed to establish order. And those who oppose the military rule especially after the military intervention and the crackdown that followed, had largely boycotted the elections and dismissed them as a farce. El-Sisi seizing power has given rise to an extremist insurgency in the country. Hundreds of people have been killed since Sisi came to power in bombings, and attacks on the military and the Christians across the country by Islamic extremists have become more brazen and frequent.

The lesson learnt from the failure of the "Arab Spring" in Egypt is that, it is difficult to make the transition to democracy in the absence of credible plan supported by strong civil institutions, including political parties, free judicial system and civil societies for governing the country. The protesters of the 2011 "Arab Spring" had no leadership or plans of action after overthrowing Hosni Mubarak's regime, and the MB filled the vacuum. They won the free elections because they were the only well-established political civil society. Egypt has not yet succeeded in fostering the institutional prerequisites of democracy, the acceptance of political opposition, protection of minorities, the free press, independent courts and universities, independent Al-Azhar Islamic institution, and the emancipation of women. Liberal economy is another prerequisite for the success of democracy, but Egypt's economy was far from liberal. The Soviet inspired central planning economy that had been used by the Egyptian government under Nasser, and the crony capitalism under Sadat and Hosni Mubarak, failed to produce free market economy. The military controls as much as forty percent of the Egyptian economy through military-run factories, food production, factories and land ownership.

6. LIBYA

The Ottomans lost Libya, the 'Tripolitania' that was part of their Empire, to Italy in the 1911–12 'Italo–Turkish war'. Once Turkey became too weak to defend its large empire, it surrendered the Libyan territory to Italy in the 'Treaty of Lausanne', and the country came under Italian control from 1912 to 1947. It was divided into three areas, Italian Cyrenaica, Italian Tripolitania, and Fezzan. The country was called 'Italian North Africa' from 1927 to 1934, and since 1934, it has been officially called Libya, a name used by the ancient Greeks for all North Africa except Egypt. The territory was run by Italian governors and some 150,000 Italians settled in the country, constituting roughly twenty percent of the population. Much of the colonial period had Italy waging war of subjugation against the people of Libya.

The colonization of Libya marked the beginning of a series of battles between Italian colonial forces and nationalist Libyan armed opposition that centered in Cyrenaica, the eastern sector of the country. Fierce resistance to the Italians by members of the Senussi political-religious order under Omar al-Mukhtar lasted twenty-two years. The Senussi order is a Sunni-Islamic-Sufi sect that, according to its critics, reduces Sufi standards to suit the harsh simplicity of Bedouin life. The founder of the order, Sayyid Muhammad Ibn Ali Senussi (the Grand Senussi) and his disciples had established a lodge 'Zawia' for his followers in the central Cyrenaican plateau near the ruins of the ancient Greek city of Cyrene in 1843. The Ottomans forced the Senussis to leave the coastal region for the desert village of Jaghbub close to the Libya's border with Egypt in 1856. The Order was successful deep in the desert because the Ottomans' authority was confined to the coastal towns, and the desert Bedouins needed some outside authority to bind them under a common symbol and resolve the inter-tribal disputes. The Senussis lived in lodges within the tribal homelands and held prayers and meeting there. They built an Islamic university for the Senussi brotherhood, mosque center and palace (which are now in ruins) where the late Senussi, the future King of Libya Idris al-Senussi was born.

The Ottomans forced the Senussis to move even farther south to Kura oasis in the Sahara Desert in 1895. They founded the village of el-Tag where the founder, Grand Senussi, died and eventually it became a holy place for the Senussi Order. Wherever the Senussis settled, they established a lodge that consisted of a mosque, school, store rooms and living quarters for the members of the Order. The lodge is self-sufficient with needed land and water to support the residents and their visitors. The Senussi Order does not impose rituals but it demands a complete identification with God that was achieved by "the contemplation of the Prophet Muhammad." Followers were urged to imitate the Prophet's life which they believe is a Bedouin faith at heart. According to cotemporary scholars, "the kinship between the Senussi Order and modern Islamic Salafists is striking."

Omar Al-Mukhtar was a follower of the Senussi Order, a teacher of the Qur'an by profession, an experienced soldier and a skilled strategist of desert warfare. He had a unique ability to keep the peace within fractious tribes and unite them by following the traditions of Islam.

His knowledge of the local geography gave him the advantage he needed in his fights against the Italians. He skillfully attacked their outposts, ambushed troops, cut their lines of communications, and faded back into the desert terrain. Italian forces waged punitive pacification campaigns using acts of repression. Resistance leaders were executed many went into exile, and thousands of people ended in concentration camps. The historian, Ilan Pappe estimates that the Italian military "killed half the Bedouin population" in Libya between 1928 and 1932.

Omar al-Mukhtar, the leader of the rebellion, was captured by the Italians after he was wounded in battle near Slonta in the district of Jabal al Akhdar, tried and hanged in 1931. Al-Mukhtar was called "the Lion of the Desert" while he was fighting the Italian colonialists and he has become an Arab, Islamic and international legend after his death. His final years battling the Italian forces were depicted in the American movie "Lion of the Desert" in 1981 a mosque in Tampa, Florida, is named "Masjid Omar Al-Mukhtar." Most Arab countries have streets named after al-Mukhtar and his picture appears on the Libyan ten-dinar bill.

Idris al-Mahdi al-senussi (later King Idris I), led Libyan resistance against the Italian occupation after the death of Al-Mukhtar. In World War II, Italy and Germany lost the war and its colonies to the British and the

French. From 1943 to 1951, Tripolitania and Cyrenaica regions came under the control of Britain, while France took over the administration of Fezzan. The UN General Assembly passed a resolution on November 21st 1949 stating that Libya should become independent state before January 1952, and Idris al-senussi represented Libya in the negotiations. Libya was declared on December 24, 1951 a constitutional and hereditary monarchy under King Idris al-senussi. The first Libyan constitution that formally established the creation of a single Libyan nation state was drafted by the Libyan National Assembly and accepted in a meeting held in the city of Benghazi on 7th of October, 1951. The constitution contained many of the entrenched rights common to European and North American nations. It set out equal civil and political rights, equality before the law, equal opportunity and equal responsibility for public duties and obligations, "without distinction of religion, belief, race, language, wealth, kinship or political or social opinions," but it proclaims Islam the religion of the State. The draft was submitted to King Idris al-senussi, then published in the Official Gazette of Libya.

The Berber

The Berbers or Amazigh are the indigenous inhabitants of Northwestern Africa and the Sahara. They had been living as predominantly but not entirely nomadic tribes. They had their own culture and Afro-Asian language with different dialectal variations before the Arab invasion, since the beginning of civilization undisturbed except when there were foreign invaders or natural calamities. The common language spread westward from Egypt across the Sahara into the whole North Africa region under the Ancient Greeks, the Carthaginians and the Romans.

Unlike other ancient peoples who lived in the ME, the Berbers did not leave recorded history because they had no written language. The Moroccan Berber language, the Tamazight, has been revived as a written language with a modified Latin script with the help of UNESCO.

Archaeologists have discovered paintings depicting farming and domestic activities in South Libyan caves. Some of them are more than a thousand years old. Before the Arabs invaded the region and forced the Berbers to convert to Islam, the majority was Animist and some followed Christianity and Judaism. The Animist Berbers believe that humans, animals and plants have their own souls that unite them all in harmony and peace.

The Arabs started raiding and settling the indigenous-Berber (Amazigh) territory after their Muslim armies conquered Egypt in 642. They called the area of North Africa west of Egypt, "Bilad al-Maghrib," which means (Lands of the West). The Arabs arrived from Arabia in big number during the early years of Islam when an expedition of Muslim warriors from the Arab Bani Muzaina tribe under the leadership of the adopted son of the Prophet, Zaid ibn Haritha, invaded North Africa in the 7th century. All North Africa became a province of the Muslim empire in 705 under the Umayyad Caliphs. Arab Muslims had much more impact on the culture of North Africa than did the region's conquerors before and after them.

The big migration of Arabs was when Libya fell to the Shi'a Fatimids of Egypt in the 10th century and the Berber Zirid tribes broke away from them and refused to accept their rule. The Fatimids brought the Arab tribes of Bani Hilal and Bani Salim to the country to assist in containing the Berber resistance. By the 11th century, most Berbers had become Islamized and many Arabized. They followed a nomadic lifestyle rearing cattle and sheep. Bani Hilal and Bani Salim were unruly Arab Bedouin tribes originally from Hejaz and Najd with the "infamous reputation" of being late in conversion to Islam. At one time they had participated in the pillage of Mecca in 930. The Fatimids had to confine them in South Arabia for years before forcing them to relocate first to south Egypt, then to Libya and the rest of North Africa.

The unfolding tales of Bani Hilal long journey became part of the Arab epic folk literature that recounts events in Arabia and during the march to North Africa. According to Ibn Khaldun, the Fatimids sent them to settle in the Maghreb accompanied by their wives, children and stock. After repeatedly fighting battles against the Berbers, they eventually coexisted with them. The Arab tribes began the process of transforming North African culture into Arabic including the nomad tribal life in areas where agriculture had previously been dominant. The vast majority of North Africans today, especially Moroccans and Algerians, are Arabized Berber, and it is impossible to trace a purely Arab lineage due to intermarriage between the two ethnic groups. While most Berbers are Muslims, they are more liberal than their co-religious Arabs. They do not have rigid segregation of the sexes as in traditional Arab tribes and they are more secular regarding religion and the state.

The Berber tribes had their own way of life and traditional internal socialized system based on egalitarian principles to achieve survival for all members of the tribe. One purpose of this system was to eliminate poverty by sharing the harvest of nature amongst all members of the community. They had a tradition of providing grain and other essential food supplies during harvest for the poor and the sick members of the tribe. Each tribe had its tribal council of elders with a representative tribal leader that include males and females. During the Middle Ages, a woman called Kabylia led the fight against the French. Due to the foreign invaders of the indigenous people in North Africa, some traditions including the egalitarian system are being weakened, but the social tribal system especially the loyalty is still an important part of the North African Berber societies. Most North Africans' surnames include the name of their tribe. Colonel Muammar Gaddafi, for example, came from the Gaddafi tribe, an Arabized Berber tribe of the ancient Greater Syrtis region, now known as Sirte.

Under the banner of Islam, the Moroccan-Berbers helped the establishment of a foothold and a great civilization in Europe that lasted six centuries. In 711–718, a large army of mostly Berber fighters led by the legendary Muslim General Tariq ibn Ziyad crossed the Strait of Gibraltar from North Africa coast at what is today known as the Rock of Gibraltar and conquered Spain and Portugal. The Christians began the long drawn-out process known in Spanish history as the Reconquista, which eventually led to the eviction of the Muslim-Moors from Spain in 1340.

In the eleventh and twelfth centuries, the Berbers established many dynasties in North Africa based on Islamic ideologies. These included al-Murabeteen and al-Muwahedeen in the Sahara and High Atlas, the Marinids at Fes-Morocco, the Ziyanids at Tlemcen-Algeria, and the Hafsids at Tunis-Tunisia.

There are hundreds of Berber and Arabized Berber tribes in North Africa and across the entire Sahara region today, but their number has not been officially verified because the tribes of the Sahara never been included in any census. They are estimated at 50% of the population in Morocco and between 10% and 23% of the Libyan population today. Some historians note that the population of the Libyan Berbers in the 1950s was close to 50% and the current drop in percentage has been due to government policies of making it easy for ethnic-Arabs to have citizenship. The increase of Egyptians and Tunisians granted Libyan citizenship by King Idris and Gaddafi led to the current drop in the Berber percentage. Libyan population was two million in 1968, and under Gaddafi's rule the population rose to more than five million.

The Berbers became an integral part of the Arab Spring movement in Libya and Morocco. The Berbers of Libya joined the rebel forces that overthrew Gaddafi the Berber tribe of Tuareg declared large swathes of the north Mali a self-rule homeland and in Morocco, they demonstrated and forced the king to make important concessions. King Muhammad VI presented reforms to defuse the Berber protests. He included a constitutional amendment to make the Berber language, the Tamazight, an official language alongside Arabic.

The Arab Spring in Libya

Muammar Gaddafi led a small group of military officers in a bloodless military coup against King Idris on September 1st 1969. He ruled Libya for forty-two years and saw himself go from a revolutionary hero to a self-centered unconventional unpredictable tyrant and international pariah. Gaddafi chose to be referred to in government statements and official Libyan press as "Brother Leader and Guide of the Revolution." He created "people's committees" vested with no power, authority or budgets, with the knowledge that anyone who criticized the regime could be carted off to prison. Gaddafi spent his political life reinventing himself from pan-Arab as an eager disciple of Egypt's President Jamal Abdel-Nasser then he became a pan-Islamist and finally he switched to a staunch pan-African advocate.

Gaddafi was an important player on the international stage because he presided over Libya with its small population (less than three million at the time) and significant oil reserves. Libya under his leadership was the first oil producer country to secure the majority share of oil revenue. He directed funds toward public education for both sexes and health care for everyone at no cost, but this was accompanied by political repression at home and controversial foreign policy. Unrestrained by any of the normal governance controls, he was able to fund militant "anti-imperialist" groups abroad that he liked and buy loyalty of African governments with his petro-dollars. Gaddafi was given the honorific title of "King of Kings of Africa" in 2008 as part of his campaign for a United States of Africa. Foreign leaders tolerated his long boring speeches in international gatherings, his unconventional behavior and outlandish clothing. European leaders visited Gaddafi in his tent, and on his official visits to Europe, they accommodated his strange needs to have his nomadic style tent erected in the center of their capitals.

Gaddafi was a ruthless ruler, never tolerated any criticism of his regime, sentence lengthy jail and execution without fair trial for dissidents, and his global intelligence network were accused of killing many of the Libyan exiles. He was accused of supporting terrorist organizations including the Irish Republican Army that was declaring attrition war against the British presence in Northern Ireland for years before the "Good Friday Agreement" of 1998. Despite conflicting evidence and dubious circumstances, in 2009 one of Gaddafi's intelligence officers was found guilty of 270 counts of murder in connection with the bombing of Pan Am 103, a passenger jet. Perhaps to placate the US, Gaddafi accepted responsibility for the bombing and agreed to pay $10 million to the relatives of each of the people killed. His governing style and the oppression did not endear him to his country-people. When the Arab Spring arrived in Libya, Gaddafi could not withstand the tide of his country's popular feelings that swept him away in a cruel undignified death.

On Feb 15, 2011, the Libyan anti-government protests began in front of Benghazi police headquarters to protest the arrest of a human rights lawyer who had represented relatives of political prisoners allegedly massacred by the government security in Tripoli's Abu Salem jail in 1996. The peaceful demonstrations turned into confrontations when Libyan military and security forces fired live ammunition on the protesters killing and injuring many. The Libyan activists formed the National Conference for the Libyan Opposition and declared a "Day of Rage" to protest the government use of force against peaceful demonstrators. The security forces panicked and withdrew from Benghazi when they lost control and many of their members joined the protesters. The anti-Gaddafi coalition established a provisional government in Benghazi, called 'the National Transitional Council' with the ultimate goal of overthrowing Gaddafi's government in Tripoli.

It developed into a brutal war between popular opposition forces and Moammar Gaddafi military and loyalists. The city was captured by the rebels, the government was overthrown, and the ruthless dictator Gaddafi, was killed by armed mob on Oct 20,2011. Gaddafi's fall put an end to Libya as a country with a functioning central government. The successful overthrow of Gaddafi, in which the West especially the US played a leading role, has left that country in chaos because his regime centered on himself and his family. There were no national institutions, and even no strong regular army to pick up the pieces and govern the country.

The primary beneficiaries of Gaddafi's ouster seem to be al-Qaida's affiliates in North Africa and the Sahara. Seven years after the death of Gaddafi, Libya today is divided into three tribal groups vying for control of the country and its natural resources.

Libya's militiamen acquired arsenals of looted weapons that outgun anything the central government could muster. The UN tried to bring peace by supervising elections when the Islamic parties suffered sharp defeat. The Islamist heavily armed militia groups formed the "Libya Dawn" coalition, seized the capital city of Tripoli and forced the new government to flee to the city of Tubruk and bunker down in its hotels. Libya's new warlords and militia chiefs were loath to forgo the inheritance they had grabbed and argued for a total overhaul of anything that had to do with the old power. They rejected the elected parliament and the post-Gaddafi fledging government demands to disband or hand over their captives or surrender their bases.

The militias turned on each other in turf wars, full-scale civil war has since raged across the country and ISIS loyalists established a foot-hold in

"Libya Dawn" territory and expanded amid the chaos. With thousands dead and towns destroyed, Libya's territory would fragment into its three tribal constituent parts: Benghazi region in the east, Tripoli Tania in the west and Fezzan desert area in the south.

Libya in 2015 was ruled by two rival parliaments, the Islamist National Salvation government (INS) based in Tripoli and the internationally recognized parliament in Tobruk, and many militia groups who recognized their lack of legitimacy, but they continued to maintain their own prisons and makeshift judicial systems. A 2015 UN-brokered peace talks established a Government of National Accord (GNA) that would be the legitimate government in Tripoli. The governments of the two competing parliaments were supposed to cede power to the new UN-brokered government, but both administrations were unwilling to hand over the reins. While a number of powerful armed groups and municipalities supported GNA government, the Islamist militias that have come to rule the city of Tripoli refused to honor the brokered peace agreement and warned the Prime Minister-designate Fayez al-Sarraj and his cabinet to stay away. The would-be prime minister was forced to travel by boat because the airspace of the city from which he planned to govern was closed. Leaders of Tripoli-based parliament even called the members of GNA government "illegitimate infiltrators."

By 2016, Libya had a third rival administration under an army led by Khalifa Hafter, a retired Gaddafi-era general, and many areas under militants loyal only to their commanders. They have been competing for territory, economic resources and political leverage. Hafter's Libyan National Army (LNA) seized key oil export terminals in the east. In 2017, his forces, with strong support from neighboring Egypt, ejected ISIS group from Benghazi after three years of fighting and liberated the city from Ansar al-Sharia Islamists who had been accused of being behind the fatal 2012 attack on the US consulate. Human rights organizations accused some of Hafter's commanders of committing mass executions.

Egypt, the chief backer of Khalifa Hafter has joined the civil war. The execution of Egyptian Christian expatriates by ISIS terrorists has turned the civil war into an international conflict. Some Egyptian security officials even toyed with hiving-off Libya's oil-rich eastern province and annexing it to Egypt. Egyptian warplanes launched air strikes on the Libyan city of Darna days after masked militants boarded vehicles en route to a monastery in the southern Egyptian province of Minya and opened fire at close range, killing more than 45 in May 2017. All the victims were Egyptian Christians and ISIS claimed responsibility for that attack. ISIS had beheaded expatriate

Christian workers in Libya, claimed responsibility for church bombings killing scores of worshipers in north Egypt and in Sinai.

After the decades of persecution by Gaddafi, leaders of the non-Arab Berber tribes built alliances with other Berber ethnic population in the mountains of Morocco, Sahara oases, Mali and Egypt to promote their separate language and culture. Along Libya's borders, warlords today are managing the smuggling routes for Africans seeking refuge in Europe, reviving the ancient entre-pots and coastal city-states. Thousands of African immigrants risking the crossing of the Mediterranean from Libya have become a major European issue especially in Italy. The journeys have claimed thousands of lives and created tension between Italy and the European Union regarding the role of rescue ships operated by humanitarian groups and nongovernmental organizations. Italian government is considering denying landing rights to rescue ships if the EU does not help. A stable Libya with a functioning government and a regular united military is the only means to defeat the smuggling networks and end the flow of refugees through the Mediterranean.

Libya has continued to descend into chaos, with factions fighting against one another. These include tribe militias, ISIS, former members of Gaddafi's military, and many other factions. And now Libyan politics have been defined by three coalitions, each claiming to be Libya's legitimate government. The General National Congress is largely MB-influenced and is supported by Qatar, and in the past it was supported by Turkey General Khalifa Hafter and his LNA Army is supported by Saudi Arabia, UAE and Egypt and the Government of National Accord is recognized by the UN as the legitimate government.

France has been trying to play peacemaker role in Libya where years of efforts by the UN and former colonial power, Italy, failed to bring stability. The French president, Emmanuel Macron has convened many face-to-face talks between the leaders of the main rival Libyan factions to restore order where lawlessness has fed Islamic militancy and instability in the wider region. Two competing leaders in Libya today are Fayez al-Sarraj, head of the UN-backed government of National Accord based in Tripoli the capital, and khalifa Hafter, head of the so-called LNA Army that controls large tracts of territory to the east. They have been unable to agree on a power sharing compromise to reunite the country.

The Arab Spring in Libya went so bad for many reasons, mainly for the lack of functioning institutions after decades of Gaddafi's one man rule, and Libya's atomized tribal structure that makes cooperation hard and creates distrust. Seven years after the start of the revolution, Libya is a failing state, torn by civil war. The non-state armed groups are expanding, there's no democracy, the country is divided, the economy is in ruins and the dreams of 2011 are shattered.

7. THE ARAB SPRING IN SYRIA

In Syria, the ruling Assad family dynasty owes its primacy and survival in power for forty years to the military establishment. Hafez al-Assad was the commander of the Syrian air force and minister of defense when he seized power in 1970. He used the military as an instrument of sectarian rule, staffing it with the minority Alawites officers who would remain loyal to his regime. Hafez created a system of divide and rule to establish a rigid intolerant of dissent police state. To end a 1982 swelling insurgency in the City of Hama, his military killed thousands of its residents. Hafez treated Syria as personalized and family business with the support of the military headed by his tribal kens. Key ministries and state agencies served as important vehicles of patronage and provided an essential link between the presidency and its support base. When Hafez died, the government institutions were so weak to govern that the regime had to recruit his son Bashar, a medical student in Britain, to inherit the presidency. His only known political qualifications were his last name.

In May of 2011, Syrians demonstrated in Dera'a city demanding the release of teenagers who had been arrested and tortured for alleged anti-regime graffiti. The government security forces opened fire, killing and injuring many demonstrators. Instead of apologizing, President Assad threatened and indulged in conspiracy theories. This was the spark that ignited anger and more protests in the cities of Damascus, Hums, Aleppo and other population centers. They were demanding free life, end to government corruption and arbitrary arrest, independent judiciary, abolition of torture, justice and genuine elections leading to legitimate authority. President Bashar al-Assad answer was arrests and violence including the deployment of tanks and harsh military crackdown on the protesters. The protests and the government response led to a widespread rebellion and continued bloodshed. Thousands were rounded up, tortured, killed or disappeared. Soldiers burned crops and killed livestock and neighborhoods were blasted by big guns, airplanes, Scud missiles and Sarin gas.

In the "Arab Spring," Syria has become the most desolate country on Earth, half its population displaced and most cities destroyed with a hodge-podge of fighters descending from all over the world. Syria had the worst of both worlds after the "Arab Spring," a divided country, the preservation of the brutal regime under the protection of Russia, and a power vacuum in territory that was filled with separatists and extremists. Israel continues to occupy the Golan Heights, the Palestinian refugees in Syria suffered with the Syrian people and the "Palestinian issue" is no more a Syrian concern.

The escalation of the regime's brutal suppression caused international condemnation and calls for imposing sanctions. After killing hundreds of demonstrators in Hama and other cities, US Secretary of State, Hillary Clinton declared in July that "Assad lost legitimacy." Vast majority of the UN General Assembly members supported a resolution asking Assad to resign. Russia blocked resolutions critical of President Assad at the UN Security Council and has continued to supply weapons to the Syrian military despite international criticism. The UN Security Council condemned "widespread violations of human rights and the use of force against civilians by the Syrian authorities," but Russia and China vetoed resolutions threatening sanctions against the regime. Many militant opposition groups were created. The Syrian National Council (SNC) and hundreds of military defectors including high level ranks established Free Syrian Army (FSA) with the aim of toppling Assad regime. The SNC was claimed as "a legitimate representative" of Syria by a collection of more than 100 countries including the US, France, Britain, and Saudi Arabia.

The situation in Syria became more complicated when foreign jihadist groups and ethnic separates Kurds joined the rebellion and the Lebanese Hezbollah and Iranian militias came to defend the regime. The International Committee of the Red Cross declared the situation in Syria a sectarian and ethnic civil war. What started as a progressive call for social and political reforms turned into a sectarian clash and became war of all against all. While Syrians were doing most of the fighting and dying, the regime and the opposition welcomed foreigners into their ranks. Iranian, Afghani and Lebanese Shiites fighters reinforced the government military, and Sunni jihadists from many countries joined the rebels.

As for the involvement of Iran in the Syrian civil war, the Institute for the Study of War concluded that "Iran has conducted an extensive, expensive, and integrated effort to keep President Bashar al-Assad in power as long as possible." Iran along with the Lebanese Hezbollah and several Iraqi Shiite militias have been heavily involved in Syria's civil war. They helped the Syrian regime consolidate control and regain completely destroyed towns lost to Syrian rebels and jihadists. With Iranian ground support, other Shiite militias and Russian airstrikes, Assad's forces recaptured the rebel-held Syria's towns including the large city of Aleppo.

Many rebel groups joined the fighting including ISIS, Jabhat Fateh al-Sham, Iran-backed Hezbollah, and the Syrian Democratic Force (SDF) dominated by Kurdish People Protection Units (YPG). The group calling itself the Islamic State of Iraq and Syria (ISIS) that had an ideology even more extreme and brutal than Al-Qaeda emerged in northern and eastern Syria after achieving military breakthrough by capturing major cities of Mosul and Tekreet in Iraq and the provinces of Raqqa and Kobane in Syria. The ranks of ISIS included a sizable number of fighters from around the world.

It was estimated that over 27,000 foreign fighters from at least 68 countries travelled to Syria and Iraq and joined ISIS and other extremist groups in the region since fighting broke out in 2011. Most non-state entities involved in the war in Syria receive various types of support from foreign countries. Many opposition groups received financial, logistic and political support from Middle East major Sunni states, most notably Saudi Arabia, Qatar and Turkey. The US, France, Canada and the UK provided political and military support to rebel groups that were not designated by them as terrorists. Iraqi Kurdistan and the US provided military and logistic support to the Syrian Kurdish 'People's Protection' group, and the US provided air support against ISIS and other radical militant groups. Kurdish groups in northern Syria are seeking self-rule in areas under their control. They have formed an arc of influence in Syria that advances the broader Kurdish project of a sovereign state carved from north-eastern Turkey, parts of Iran and the existing Iraqi Kurdistan. This raised alarm in Ankara because it emboldened its own separatist Kurdish rebels who have been challenging the state for years.

The conflict in Syria is widely described as a series of overlapping wars of Shi'a against Sunni, Iran against Saudi Arabia, US against Russia and Turkey against the Kurds. Analysts anticipated Syria's disintegration into a Sunni central area running north-south linking Syria's most populous cities, and Alawite territory that runs from the Syrian Mediterranean coast through Lebanese mountains to southern Lebanon. Syria's northern Kurdish towns feed Kurdish aspirations not only for autonomy, but a pan-Kurdish state which links neighboring Kurdish zones in Turkey and Iraq. And in 2015,

Russia intervened directly in the Syrian civil war in support of Assad regime the US armed the Kurds and provided them with advisors in 2017 while Turkey had declared war against the Kurds, thus transforming the conflict from regional conflict into a direct geostrategic war.

The rise of armed Islamist groups is linked to the organic crisis of the Arab states, a crisis of failed political and economic governance decades in the making under secular regimes manipulated by foreign powers. The fragility of the Arab states regimes created a free-for-all struggle for influence and hegemony advantage by regional and foreign powers and the rebirth of the non-state actors, including ISIS. Syria has become a place of "proxy wars": the Sunni theocrats of Saudi Arabia and the Gulf States against the Shiite mullahs of Iran Turkey against the Kurds to prevent the establishment of Great Kurdistan Arab nationalists against Turkey over the attempted restoration of Turkey's old dominance and Russia for control over the strategic ME region that had been for too long under US hegemony.

The war created so much suffering, thousands died and wounded, families were buried alive, babies died in their cribs, children became orphans, neighborhoods and entire cities were destroyed and millions have become refugees seeking safety in neighboring countries and in Europe.

Without Russian military support, the Syrian regime might well have crumbled against the rebel groups. Assad accepted Iran, Russia and Hezbollah armed forces to rescue his regime from collapse. Their support has kept Syria from becoming a failed state altogether, like Libya. But large areas of Syria are held by beleaguered democratic nationalists, Arab or Kurdish, and a lot is strangled by transnational jihadists.

The US says its military involvement in Syria's civil war has been limited to small numbers of Special Forces supporting the Kurds against ISIS and other jihadist groups. The US wars in Iraq and Afghanistan have been very costly in terms of lives and resources destroyed this has eroded the American people's confidence in their government's actions. They have become weary of war and skeptical about promises of easy military engagements with positive outcomes. The Obama administration understood that there was little domestic appetite for becoming embroiled in another ME war.

President Obama drew "a red line" that would have "enormous consequences" and "change my calculus" for the Syrian government against the usage or the transfer of chemical weapon in the war, only to back away from it when the Syrian regime crossed his red line. The Syrian military attacked rebel-controlled areas of Damascus suburb with chemical weapons on August 21, 2013 killing more than 1,600 civilians, including 400 children. Videos showed victims twisted bodies sprawled in hospital floors after being exposed to Sarin gas, a nerve agent that causes lung muscle paralysis and results in death from suffocation. Because this Syrian assault had clearly crossed Obama's "red line" the US was expected to retaliate, but instead of ordering air strikes, the President wanted first to ask Congress for explicit authorization. The American people and Congress were strongly opposed to have their armed forces involved in another Middle East conflict.

Finally Russian President Vladimir Putin gave Obama an escape hatch by offering to force Assad to surrender his chemical arsenal if Obama promised not to strike. The Obama administration accepted Russia's offer to remove all Syria's chemical weapons that was estimated at 1,300 tons. But chemical weapons kept being used in rebel-held areas, and according to the US government and Human Rights Watch the Syrian government forces were responsible.

The US administration under Obama had repeatedly stated its opposition to the Assad regime even before its alleged usage of the chemical weapons. The US and the European Union have accused the Syrian government of conducting several chemical attacks including dropping chlorine bombs on the towns of Ghouta in 2013, Talmenes in April 2014 and Sarmin in March 2015. The Syrian military used chemical weapon against the rebels in 2016 during the final weeks of the battle to retake the city of Aleppo, killing and injuring hundreds of civilians. But in keeping with his strategy of leading from behind as he did in Libya, Obama chose international cooperation rather than direct military action. Once President Trump came in office, he placed the US policy in hopes of having as big a stake as possible in Syria by defeating ISIS and countering the growing influence of Iran. The US brought its forces in conflict with Russia and Iran by expanding its military presence in southern Syria near its borders with Jordan. More US military forces supported the Syrian Democratic Forces fighting ISIS in northern Syria.

On April 7, 2017, President Trump ordered the first US direct attack on a Syrian government target. US warships launched fifty-nine Tomahawk missiles on the Shayrat Air Base that was said to be the source of a chemical attack which the Syrian government carried out on the rebel held town of Khan Shaykhun on April 3. But the big event in Syria's civil war was the defeat of ISIS in October 2017 when the Kurdish-dominated Syrian Democratic Forces established full control of the city of Raqqa in north Syria that was the de facto capital of ISIS. This was after months of fierce fighting and daily US-led coalition's bombardment and after establishing full control over Deir ez-zor and capturing the Abu Kamal in eastern Syria.

In seven years of war, more than half million Syrians lost their lives in the conflict, more than a million injured, and more than half Syria's population have been forced to leave their homes and seek safety internally, in neighboring countries and in Europe. The war destroyed Palmyra's temples and Aleppo's Umawi mosque minaret, monuments that survived earthquakes and Mongol invasions are now razed, and the social fabric of the country irreparably torn.

The countries involved in the Syrian civil war have failed to negotiate a comprehensive political solution especially after the direct involvement of Russia in support of Assad regime and retaking back most of the territory that was lost to the rebels. The Russians have saved the Syrian regime from collapse, but the country has been fragmented into many semi-autonomous regions that will continue to defy the central authority of the regime.

After routing the ISIS in Syria and Iraq, and if there will ever be a negotiated settlement in Syria, a new reality will be established for a long time to come. The Syrians had lost and would continue to lose their sovereignty and independence over their country. Many international and regional players including major global powers and myriad of rebel groups with conflicting interests were involved in the Syrian conflict they will be seeking a return on their costly investments. Russia is the most important international backer of President al-Assad his regime survival is critical to maintaining Russian interests in Syria. Russia will become more involved in Syria's security and defense to protect its only Mediterranean naval base facility which it had leased at the Syrian port of Tartus to support its Black Sea fleet.

The US supported Syria's main opposition alliance, the National Coalition, and provided military assistance during the war. The US will keep its more than 2000 military personnel in northern Syria to balance the Russian presence and Iranian influence on post-civil war Syrian regime. The present US administration national security interests in Syria is beyond just defeating the "Islamic State." It includes making sure any future political settlement of Syria's civil war would not surrender the country to Russia and Iran. The US has to shore up its most important Syrian partner, the Kurdish-dominated Syrian Democratic Forces and Syria's Kurd ethnic population's nationalists who aspire to have a Syrian Kurdistan as a repayment for helping in defeating ISIS.

Saudi Arabia, a provider of military and financial assistance for many rebel groups and a critic of Iran's meddling in the Arab states affairs will oppose any settlement that gives Iran a role in Syria. Israel has big stakes in Syria's civil war across its borders. It will do anything in its power to prevent the Lebanese Hezbollah from establishing a foothold on its borders with Syria. Its air-force penetrated Syrian airspace several times attacking many Hezbollah targets that included its weapon storages in Syria and weapon convoys destined for its fighters in Lebanon. Israel has acknowledged carrying out at least 100 clandestine strikes in Syria since 2011.

Turkey was a full-fledged party in the civil war by its military incursions into Syria and occasional shelling and airstrikes against the Syrian Kurdish militant group with ties to Turkey's Kurdish Workers Party (PKK). Turkey has been a key supporter of the Syrian opposition and it has faced the burden of hosting millions of the refugees. It allowed the US-led coalition against ISIS to use its air bases for strikes on Syria, but it had been critical of the coalition support for the Syrian Kurds Popular Protection Units (YPG), an affiliate of the banned PKK and the Kurdish-dominated Syrian Democratic Forces (SDF). Turkey also has territorial ambitions in north Syria, a border area it likes to annex. Should Turkey insist on keeping Syrian territory under its control, it may trigger direct confrontation with Syrian regime allies, Russia and Iran and even the US. The US has built bases in Kurds controlled territory in North Syria at the border with Turkey and announced to form a 30,000 strong Kurds-border-force. Turkey sent tanks across the frontier to take over the Syrian towns of Afrin and Manbij from the YPG units, and in the process, the Turks may be confronted with the US military stationed in the area.

There is talk on finding a comprehensive political settlement in Syria, but peace and normality there is a remote possibility. Should peace come, the challenges facing the future Syrian regime would be enormous. These include the task of reconciliation with the millions of aggrieved, injured and displaced, reintegrating the different regions of the country, the question of Syria's Kurdistan, deciding the status of the foreign troops remaining in the country, the future of millions of Syrian refugees who wish to return, and the cost of national reconstruction and development of cities, towns and infrastructures that are in ruin. But for now, the regime is effectively terrifying its civilian population.

The Palestinian Refugees in Syria

Before the Arab Spring, there were more than 600,000 Palestinian refugees and their descendants, both registered and unregistered in the UN Relief and Works Agency (UNRWA). They have been living in Syria before the civil war with160,000 living in the Yarmouk, the largest refugee camp. As the civil war gripped the country, the Palestinian refugees suffered like the rest of the Syrian people. Residents of the Yarmouk were caught in the fighting especially when members of ISIS infiltrated the camp and the government destroyed it in repeated attacks. After months of siege and bombardment, the camp has been reduced to piles of concrete rubble. The surviving refugees were forced to seek a new refuge once again. Some moved internally in Syria and many had to venture across the borders into Lebanon, Jordan, Turkey and Europe, much like their Syrian counterparts. More than 280,000 Palestinian refugees had to be displaced inside Syria as a result of the war, and another 110,000 left Syria, by 2017, according to the UNRWA.

Palestinian refugees who fled Syria to neighboring countries have found it harder than their Syrian counterparts. They were not welcome in the Arab countries. They faced hostilities, discrimination and stigmatization within the host countries because of their conditions as "stateless." They could not legally live in camps designated for displaced Syrians. Jordan announced in 2013 a non-entry policy for Palestinian refugees coming from Syria, leaving them vulnerable to arrest, exploitation and involuntary deportation back to Syria. The Lebanese treatment of the Palestinian refugees from Syria was even worse. Lebanon opened its doors to Syrians fleeing the conflict, but it met the Palestinians fleeing Syria with hostility and in 2014, it officially closed the borders to them. Egypt as well as the Gulf States does not issue entry visas for Palestinian refugees from Syria either. They cannot register with the UN High Commission for Refugees agency, and the underfunded UNRWA agency for assisting and protecting Palestinian refugees has been unable to provide for basic needs of Syria's Palestinian refugees in Jordan and Lebanon.

8. LEBANON

Lebanon is a small Mediterranean country with rich history, home of a multitude of ethnic and religious groups including Muslims (Sunnis and Shi'as), Christians (Maronites, Greek Orthodox, Greek Catholics, Protestants, and Armenians), a Druze community, Alawites and Ismailis. The different groups interact within the state and society with particular belief-systems and ways of life. They deploy methods that include violent resistance if necessary to protect or advance their right to practice their belief, and their political rights in their particular spaces. Sunni-Muslims and Christians are the majorities on the coastal cities, Shi'a-Muslims are mainly based in the south and the Beqaa to the east, and the mountain populations are Druze and Christians. Unlike the rest of the Middle East countries where Muslims are overwhelming majority, Lebanon diverse mix of Muslims and Christians, each make up approximately half the population. But both Christians and Muslims are sub-divided into many splinter sects and denominations.

Although Lebanon is considered the most liberal Arab country, its people practice a consensual democracy that deals with its multi-confessional diversity one that tries to accommodate all religions. It is faith based democracy. Their form of democracy had been inherited from the 1920–1943 French colonial period where the parliamentary structure, the presidency, and the hierarchy in the military are distributed among the different faiths and sects, granting Christian groups some privileges. Based on its demography today, the Lebanese democracy favors the Christians even more.

For centuries, Lebanon has been the Maronite and the Druze communities home, retreat and fortress. Both groups survived invasions and repression for over hundreds of years in Lebanon while preserving their religions and cultures. They sometimes were allies and in many other times fought each other. Many clans that had originated from Arab tribes settled between Tripoli and Beirut centuries ago, then some of them moved to Bekaa' region where they continued to live. The Lebanese clans have members trained to take up arms if needed when the government does not protect them. The Lebanese Christians had their "Lebanese Forces" mainly staffed by Maronite s and comprised of "Phalangists," the "Tigers," "al-Tanzim," "the Guardians" and "al-Kata'eb" militias, the Sunni-Muslims had the "Lebanese Front," the Shi'a formed "Hezbollah." Lebanon's recent history is that of its faith and ethnic based minorities, the Maronites, the Druz, the Sunni and Shi'a, and the Palestinian refugees.

The followers of its eighteen recognized sects corresponding to different religions range from fanatic to agnostic or even atheists. Compared to other Arab countries, the Lebanese are not religious, but religion for every Lebanese is a tribal identity not necessary a faith to practice its rituals and teachings. Officially, religion and sect defines the rights and obligations and the limits of the individual political ambitions. No official census has been taken since 1932 when the population was only 875,252 with around 53% as Christians. Conducting a census today is a very sensitive issue due to the sectarian divisions and the pressure that some groups may exert for more political power in case there was a shift in the demographics. It is estimated that the population today exceeds six million the majority is Muslim with the Shi'a the single largest group. The Palestinian refugees in Lebanon, victims of 1948 and 1967 Arab-Israeli wars are not accorded the legal rights enjoyed by the rest of the population. They exceed half a million registered with the UN Relief and Works Agency (UNRWA).

Lebanon and Syria are twines and we cannot talk about one without including the other in the discussion. By the end of World War I, the French put together a state in Syria, but failed to create nationality to go with it. The Syrian Arab nationalists refused to accept the French mandate. They revolted and demanded independence for 'Great Syria' that includes Lebanon, Palestine and Trans-Jordan. For a brief time, they had a kingdom under Prince Faysal with its capital in historical Damascus, once the seat of great Umayyad caliphs. The 1925 uprising against the French that lasted two years, provoked the French bombardment of Damascus, destroyed the kingdom, then the French established five mini-states including Lebanon on Syria's territory. In addition to Lebanon, the French established four Syrian states: the State of Aleppo, the State of Damascus, the State of Alawites and the State of Jabal al-Druze. Local Arab nationalist leaders who failed to establish the kingdom under Faysal used the strong popular sentiment for unity against the French to force four of the mini-states to merge and form the Syrian Republic. From the Arab nationalist view, the Syrian Republic did not satisfy the aspiration of its people because it does not include all the Arab land east of the Mediterranean. Lebanon and Syria as sovereign states today are the outcome of the great powers design in the 1916 Sykes-Picot Agreement, the San Remo Conference and the 1920 League of Nations decision to grant the mandate for the two countries to France.

After independence, Lebanon enjoyed periods of prosperity built on tourism and Beirut's position as a regional center for education, publishing, finance and trade, but other areas of the country, notably the South, North, and Bekaa' Valley, remained economically poor in comparison. The relative calm was intercepted with periods of political turmoil. An insurrection broke out in 1958 and US forces were briefly dispatched to the country in response to an appeal by President Camille Chamoun. In 1970, problems arose over the presence of more Palestinian refugees and the arrival of the PLO armed groups from Jordan that triggered Muslims vs. Christians' conflict, Syria's military intervention and Israeli invasions. Lebanon became a hopeless country at war with itself. It was engulfed in a bloody sectarian civil war that lasted from 1975 to 1991 Israel invaded the country in 1978, and its military units reached Beirut in 1982.

The 1982 Israeli invasion of Lebanon during the civil war and its collective punishment added more misery and torn the country to shreds. The PLO resistance was the alleged target of the invasion, but Israel's military smashed its way to Beirut, destroying 20,000 Lebanese lives and injuring many more. The New York Times reported "indiscriminate" bombing of Beirut. Israel's reign of terror fell over this defenseless country Israel dropped bombs all over civilian infrastructures including hospitals. The Israelis forced Yasser Arafat and the 6,000 PLO fighters to leave Lebanon and go mostly to Tunisia on September 10, 1982.

On September 16, 1982 and one day after the assassination of President-elect Bashir Gemayyel, the Israeli army encircled and sealed Palestinian refugee camps Sabra and Shatila which were home for hundreds of thousands, and allowed the Phalange militiamen to enter the camps with their weapons. The Phalanges massacred thousands of unarmed civilian Palestinians, mainly women, children and elderly. The Israeli forces provided support to the Phalanges armed gangs by preventing civilians from leaving the camps and illuminating the night by launching flares.

The spark that started the 1975 civil war was the killing of four members of the Phalanges Party during an attempt to assassin the Maronite leader Pierre Jumayyil. The Phalangists accused the Palestinians of the crime and retaliated by attacking a bus carrying Palestinian passengers. Fighting and random killing erupted in earnest and the country fragmented into a system of religion based militias with shifting alliances. Leftist, pan-Arabist and Muslim Lebanese groups formed alliance with the Palestinians. Foreign powers, Israel and Syria, became involved in the war and fought alongside different factions. It was the beginning of a war that lasted 15 years until a committee appointed by the Arab League, chaired by Kuwait and including Saudi Arabia, Algeria, and Morocco formulated a solution to the conflict. It led to a 1989 meeting of Lebanese parliamentarians in Ta'if, Saudi Arabia, where they agreed to a national reconciliation accord. The Chamber of Deputies was expanded to 128 seats divided equally between the followers of the Christian Faith (who included Roman Catholics, Maronites, Orthodox, Protestant and Armenians), and the followers of the Islam Faith (who included Alawites, Druze, Shi'a and Sunnis). The president remained a Maronite Christian, the prime minister a Sunni-Muslim, and the speaker of the Parliament a Shiite-Muslim. October 13, 1990 marked the official end of the Lebanese civil war and in 1991, the parliament finally passed an amnesty law that pardoned all political crimes prior to its enactment. It has been estimated that more than 150,000 most of them civilians are believed to have perished in the fifteen year war. Another 100,000 left handicapped and about one million were displaced from their homes. Much of the once beautiful city of Beirut was reduced to rubble, and the city was divided into two separated sectors, Muslim and Christian.

So many lives were wasted in Lebanon's civil war including civilians, political, religious and other civil society leaders who were assassinated in cold blood. This is a partial list of prominent Lebanese, whose lives were cut short by the civil war:

Maarouf Saad, Mayor of Sidon and founder of the Nasserist Party

Kamal Jumblatt, Druze leader and founder of the Progressive Socialist Party

Tony Franjieh, son of former President Suleiman Franjieh

Salim Lawzi, a prominent journalist

Riad Taha, journalist and president of Lebanese Publishers Association

Bashir Gemayyel, President-elect and son of Pierre Gemayyel, founder of Lebanese Forces

Sheikh Ahmad Assaf, a distinguished Sunni cleric

Subhi Saleh, head of the Sunni Islamic Higher Council

Rashid Karami, former Prime Minister

Muhammad Choucair, adviser to former President Amine Gemayyel

Hasan Khaled, former Grand Mufti of Lebanon's Sunni Muslim community

Nazem el-Qadri, member of the Lebanese Parliament

Rene Moawad, former Lebanese President

Dany Chamoun, son of the former Lebanese President Camille Chamoun

Seventeen years after the Ta'if Agreement of 1989 that ended the bloody civil-war, Lebanon suddenly faced a new political crisis in 2006 when the government decided to control Hezbollah unauthorized activities. The government ordered the removal of security surveillance network installed by Hezbollah in Beirut International Airport. Hezbollah objected, riots and heavy clashes between supporters and opponents of Hezbollah followed in several areas in the country especially in the North. Weapons were used and more than 300 Lebanese died before the Arab States acted to stop the violence. The 'Doha Agreement' among the rival Lebanese political factions was reached in Doha, Qatar on May 15, 2008 to end the eighteen month long fighting under the aegis of the Arab Ministerial Committee. This agreement like previous agreements, failed to tackle the root of the political crisis, the structural problem of Lebanon's system of government that has been institutionalized and cannot be solved by dealing with the symptoms.

Since the Doha Agreement, the Lebanese government collapsed twice in 2011 and 2013, the presidency was vacant for 29 months from 2014 to 2016, and the parliament extended its mandate several times. The Lebanese elected a new parliament in 2018 after nine years of the last elections, 49 percent of eligible voters turned out. The militant Shiite-Iranian backed Hezbollah won more seats than ever. Supporters of Sunni candidates took to the streets protesting Hezbollah victory while the militant party supporters stormed into Sunni neighborhoods, shooting guns in the air celebrating their big gain in the parliament. Religion or more precisely, sect-identity defines the rights and obligations of the individual in Lebanon, and that has bedeviled the country's notion of citizenship.

Lebanon and Israel

Lebanon joined other Arab countries against Israel in the 1948 war and never signed a peace treaty with it. The two countries are still technically in a state of war, but they have been bound by an armistice agreement which regulates the presence of their militaries at the border since 1949. Lebanon was considered the least hostile Arab state to Israel, but it has proven in recent decades to be a deadly arena of bloodshed and war. Lebanon played no role in the 1967 war, but Lebanese lands were occupied in the war.

In the Cairo Agreement of November 1969, the Arab states gave the PLO special status in Lebanon, and in 1970, the entire PLO armed groups moved to Lebanon. The PLO used the country as a launching pad for military actions against Israel and Hezbollah militias established bases in the Shi'a majority south to defend against Israel's cross-border attacks. There were occasional skirmishes and serious confrontations, and Israel's military had a history of crossing the borders especially when the PLO made attacks on Israel from bases in Lebanon. In 1968, Israeli Commandos landed at Beirut airport and blew up the fleet of Lebanon's airline in retaliation for Palestinian militants firing on one Israeli airliner in Athens, Greece. As described above, Israel invaded Lebanon in 1978 and again in 1982 to drive the PLO out during Lebanon's civil war.

When the Israeli forces withdrew from Lebanon in 1978, they established a "security zone" north of the border manned by elements of Christian Lebanese willing to serve as Israel's proxy in "South Lebanon Army" under the command of Major Saed Haddad, a renegade Lebanese Army officer. In 1996, Israel accused Hezbollah of shelling northern Israel and launched a massive air and artillery attack on southern Lebanon. During the two weeks offensive, a UN shelter for Lebanese civilians at Qana village, Lebanon, was the target of Israeli shelling, killing 118 Lebanese civilians and wounding 350. Hezbollah responded with more than 600 rockets targeting Israeli settlements wounding more than 50 civilians. Saed Haddad's "South Lebanon Army" also engaged in the fighting against Hezbollah.

After the Hezbollah Lebanese Shiite militia forced Israel to withdraw its military from southern Lebanon to its side of the UN designated border in 2000, mines in the border area continue to take Lebanese lives and injure farmers. The Israeli military retains control over Lebanese Sheba-Farms, claiming this as Israeli territory as part of the Golan Heights which was captured from Syria in th1967 war.

The IDF soldiers and Hezbollah fighters eye each other over the border. Border wars broke between Hezbollah and Israel in 2006 and in 2018. In July of 2006, a thirty-three day war broke when Israel accused Hezbollah of killing three of its IDF soldiers in a cross-border raid. It sent thousands of ground troops into south Lebanon to destroy Hezbollah bunkers and rocket-launching sites. Vicious fighting took place where 119 Israeli soldiers and 40 civilians lost their lives more than 1,000 Lebanese, mostly civilians, died over the course of the fighting before a UN cease fire took hold. An Israeli committee appointed by Prime Minister Ehud Olmert to examine the conduct of the 2006 war concluded that the war was a "severe failure" on the part of Israel.

Lebanon and Israel have maritime border disputes over a 325-square-mile triangular area of the Mediterranean along the edge of gas energy blocks that Lebanon put to tender in 2017. The dispute started in 2010 when Israel and

Cyprus signed a maritime border agreement that, according to the Lebanese, overlaps with parts of its Exclusive Economic Zone.

The Maronites

A small rebellious self-identified ethnic group united by confessional identity seeking independence and freedom, the Maronites inherited the virtues of hard work and ingenuity. They are named after a fifth-century hermit called 'Maroun' or Maron, who later on became a saint. He preached the word of God and attracted pagan people from the mountains of his retreat who were drawn by his wisdom and desired to live under his spiritual guidance. As his disciples increased in numbers, they began to be called 'Maronites'. A priest and one of Saint Maroun's disciples, called Abraham of Cyrrhus, set out to convert the area's pagans to Christianity. He founded an eremitic community, a place for hermits, on Mount Lebanon in Aqura near the river Adonis (named after the Phoenician god). After the community in that region was converted to Christianity, the river was renamed the 'Abraham River'.

A Maronite monastery called Beth-Maroun that was built near Maroun's tomb became the nucleus of the community where the spiritual leaders guided and protected their faithful with wisdom. Until today, their spiritual leaders have kept watch over the political and social rights of their flocks. Some Maronites claim they are the true Lebanese people and their heritage is of ancient Phoenicia, predating the Arab heritage by thousands of years, and that "none of their neighbors ever had its historic experience." Theirs, they claim, was an ocean navigation heritage once shared with Greece and Rome and which now they share with Western Europe. But not every Lebanese, including many Maronites or Christians, thought or felt as these did.

Many of the early Arab national movement leaders were Lebanese Christians, who promoted Arab nationalism rather than sectarianism. Lebanon has been for long time the center of Middle East intellectual activities and the Christian Lebanese were the first to achieve the social status of bourgeoisie, due to their easy access to education in the missionary schools. The Syrian Protestant College, which was opened in Beirut in 1866, was the first high education institution that trained Arab students in education, science, literature and medicine. It has been credited with graduating many Arab nationalist pioneers.

George Antonius (1891–1942), the son of Christian parents, argued in his book Arab Awakening that Arab nationalism and the call for Arab unity and renaissance has been sustained by the common language and not by the Islamic religion. The "Syrian Social National Party" was established in Beirut in 1932 by Antun Sa'adeh (1904–1949), a Christian. It advocated the establishment of a secular state that included Syria, Lebanon, Palestine, Sinai Peninsula, Cyprus, Jordan, Iraq, Kuwait and part of southern Turkey. Michel Aflaq (1810–1989), a Syrian Christian Arab nationalist philosopher established the Baath Party as an ideological movement of protest against French colonial control. He chose Lebanon for its free and intellectual environment to publish his books when he felt that his party in Syria lost the intellectual independence and became the police arm of the ruling mix of unruly sectarians and military coups.

The Lebanese Maronite achieved self-rule in Mount Lebanon, and sometimes total independence, several times under the Ottoman rule. The Druze tribal leaders were the rulers of Lebanon before 1860. A civil war erupted in Mount Lebanon between Maronite peasants and their Druze overlords in 1860 which culminated in the deaths of thousands of Maronites and the destruction of 500 churches. The killing was halted only when the great powers decided to act. Several thousand French troops landed in Beirut and an international commission composed of France, Britain, Austria, Prussia, and the Ottoman Empire agreed to the dispatch of up to 12,000 European soldiers, half of them French, to establish order. Under the French government pressure, the Ottomans granted the Maronite community a special political status in 'Mount Lebanon' area as a privileged self-rule administrative region under international guaranty within the Ottoman Empire in 1861. The autonomy of Mount Lebanon from Ottoman-Syria was established, and an Armenian Christian named Daud Pasha was nominated as its governor.

But with the outbreak of First World War in 1914, the Turkish government abolished Lebanon's autonomous status and appointed Jamal Pasha as the commander in chief of the Turkish army in Syria and Lebanon. Jamal Pasha dealt harshly with the Lebanese, who were considered the most disloyal subjects to Turkey, and the Turks were not willing to tolerate anything that might lead to the break-up of their empire. A military court was established in the Town of Aley, many Maronites were jailed or exiled, and on May 6, 1916, the Turks publicly executed 16 nationalist Lebanese of all religions in Beirut. The date of the massacre has been commemorated annually as Martyrs' Day, and the site in Beirut has come to be known as "Martyrs' Square."

The Maronites enjoyed their freedom for half a century before the First World War and argued for the need to annex the rest of what they considered their historical home-land, 'Great Lebanon'. They wanted it to be under their paramount control, separate, distinct and independent from the rest of Syria. The Maronite Patriarch Elias Hoayek accomplished his mission and obtained satisfaction to the Maronites' national aspirations when he went to the 1919 Conference of Versailles to demand independence on behalf of Great Lebanon. The 1920 San Remo Conference in Italy gave France a mandate over Lebanon and Syria.

The political institutions of the state were set out in unwritten 1943 National Covenant which uses the 1932 census to distribute seats in parliament on a ratio of six-to-five in favor of Christians. It was designed to accommodate the country's primary religious groups, whose coexistence required delicate balancing. This quota was later extended to other public offices. The president is to be Maronite Christian, the prime-minister a Sunni Muslim and the Speaker of the Chamber of Deputies a Shi'a Muslim. In 1926, the Lebanese Representative Council approved a constitution and the unified Lebanese Republic was declared, but still under the French mandate.

The French management style of their mandated territory in Lebanon was similar to that of the British in the Arab lands. The British used the Hashemite princely dynasties to anchor their mandate authority in their newly acquired territory, and the French used the Maronites, a Christian community with a long tradition of union with the Roman Catholic Church in France, to cement their control on Lebanon.

The Maronites were the only group in the newly Arab conquered land after First World War to continue enjoying the sort of autonomy they had enjoyed under the Turks before the war. The French created 'Great Lebanon' out of Mount Lebanon, north Lebanon, south Lebanon and the Bekaa where the Maronites had formed a clear majority of the population. They did not give their Maronite allies the Syrian territory that they had claimed as part of their historical homeland because the Maronites would be outnumbered by the Muslims. The "Greater Lebanon" that had a different character from its surroundings for the Maronites made it imperative for France to help establish it as an independent state. In 1944, the French High Commissioner in Beirut declared the independence of Lebanon and the transfer of all the mandate powers to its government in Beirut. The concept of Lebanese nationality was meaningful to the vast majority of the Maronites but not to all Lebanese.

The Druze

The Druze faith adherents belong to a Middle East religious sect that exceeded one million in the early 21st century. Majority of them live as communities in Lebanon, Syria, Jordan and Israel and they call themselves Muwahhidun (monotheists in Arabic). Jabal al-Druze in Lebanon, especially Chouf region, is the most densely populated area with Druze followed by Hooran District in south Syria. Living in close-knit communities according to the principles of their faith has enabled the Druze to maintain their distinctive faith for centuries.

Druze people practice a mystic Unitarian faith related to Islam that began as a movement in the Ismaili sect in the 11th century. The Ismaili sect of the Shi'a acknowledged the claim to the imamate of Ismail, the eldest son of the sixth imam, Ja'far As-Sadiq. The Druze faith was preached by the Ismaili scholar Hamza ibn Ahmad who came to Egypt in 1014 and assembled a group of scholars to establish the foundations of the faith. The sixth Fatimid Caliph al-Hakim be-A'mr-Ellah who ruled Egypt between 996–1021 sponsored the faith doctrine in 1017. The name "Druze" came from the name of a preacher who was promoting the faith then he was expelled from the movement because he referred to Caliph al-Hakim be-A'mr-Ellah as a divinely appointed caliph which caused riots in Cairo.

Access to the secret religious teachings of the Druze scriptures, Al-Hikmah al Sharifah and participation fully in the religious services is permitted only by few elders, known as Uqqal (the wise). The Druze people discourage marriage outside their faith and they do not permit conversion to-or-from their religion, but they blend with the communities of other religions. Druze moral system includes strictly following their religion and accepting the unity of mankind. The political leader of the Druze community in Lebanon, Walid Jumblatt made an exception to the inter-marriage restriction. He welcomed the marriage of the Druzi-born Amal Alamuddin to the American movie-star George Clooney in 2014. The Druze community has been at the front of all the big events in the Middle East history although they constitute little more than five percent of the population. They joined the armies of the Ayyubid and the Mamluks in the fight against the Crusaders in Lebanon. They had local autonomy in Lebanon under the Ottoman Empire, and in the 17th century, the legendary Durzi Prince Fakhr al-Din II (1572-1635) forged a coalition with the Maronites, fought other Lebanese families and sought independence from the Ottoman Empire for Jabal Lubnan (Lebanon Mountain). He failed to achieve independence but he was the first Lebanese leader to seek sovereignty for modern-day Lebanon. Prince Majid Arslan (1908-1983) was a national political figure with a big role in Lebanon's independence.

Palestinian Refugees in Lebanon

The Palestinian refugees in Lebanon are better viewed in context. Palestinians have been victims to various types of forced migration since 1948. Israel does not recognize the Palestinian right of return, ultimately preventing them from returning to their homes. They were expelled or ran away for their lives from their homes in Palestine into neighboring towns and countries, such as Gaza, the West Bank, Lebanon, Syria, and Jordan, while smaller numbers fled to Egypt and Iraq. Some 150,000 Palestinians managed to remain in Israel, many are considered internally displaced as they are prevented from returning to their original villages. The second large-scale displacement occurred in 1967, pursuant to the Six-Day War between Israel and its neighbors, during which Israel occupied the West Bank, Gaza, East Jerusalem, the Syrian Golan Heights, and the Egyptian Sinai. The Sinai was returned to Egypt as part of an agreement in September 1975, while the rest of the areas remain occupied territory. By the end of the war, more than 300,000 Palestinian refugees fled or expelled to Jordan, almost half of them were victims of secondary displacement. They were originally displaced in 1948, and uprooted for the second time in 1967.

The treatment of the Palestinian refugees varies depending on the host-country. In Lebanon, the Palestinian refugees face significant discrimination and are excluded from many areas of public life as a result of a law that distinguishes between Lebanese citizens and foreigners, defining a foreigner as "any natural or juridical person who is not a Lebanese subject." Because Palestinians do not have Lebanese citizenship, they are considered foreigners with limited civil rights. The government controls where they live and where they work. They cannot own businesses or property in Lebanon and are banned from more than 30 professions including most decent-paying professions like medicine and law.

Lebanon has twelve refugee camps housing generations of Palestinians cleansed from their homes after the founding of Israel. Many camps lack basic services, such as electricity, sewage and waste disposal networks. Palestinian refugees in Lebanon are treated as second class residents, forced to live in run-down camps and barred from formal public education. The government does not give citizenship rights to them for fear it could change the demography of the country in favor of the Muslims. Generations of Palestinian refugees have grown up in limbo, without basic protection.

The Arab Spring in Lebanon

In the Arab Spring of 2011-12, Lebanon known for its polarized population based on religion and ethnicity was apparently fatigued from previous bouts of unrest. Lebanon had climbed out of its own last civil war twenty years earlier and ended with no meaningful reform. The idealists, then, who demanded structural change to the confessional system of allocating power, lost ground to the partisans of sectarian identity. Unlike other Arab states, the Lebanese central government is a parliamentary democracy where political power and senior positions in the government bureaucracy are allocated to different segments of the population based on their confessional identity. It is not a monolithic dictatorial repressive regime against which the people may rebel and lose life for. But the Syrian conflict pulled at Lebanon's communal seams and because of its proximity to Syria, the negative aspect of the Arab Spring pulled down roots in Lebanon. The inability of the Lebanese society to cope with the spill-over of the Syrian struggle infused life into old tensions that have the potential of creating economic, political and social instability. Lebanon hosts nearly 1.5 million Syrian refugees, most languish in sever poverty and several thousand live in makeshift camps in a barren mountainous region. The country had to absorb the impact of receiving around a quarter of its population, mostly Sunni Syrian refugees, a financial burden and a demographic threat that makes many Lebanese resent and feel victimized by the Arab Spring. Majority of Lebanon's communities had no desire to hurt themselves by entering into the Arab Spring conflicts, but the central government could not completely inoculate the country against involvement in the civil wars that raged in neighboring Syria and Iraq.

Fighting from Syria's civil war spilled over into Lebanon as opponents and supporters of the Syrian rebels came to Lebanon to fight each other on Lebanese soil. Seven people were killed and more than fifty wounded in fights between gunmen in Tripoli, and during the summer of 2012, there were deadly clashes between Sunni Muslims and Alawites in Tripoli and Beirut. In May of 2013, at least 10 people died in further sectarian clashes in Tripoli between supporters and opponents of the Syrian regime. Lebanon's army successfully quelled many instances of communal fighting but could not completely prevent fighting between the pro and the anti-Syrian government groups. It could not stop Hezbollah (the party of God) military wing from joining the war in Syria in support of the regime.

Hezbollah is a Lebanese Muslim-Shi'a political party, established in 1982 with a military wing to fight against Israeli occupation of Lebanese lands. When Israel invaded Lebanon in 1982, the Shi'ates, who make up the bulk of the population in south Lebanon, were the first to take the brunt of Israel's aggression. Hezbollah emerged to defend these defenseless Lebanese people. It has been led by the charismatic Shi'a cleric, Hasan Nasr-Allah since 1992 after Israel killed the group's cofounder Abbas al-Musawi.

Hezbollah militia is no match to Israel's military but it is determined to defend South Lebanon, home of its constituents against Israeli incursions. According to US press reports, its military wing has anywhere from 2,000 to 3,500 fighters armed with small weapons and short to medium range rocket launchers received from Iran government and the international weapons markets. Hezbollah provides social services network and it is also one of the largest employers in Lebanon-schools, clinics, transport, farming and stores.

Hezbollah resistance to Israel's intrusions gained its political party and military group broad support beyond its Shi'at base. Its members participated in Lebanon's parliament elections for the first time in 1992, winning 8 out of 128 seats, and it has been winning more since then. The party has continued to play an important role in Lebanese politics. Its political strength grew more in 2008 after it was effectively granted veto power over forming the government in the 'Doha Agreement' Accord to end eighteen-month-long political crisis. But because of its increasingly involvement in the Syrian civil war, it has alienated many of its Lebanese constituents. The US has labeled Hezbollah as a terrorist organization since 1997 and in 2011 the UN's Special Tribunal for Lebanon issued arrest warrants against four Lebanese over the murder of Prime Minister Rafik Hariri. The accused are members of Hezbollah, which says it won't allow their arrest.

For decades, Hezbollah claimed its military was to protect Lebanon from Israel's attacks. It built tunnels and bunkers on the border with Israel and trained its fighters to deal with Israel's military. But with the conflicts in the Middle East after the Arab Spring, Hezbollah military arm changed from a Lebanese militia to a regional military player. It has developed new power and reach that has not been widely recognized. It has sent legions of fighters to Syria and it has provided trainers to Iraq. There are reports that Hezbollah has backed al-Houthi rebels in Yemen, and it has helped organize a battalion of militants from Afghanistan armed by Iran that can fight anywhere. It has been described by some Arab politicians as not just a power unto itself, but is an instrument in the drive for regional supremacy by Iran. While most Lebanese Christians naturally support the need for Hezbollah to hand over its weapons to the state, they are not hostile to Hezbollah for one reason: It had a role in protecting Lebanon from ISIS and other extreme Islamists across the borders in Syria.

9. JORDAN

Jordan, an Arab state, is a British creation. It is ruled by the Hashemite family that claims to be descendant of a noble ancient Arabian tribe. The history of the Hashemite kingdom of Jordan started in 1921 when the Colonial Secretary of Britain, Winston Churchill, offered the territory of Trans-Jordan to Prince Abdullah ibn al-Hussein as a reward for his support to Britain against Turkey in the First World War. During the war, representatives of Great Britain and France reached an accord in 1916, known as Sykes-Picot Agreement. It divided Arab lands under the rule of the Ottoman Empire that included the provinces of the historical Mesopotamia (Iraq) and Syria between British and French spheres of influence with the understanding that the holy Land of Palestine would have an international status. The British occupied Palestine during the last months of the war and opened its doors for East European Jewish settlers. When the Ottoman Empire had virtually ceased to exist after the war, the League of Nations approved Sykes-Picot Agreement and mandated the Arab provinces territory, with the provision that they would be prepared by Britain and France for independence.

The Western allies felt they could ignore the national sentiments of the Arabs in the newly mandated territories as they set out to divide them into states. The Arabs found themselves exchanging domination by the Turks for domination by the British, the French and the Zionists. The allies redrew the political map of the Arab world in the manner which suited them. The strategic importance of oil and the means to transport it were the principal considerations taken into account. Britain biggest prize was gaining access to the proven Mesopotamia oil resources.

The interest in the petroleum of the Gulf and Mosul area and its transportation through pipelines to the Mediterranean played an important role in the British policies. To meet the need for oil to run the newly installed combustion engines of the royal navy ships, the British government formed a special committee, the "Petroleum Imperial Policy Committee" in 1918 to draw a plan for securing control of adequate world oil resources. The plan that was later on implemented, included building a modern port in Haifa with large oil refinery to process the pumped oil from Iraq through the pipeline and facilities to export the refined oil to Britain. The politics of the big powers toward the Middle East since the 20th century has been always for oil. For almost 100 years, the British and then the US have declared wars, dispatched navy armadas, stationed troops, installed friendly regimes and toppled others to secure the region's oil.

Syrian Arab nationalists and Prince Faysal, son of Sharif Mecca, al-Hussein Ibn Ali rejected the Sykes-Picot Agreement. He established a short-lived Arab kingdom in Syria that was defeated by overwhelming French army, and forced Faysal to relinquish his Syrian kingdom. Almost two years earlier since he had proclaimed the rising outside Medina against the Ottomans, Faysal struggle was hard, dangerous and, in terms of the Arab state that was promised by the British, futile.

In November of 1920, Prince Abdullah, the younger brother of Faysal came to Ma'an, a Hejazi Province town at the edge of the Syrian Desert. He was leading two thousand armed Arabian tribesmen with an ambitious plan to fight the French and restore his brother's kingdom. The British decided to install Faysal a client king of the newly invented British mandate of Iraq and his brother, Prince Abdullah, as ruler of what then became known as Trans-Jordan.

The British policy was to create small states under members of the Hashemite family, a respected clan by reason of their lineage. The British exploited the Hashemite considerable power over the tribesmen, as a means to administer the area and control its resources. The Hashemite claim to be a noble family descended from Fatima, the Prophet Muhammad daughter, and her husband, Ali, the fourth caliph and scion of the house of Bani Hashim, the noblest of the ancient Arabian Peninsula tribes. The mini-independence given to Trans-Jordan then was a form of indirect colonial control mechanism modeled after the qualified independence of the Persian Gulf states that were ruled by leading families where Britain provided protection in return for allowing London to control their foreign affairs and natural resources. The north Arabian Desert territory that became part of Trans-Jordan secured for Britain the required contiguity between its Iraq and Palestine mandates.

Trans-Jordan Emirate was not a natural self-sustained country. It consisted mostly of open desert with a few towns, small cluster of villages scattered along the highland east of the Jordan valley, and some pastoral areas and grain-lands here and there. The territory that became Trans-Jordan was close to the hinterlands of such major cities as Jerusalem and Damascus, but it participated only marginally in the social and intellectual changes that began in the Arab world prior to the First World War. The basic form of social organization was tribal and the social relations among the various nomadic tribes and between them and the villagers was based on trade and the exchange of tribute for protection. The economically poor and perennially insecure state of Trans-Jordan Emirate was completely dependent on financial support from London. Its elite military force called "the Arab Legion" of Bedouin recruits was under the command of and trained by British officers.

The British knew Prince Abdullah when he was the emissary of his father negotiating with them on the future of the Arab lands. Abdullah came up with the idea of seeking alliance with the British against the Turks in the War. His father,Sharif al-Hussein Ibn Ali, never had the military and financial resources to challenge the Turks until his son Abdullah convinced him to gain the support of a great power in his rebellion against Turkey. The British decided to exploit the rift between the Arabs and the Turks by considering the offer made by Prince Abdullah to participate in joint military effort with the Hashemite against the Turks. Negotiations were conducted in several letters exchanged between Sharif Hussein and Sir Henry McMahon, the British High Commissioner in Cairo. The direct correspondence led to an agreement that was written in general terms. To the Arabs in Mecca, it was treated as a firm commitment by Britain to give independence to the Arabs in exchange for Arab revolt against the Turks. But by the end of the war, Britain had entered into several conflicting commitments regarding the conquered Ottoman Empire. There was the agreement with France to share colonization the Arab lands, a promise to support Arab independence, and the promise of a homeland for the Jewish people in Palestine. And in conflict with the wartime alliance with Sharif al-Hussein Ibn Ali, there was a standing British alliance with Abdul-Aziz Ibn Saud of Najd in central Arabia, who subsequently forced Sharif al-Hussein out of Hijaz and founded the Kingdom of Saudi Arabia.

Naturally, it was impossible for Britain to honor simultaneously all these conflicting commitments. The British allowed Sharif al-Hussein, the senior Hashemite and the guardian of the Islamic holy shrines of Mecca, to have the title of "King of Hejaz" with a provision that gave Great Britain the exclusive responsibility of defending the Muslim holy places against external aggression. When Sharif al-Hussein refused to accept the commitment of the

British mandate on Palestine regarding the Balfour Declaration, the British abandoned him and supported his rival, Sultan Abdul-Aziz al-Saud of Najd, in his effort to conquer Sharif al-Hussein's kingdom in 1924.

When Trans-Jordan was established by the British, it was sparsely populated mostly by nomad Bedouin tribes whose livelihood was based on camel herding. Arab tribes used to attack each other, but their rules prevented the attacks from turning into random violence. Clans defected from their tribe if they felt treated badly by other higher hierarchy clans. Each tribe is a self governing group of people that claimed descent from a supposed founding ancestor. The tribes have their own system of justice to settle disputes among their members and other clans, impose penalties and determine settlements of blood money. The Bedouins were dependent on few settled communities for trading their animals and their products for goods that they need.

Nomad tribes in Trans-Jordan began building settlements and taking up agriculture after the establishment and the consolidation of the Trans-Jordan Emirate and the creation of a standing army that recruited the young nomads and reduce the labor once available for herding. As the nomads took titles to land and education became available to their young, their traditional relationship to tribal territory as a pastoral way of life was weakened. They increasingly chose alternative occupations, particularly in the government and the military. Government policies of providing schools, medical services and developing water resources encouraged more settlements.

By the 1970s, substantial numbers of nomads had adopted a sedentary way of life and the roaming Bedouin tribes constituted no more than 5% of the population. But their small numbers does not correspond to their cultural and political power in Jordan. The Hashemite regime gets its most significant political support from people of Bedouin origin. They also constitute a disproportionate share of the army including at the high command level. Mindful of the intensely personal nature of the Hashemite ties with the Bedouins, the late King Hussein and his son King Abdullah II visited them often, socializing in their tents and playing the roles of paramount tribal sheikhs.

Beside army careers, the government made it easy for Bedouin children to acquire education in public schools and high education institutions. Bedouin parents discovered the best future lay in education and living and working in settled societies close to the urban centers. The educated generations of Bedouin children rejected their ancestors' life style but they have not abandoned their allegiance to their families and tribes and the enthusiastic support to the Hashemite monarchs. Jordan continues to be an absolute monarchy with the Trans-Jordanian indigenous tribal population as its main constituents despite the existence of modern constitution and elected parliament. Jordan's biggest challenge today is the political competition between the Trans-Jordanian rural Bedouin tribes and the urban ethnic Palestinians. All electoral laws in Jordan, including the latest, gerrymander the seats to favor the tribes.

Jordan today is an independent Arab country, a kingdom member of the UN, with modern civil state institutions and a military under Jordanian officers. But Jordan is still governed as an absolute monarchy that Prince Abdullah Ibn al-Hussein established a century ago, although it is not the mostly desert country that was created by the British and the Hashemite royalty in 1921.

Amman, the capital of Jordan, is not the sleepy town that existed in the early days of the 20th century and the Jordanians are not a homogeneous community as they were a century ago. With its high rising buildings, congested highways, international airport, busy malls, local and international banks, active stock market, public and private universities, modern hospitals, overbooked hotels and crowded restaurants and cafes, is not the city we knew even two decades ago. Despite modernization, the rapid development in Jordan has not reduced the tribes as a primary source of social identity among the ethnic Jordanians. But Jordan is still dependent on financial support from foreign donors exactly as it was when the British installed Prince Abdullah as its Emir a century ago.

The descendants of the Jordanian generation, who had the original social contract with the Hashemite royalties, today make up less than 30 percent of Jordan's population and those of them who live in the capital are less than 10 percent, but they are still the most politically powerful segment of the population. They, whether in the desert tending their livestock and farms or college graduates, professionals or military officers, their first loyalty is to their ethnic tribes and to the Hashemite Throne. The ethnic East Bank Trans-Jordanians are still the backbone of the monarchy's support that institutionalized the patron-client system which has dominated the national politics since its early years.

The Arab Spring in Jordan

The Arab Spring of 2011-2012 highlighted the need for political and economic reform in Jordan. The Jordanians complain about ethnic tension between Jordanians and Palestinians, Islamist versus secularist issues, lack of genuine democracy, perceived government tolerance of corruption and economic woes that could become reasons for agitation and protest. Jordan faces serious external challenges including the spillover of Syria's civil war and the possibility of entanglement at its border, the spread of Islamic radicalization and the cost of sustaining the refugee population. The MB, professional associations and leftist parties dominated Jordan's opposition political scene. They called for economic reform, social justice, passing anticorruption laws, and revise the 1993 election laws.

But unlike the Arab Spring that has swept many of the Arab countries, the Jordanian Spring was limited in scope and end game. When most other Arab countries swept by the Arab Spring uprisings demanding radical political and economic reforms, the protest in Jordan was manifest mainly in social media activities and in frequent, but relatively small, nonviolent protests in Amman and other towns. They neither mobilized en masse nor called for the ousting of the monarchy. The protesters maintained a hope that they can work with the King to achieve change and King Abdullah II did not face the same pressure as other rulers throughout the region.

Those who took to the streets called for fixing rather than changing the regime. The protests of 2011 attracted no more than 4,000 from the MB, trade unions and secular opposition parties. They were protesting the rising food and fuel prices, inflation and unemployment, and they demanded the prime minister to step down. The most serious confrontation with law enforcement took place in 2012 when the government abolished the fuel subsidy as demanded by the IMF as the condition to provide Jordan with a badly needed loan. In the last decade, Amman experienced an economic downturn, inflation sky-rocketed from 1.6 percent to 13.9 percent unemployment is officially at 12 percent, but unofficially estimated at 30 percent and poverty rate jumped to more than 19 percent. Ironically, the ethnic East-Jordanians, the traditionally leading supporters of the monarch were hit hardest by the economic crisis.

The King sacked his cabinet in February 2011 and asked the new prime minister "to take practical, quick and tangible steps to launch political reform." In the next month, he established a 50 member National Dialogue Committee to draft electoral law and he set up another committee to revise the constitution to bring about the desired political reforms. While Jordanian activists cautiously welcomed the recommendations of the two committees as a positive step forward, the Prime Minister Marouf Bakhit was viewed as the wrong person to implement them. Bakhit is, in the eyes of his critics, a status quo personality with no interest in reform. The people remembered him from his previous term in office as the one who presided over a government that rigged the two 2007 elections, the Parliament election and the municipal election. Observers and opposition activists questioned the integrity of the parliamentary elections of 2007. They alleged that fraud and gerrymandering had been used to disenfranchise ethnic Palestinian Jordanian voters to ensure that pro-government representatives from the Trans-Jordanian tribes retain substantial majority in the House of Representatives.

Prime Minister Bakhit had to resign and the King met with leaders of the MB he provided $500 million into salary increases for government employees and subsidies for food staples and fuel, and pledged additional government reforms. The King insisted he would lead the transition to democracy, but the basic premise of his plans was to ensure that power would not be delivered to Islamists. Since his inauguration in 1999, King Abdullah II who was educated and trained in centers of Western liberal democracies, promoted himself as a reformer, but after more than a decade of his rule and seven prime ministers he had entrusted to form governments, there was little progress toward democracy. The king insists on preserving the electoral law that favors the Trans-Jordanian minority from which the monarchy traditionally derived its support at the expense of the urban Palestinian majority who are better educated and economically more productive. Palestinian-Jordanians feel they are treated by the government as second-class citizens. This fault-line has the potential to be as dangerous to the Kingdom as those sectarian and ethnic divisions now playing havoc in neighboring countries. The ruling-elites' disdain to democracy and the will of the people was demonstrated by suspending the parliament for more than two years between 2001 and 2003 for no reason.

Jordan's geo-strategic location at the center of a volatile region and unending of its neighboring states instability has been a challenge that remains the hallmark of Jordan's political, economic and social life since its establishment. It has become the destination of the newly displaced refugees from war-torn neighboring countries and beyond Syria, Iraq, Egypt, Libya, and Yemen. Jordan had been already a country of refugees even before millions continue to pour from Syria and now again from Iraq. Its monarchs had created a cohesive support base and a security organization loyal to the existing political order to deal with the consequences of doubling its population with the Palestinian refugees' influx of the 1948 and 1967 wars. The regime has shrewdly taken advantage of the country's humanitarian involvement in sheltering the victims of the region's conflicts to secure foreign aid from Arab rich countries and international organizations to help Jordan to make up for the lack of strong indigenous economy. Jordan receives billions of dollars in financial aid from the US, Europe, Japan and

Arab Gulf States every year to handle the financial and social needs of the refugees and to close the annual budget deficits and maintain a balance sheet. Given Jordan's pro-West strategic orientation, commitment to peace with Israel, and cooperation on counter-terrorism and security matters, the US and the Europeans have compelling interest in helping King Abdullah II manage potentially destabilizing factors.

The Jordanian populace sympathizes with the refugees and shares with them many of their concerns. Jordan like its neighboring countries has failed to develop a democratic system based on rotation of power through ballot box. Jordan is an absolute monarchy, and for years, the king has been relying on a few politicians to carry out his policies, many of whom were accused of being corrupt. In the first decade of the twenty first century, rampant corruption without effective monitoring bodies reached a point unprecedented in the history of Jordan.

Arab Spring protests in Jordan were organized and planned by political activists in a way that is different from the seemingly spontaneous protests that emerged in other Arab cities. The protest movement in Jordan did not develop into a popular uprising or a revolution as the case in other Arab countries because majority of the Jordanians preferred the stability of the status quo over the anarchy and civil wars that engulfed the region and victimized the millions.

The passive role of the emergent middle class, the ethnic Palestinians anti-revolutionaries, and the threat of ISIS shaped the national politics and contributed to the stability of the country. Middle class and aspiring cosmopolitan Jordanians, who form a significant social class in the prosperous section of Amman, saw the Arab Spring "not their fight." Arab Spring was being fought only by those who have not participated economically. And majority of ethnic Palestinian-Jordanians prefer not to protest because the change to the status quo may provide justification for transforming Jordan into the talked about "alternative country for the Palestinians" and the expulsion of the Palestinians from the West Bank, Gaza and Jerusalem to Jordan. The ethnic Palestinians who strongly feel the political system is biased against them to favor the ethnic Jordanians hesitate to protest alone to avoid reinforcing the Palestinian's stigma in Jordan as the "the complainers and trouble-makers."

The threat of ISIS since 2014 and the terrorist attacks in Amman and in al-Baka'a refugees camp contributed to the rising concerns about terrorism and the need for security. This environment reorients majority of Jordanian populace away from failed political reforms and reinforces the status-quo and with it, the powerful state-security apparatus' firm grip on the country and a media that serves as a reminder of the problems of getting out of control. The government used state security courts to try civilians for participating in peaceful protests. Some activists were arrested and tried in the security courts for a range of charges including disturbing the peace, insulting security officials and "undermining royal dignity."

The King recognized that his country had no political issues, but only security issues and developmental challenges which need a responsible government to be held accountable by elected parliament. He managed to transfer the protest and anger into positive energy and reconciliation by providing some "political reforms" led and promoted by him personally as a transition to democracy. Parliamentary elections were held in January 2013, two years early, with the promise to have the parliament participate in choosing the prime minister and have the power of no confidence in the government. All political factions participated in the elections except the Islamic Action Front which boycotted the polls in two elections since 2011 because they claimed the electoral laws favor the rural indigenous Trans-Jordanian tribes against the towns' population who are predominantly Palestinians. The MB electoral strongholds have been in areas of high Palestinian concentration. It has been seen as representing much of Palestinians' political grievances in the country at the expense of the ethnic East-Bankers. Historically speaking, the MB has been the main political opposition force it had opposed some government policies but largely cooperated with the regime. Jordan's lower house of parliament never had political power or influence over the government's policies any way. Vast majority of its 130 members have been always strong pro-monarchy loyalists. The king appoints the prime minister, cabinet members and members of the upper house of the parliament.

After the Arab Spring, the demise of the MB in Egypt, the rise of ISIS in Syria and Iraq, and the regional political chaos, the MB in Jordan had their own crisis. They were divided among themselves over the need for internal reforms to enhance their relevance in the country's politics and pull its supporters away from extremist groups. When Jordan passed the 2014 law requiring parties to renew their licenses, only the MB wing that is solely East-Jordanian and loyal to the throne was granted a license in 2015. The government stripped the old Brotherhood of its official registration and prevented its members from holding rallies. In the 2016 elections, members of the MB and other Islamists not affiliated with the MB won only 16 seats out of 130.

The real danger to the regime in Jordan is not the Islamists. It would be a development that may cause mass disaffection among the regime's traditional ethnic Trans-Jordanian supporters. These are still living in and around the

East Jordanian tribal centers like Karak, Tafilah, and Ma'an who supply the manpower of Jordan's armed forces and security services. Such opposition has begun among the young unemployed and the poor who complain about the regime's apparent indifference to tribal grievances and royally sanctioned corruption. Some isolationists resent the deepening involvement in Syria and the deployments of US troops. The Trans-Jordanian tribal-based opposition who has lost confidence in the regime's ability to deliver patronage at traditional levels has recently coalesced around a political organization, Hirak. Its members have staged street demonstrations in their cities demanding reforms. Hirak or any Trans-Jordanian organization does not pose a threat to the monarchy because lack of political reform is not their leading grievance, nor one that unifies the opposition. The popular discontent of the Trans-Jordanians is focused more on economic issues and the perception of corruption. The political reform in the sense of fair demographic representation in voting would reduce the privileged role and the political empowerment of the ethnic Trans-Jordanians.

President Trump recognized Jerusalem officially as Israel's capital despite warnings from Arab and European leaders. Jerusalem is home to holy sites for the three monotheistic faiths, and controlling the city is one of the most controversial issues within the Israeli-Palestinian conflict.

The status of Jerusalem has been at the center of the Palestinian–Israeli conflict where both parties the Palestinians and the Israelis want it as their capital, and Jordan has an acknowledged role in managing the Jerusalem's Islamic worshipping cites. One of the articles in the Israeli–Jordanian peace treaty states that: "Israel respects the present special role of the Hashemite Kingdom of Jordan in Muslim Holy shrines in Jerusalem."

Israel claims the whole city as its "eternal" capital, but the Palestinians have strong religious and historical attachments to the city as well. They feel entitled to have East Jerusalem as the capital of their future state. The dispute over the city has derailed all previous attempts at brokering a two-state solution to the decades-old crisis.

This move has ended decades of US policy and it could stymie the Middle East "peace process." It has caused indignation in the Islamic and Arab countries, especially in Jordan, which oversees al-Aqsa Mosque in East Jerusalem. A large percentage of Jordanians are Palestinians. Jordan has more than one million Palestinian refugees and the Jordanians feel betrayed by their most important ally, the US. Trump's provocative decision has sparked mass outrage because it could ultimately hamper efforts to get the peace process moving. The Jordanian people may lose faith in their government for being a junior ally with the US that does not listen to their concerns.

10. MOROCCO

Morocco was one of the Arab countries that never been subject to the Ottoman rule. It had a thousand year tradition of sovereign state, and in the last three hundred years, it has been ruled by an Alaouite dynasty, making it the Arab world's oldest monarchy. Like the Hashemite royal family in Jordan, the Moroccan royalty claims to be descent from the Prophet Muhammad through his daughter Fatimah and her husband Ali Ibn-Abu-Talib. Morocco's proximity to Europe, its strategic location on two oceans, and the potential of its natural resources created special relations with the continent and that made it easy target for the colonialists to interfere in its affairs. Much of the 19th century history of the European colonialism in North Africa was made in and about Morocco. Whenever Morocco's rulers showed weakness, conventions were held, treaties were signed and armies were dispatched by the powerful European nations to advance their colonial interests in the country and grab the spoils.

The European colonialists who were competing over the exploitation of Morocco held an international convention in Madrid in 1880 to determine the future of the country. The US and Germany, wary of Spanish and French power in the region, joined the convention to make sure Spain and France do not dominate the conference. The convention official declaration guaranteed the independence and integrity of Morocco and to maintain equal trade opportunities for all, but what followed suggest the convention gave the European colonialists equal privileges in Morocco's territory. The policy was similar to the "open door" policy which the Western powers and Japan had in China in 1899 to exploit its resources.

Europe was interested in Morocco's iron ore and other mineral wealth. The European imperialists had a history of conferring with each other about dividing up colonial lands among themselves, most of the time in secret and sometimes in open conferences. In 1916, Great Britain and France secretly reached an accord, known in history as the Sykes-Picot agreement to divide Arab lands under the rule of the Ottoman Empire into British and French spheres of influence with the conclusion of World War I. The same had happened between the two European imperialists twelve years earlier to divide North African countries between them, but this time it was in an open conference.

The Entente Cordiale conference was held in 1904 to settle long – standing imperialist rivalry between Britain and France, two of Europe's most powerful colonialist nations, over North African countries. By the conference terms, Britain could pursue its interests in Egypt, and France was free to expand its influence westward from Tunisia. France promised not to challenge Britain control over Egypt and Britain recognized France's right to preserve order, provide assistance and bring about whatever reforms in the government, economy or military it deemed necessary in the countries under its control including Morocco.

And in the 1906 Conference of Algeciras that was held by the European colonialists and the US at Algeciras city in Spain, Morocco's Atlantic and Mediterranean coasts were given to Spain's sphere of influence and the rest of the country was given to France. On May 21, 1911, French troops occupied the Moroccan City of Fez and in 1912 officially established a protectorate over Morocco with the Treaty of Fez that was signed by Morocco's Sultan Abdel-hafid. Moroccan nationalists including thousands of military men rebelled against the French. They took over the French garrison headquarters in Fez, but they could not take over the city, then they were defeated by more powerful French military. The French colonialists allowed the sultan to retain his ceremonial powers of issuing decrees in his own name and seal and he remained the religious leader of Morocco. The French used to claim that there was only one government in Morocco, the sultan government, which was protected and controlled by them.

The frequent uprisings against Spain and France by Moroccan nationalists, especially the ethnic Berbers, forced the French to move the government courts from Fez, where majority are Berbers, to Rabat, which became the capital of the country since then. Nationalists formed Moroccan Action Block and political parties and made the Sultan aware of and sensitive to their aspirations. They proposed plans of political reforms including the establishment of representative councils and they called for independence.

After World War II, the influence of European powers waned, the decolonization of Africa began, and the nationalist movement became more cohesive. In 1944, the Istiglal Party released a manifesto that was approved by Sultan Muhammad V demanding political reforms which included full independence, national unity and democratic constitution. France refused to consider the reform, and when the Sultan's popularity grew and became too threatening in his opposition to the French protectorate, the resident military general exiled him to Madagascar in 1954. The French replaced him with a member of the royal family who was pressured by the people to abdicate. Sultan Muhammad V returned to the country in 1955, greeted by delirious crowds as a national hero and immediately declared independence. France recognized the independence of Morocco in 1956 and Muhammad V took the title of king in 1957. Moroccans succeeded in controlling certain areas of the Spanish protectorate, but attempts to recover all the area was less successful. King Muhammad V forged national unity around the throne and established a governmental structure in which he would exercise an active political role, and he prevented the extreme elements of the Istiglal Party and liberal activists from challenging the monarch's authority. He also gave himself the title of Imam al-Mu'mineen "Commander of the Faithful." His son, King Hassan II, who inherited all the titles, was a close friend of the Western democratic countries, but he turned his country into an absolute monarchy and he was accused of being a ruthless ruler.

According to the journalist Robert Fisk, there was a "tendency to regard him as an 'Honorary European' while having his political opponents imprisoned without trial for decades in 'secret mountain prisons'." Amnesty International reported many incidents of torture and ill-treatment by his security police. He once said, according to Robert Fisk, that "there are no political prisoners, only traitors." King Hassan II survived two coup attempts and many plots during his four decades on the throne. People from his own air-force tried to shoot him down and in July 1971, army officers angry at the Monarch's abandonment of large area of Morocco territory in the border war with Algeria, organized a coup where 2,000 armed men overran his birthday killing more than one hundred guests, but the King escaped.

Some describe King Hassan II as a pragmatic politician, but his counseling to the Palestinian leader, Yasser Arafat when he was confined in his headquarters in Ramallah by the Israelis, suggests the King was too pragmatic to the point of cynicism. According to the Egyptian journalist Muhammad Heikal, the King told the PLO leader to find a way to accommodate Israelis' demands rather resisting them because of the things they did for him [Arafat] personally. He told Arafat: "Those people [the Israelis] are very powerful. Consider what they have done for you. In 24 hours they have changed your image from terrorist to peacemaker, enabling you to go to the White House, to dine at the State Department, to have lunch at the World Bank, to enter 10 Downing Street."

When Muhammad VI became monarch in 1999 after his father's death, he initiated political and economic changes and he ordered investigations into alleged human rights abuses during his fathers' rule. One of his liberal achievements was enacting laws that granted more rights to women despite opposition by some conservative religious leaders.

The Arab Spring in Morocco

In the 2011 Arab Spring, Moroccans had more reasons to protest than their neighbors in Tunisia where the Arab Spring was triggered. They had many economic and government mismanagement grievances to complain about. Their per capita income is almost one half that of Tunisia, youth unemployment is close to fifty percent, the unusual dry winter in the last few years cut the country's wheat harvest in half, a mounting budget deficit, a downturn in tourism, and like the rest of the Arab countries, government corruption, nepotism and cronyism through the palace were endemic. World Bank classified Morocco as a lower-middle-income country. But the king and the royal family were rich French journalists describe the monarch of this impoverished country as more wealthy than Britain's Queen Elizabeth II.

Thousands of people took to the streets in Casablanca and other cities in 2011 to protest their government's failure to deal with the country's social and political issues. Few weeks after Tunisian Bin Ali's exile, the Moroccan King Muhammad VI listened to the desires of his people for a better life and political participation and unveiled a new constitution that shifted the responsibility of governing from his royal court to a parliamentary government to be chosen by the people. To that end, he first delivered a speech to the nation pledging to open a new page.

He gave up his claim to divine rights as sovereign and retained his status as the spiritual "Commander of the Faithful." And he authorized a commission, approved by national referendum, to propose constitutional amendments that would give the prime minister the power and independence needed to govern.

The king revived the monarchy's legitimacy while holding the people accountable for the policies of the government they elect, not the monarch. At the same time, he retained considerable power as a chief executive. He remained head of the Council of Ministers, the Supreme Security Council, and the Ulama Council, which runs the mosques. He runs the military, the security and the intelligence forces. Moreover, under Article 41 of the new constitution, the laws can be overruled by royal "dahir," or decree. The King's critics say that the changes made by him were cosmetic and real democratization is needed to save the monarchy in the long run. The Islamist Justice and Development Party (PJD) actively participated in Morocco's political life for the first time and won 107 parliament seats out of 395, followed by the former ruling Istiglal Party which won 60 seats in the first elections to be held after the constitutional reforms of 2011 which granted the prime minister more powers. King Muhammad VI appointed the PJD Islamist party leader, Abdel-elah Benkirane, as the prime minister and trusted him to form a government for the first time in the modern history of Morocco.

Even with the king retaining considerable power, Benkirane held more power than any previous prime minister in Morocco. He was a popular leader liked even by the opposition for his honesty and simple lifestyle. Benkirane declined to leave his aging town house in an ordinary middle class neighborhood for the stately home with his office. And unlike the more high-falutin Arabic of traditional courtiers, he spoke in a language all Moroccans understand, a dialect called 'derija', which mixes the various cultures that have swept through the country's mountains: Tifinagh, Berber tongue, French and Spanish. Majority of Moroccan population is believed to be Berbers or Arabized Berbers. Benkirane's common touch made him unusually popular even among those who disdain the Islamist busybodies in a country often depicted as feudal. According to reporters, "Benkirane's ministers arranged meetings in cafes wearing duffle coats and insisted on paying their own bills." The Moroccan PJD Islamists demonstrated their open-mindedness and reconciling attitude toward other parties. They formed a government coalition led by the PJD embracing various parties including the right-winged Istiglal Party and the Progress and Socialist Party. Benkirane has verified the claim that political pluralism can be navigated with an Islamist party at the helm in an Arab country. The smooth transition to a constitutional monarchy with an elected parliament in Morocco was good news, but that has been lost amid the hustle and bustle of the civil wars and the chaos in the rest of the Arab world.

Morocco has gone through the "Arab Spring" and the ensuing Islamist power takeover unscathed mostly because of the predominance of Sufi-Islam culture in the country. The majority of Moroccans follow Sufi-Islam which is almost as old as the monarchy itself. There are dozens of Sufi orders in Morocco that owe allegiance to the monarchy and give it religious legitimacy. Moroccan Sufi-Islam follows Murabitoun tradition of tolerance and accepting the others. Its philosophy is taught in "Imam Academy of Rabat" where local and many foreign Imams who like to benefit from its religious experience are trained. It is considered as a tool to get out of the framework of strict form of Islamic orthodoxy and power tool to fight extreme ideology. King Muhammad V gave donations on many occasions from his own money to Sufi organizations across Morocco.

Protest against the government started again in 2017 in Huceima, Morocco north east Rif area when Mouhcine Fikri, a poor fish vendor was crushed to death in a trash-collecting truck while trying to recover his stock that was confiscated by police. The protests were Morocco's biggest since the "Arab Spring" that only intervention by the king could have defused the deepening crisis. The death of Fikri became a symbol of "hogra," a colloquial term of the deprivation of a person's dignity by the state due to the abuse of power and injustice. The Rif is a northern mountain region with a history of rebellious streak. It is home for a large indigenous non-Arab-Berber community, has been always a hotbed of anti-government dissent and unrest since the colonial occupation era.

The people of the Rif region revolted under the leadership of the legendary nationalist Muhammad Ibn Abdel-Kareem al-Khattab against the Spanish colonial occupation in 1920 and established the "Confederate Republic of the Tribes" that lasted five years. The Spanish colonial army of 5,000 suffered a major defeat at the hands of al-Khattab and his Berber 3,000 irregular combatants on July 22, 1921 in "the Disaster of Annual" battle as referred to by Spanish historians. At the end of 1921, Spain lost to the Rif rebels all its Protectorate territory in Morocco that it had colonized since 1909. This rebellion began in the Spanish controlled area, then it reached the French controlled sector until a coalition of well-armed French and Spanish army defeated the rebels in 1925.

The tragedy of Fikri's death cannot be erased from the collective memory of the Rif people unless there is true reconciliation initiated by the government. Moroccan authorities arrested responsible people over Fikri's death and government spokesman stated that more major development projects of the region were underway. But in 2017, the protest became a large-scale movement "Hirak al-Sha'bi," Arabic for "popular movement" with demands for political, social and economic reforms. The demands included the end of the 1958 designation of the Rif region as a military area during the rule of the late King Hassan II.

King Muhammad VI had sought conciliation with the people there since the start of the 2011 "Arab Spring." He promised to launch development projects in 2015, but the progress has been slow and the mistrust between the local population and the government is still prevalent. The area still lacks civilian infrastructure such as good roads, airports, universities and hospitals that would encourage tourism and investment in industrial projects. For months, Moroccans in the Rif region have been staging the biggest protest since the "Arab Spring." What aggravated the situation is the massive security presence and detention of activists in the region where many have been prosecuted on charges including "threatening national security" and "receiving foreign funding." Civil rights groups have criticized the arrests, alleged torture, beating and lack of immediate access to legal counsel in the region.

So far, the demonstrators have directed their rage at the government, not at the King himself, but they believed he must act rapidly. The protest intensified and spread to the capital city, Rabat, largely led by the banned Islamist "Adel-wal-Ihsan" movement. It echoed the demonstrations of "Arab Spring" in February 2011 that was inspired by the revolts in Libya and Egypt. King Muhammad VI, then, managed the protest with a combination of limited constitutional reforms that included ceding some powers to parliament and promised public spending. While government officials trade blame over the responsibility for the unrest and for delayed projects, many activists called for the King to intervene.

The King, who heads the Muslim world's longest-serving dynasty, presents his kingdom as a beacon of stability in a turbulent region even with the daily and occasional clashes. He is credited for trying to weather the crisis by fulfilling many of the social demands that motivated the "Arab Spring." He increased spending on subsidies, wages, and pensions in order to improve living standards and underpin the shift toward more open political system. Meanwhile, dissident Islamists and the Berber tribes have reduced their public protest, but they continue to agitate for change more quietly. There are peaceful demonstrations in different places for social and economic reforms including the poor town of Jerada calling for state aid and alternative jobs since two coal miners were killed in an accident. They are far from the mass protests which rocked the country in 2011, but it poses a challenge to a constitutional monarchy in which the king has far-reaching powers.

11. IRAQ

Iraq is another artificial nation-state. The British forces seized Baghdad in 1917 First World War, and the League of Nations approved British mandate in Iraq in 1920. To create an order that would serve the British colonial interests for a long time, in 1921 the British offered the throne of the oil rich Iraq to Prince Faysal and that of the Trans-Jordan territory to Prince Abdullah as rewards for their support to Britain in the war. The offer was a form of an indirect colonial control by providing lucrative and powerful positions to two influential Arabs who would owe their titles to the colonial power.

The newly established country included parts of two pre-existing Ottoman provinces, a majority Shi'a native Iraqis and Arabian Peninsula Bedouin tribes, without the loyalty of the people within them. To the north, Kurdish land was splintered from Kurdistan Province by arbitrary division, forcing the unwilling Kurds to submit to Arab dominance. In the south, a native population was divided between Iraq and Kuwait. And in the west, the area was populated by mostly Arab Bedouin nomads with no tradition of allegiance to any central government. The borders were determined by a scramble of the region's oil wealth and colonial policy of ruling by pitting various ethnic and religious groups against each other. The first British administrator of Iraq observed that, "What we are up against is anarchy plus fanaticism."

King Faysal of Iraq surrounded himself with Syrian veterans of the Arab rebellion. His regime was more Arab nationalist and less inclusion of Iraqi ethnic and sect groups. Faysal's government was dominated by Sunni Arabs and less participation by Iraq's majority, Shi'a Arabs and Kurds. Thus the sense of loyalty to the state among the people of Iraq remained rudimentary and confused. He established an Arab Sunni nationalist regime and ignored two of his constituents, thus planted the seeds of Iraq's future sectarian and ethnic conflicts.

Iraq became an artificial nation-state comprised of an amalgam of mutually conflicted ethno-confessional and ethnic groups. Most Iraqis see themselves as members of their tribe, a religious sect, and an ethnic community. There are more than hundred Arab tribes in Iraq, seven Kurdish tribes, Turkmens tribes, Sunni Muslims, Shi'a Muslims, Eastern Aramaic Christians, Yazidi Christians, and Armenian Christians. The British government plan was to integrate the autonomous territories of many tribes connecting Basra's oil fields in Southern Iraq to the port of Haifa in Palestine through Trans-Jordan. The three countries were under the post-World War One British mandate. There has been overlap in maps between the tribal and the colonial: the first was based on kinship and loyalty in the old tradition of Arab tribalism and the other was based on Sykes-Picot and the interests of the colonials and their Arab urbanite protégés. The British succeeded in winning over few tribes in the territories they needed for their project, but they could not integrate all of them. In 1932, the mandate ended and Iraq gained independence but Britain retained military bases in strategic locations to insure the flow of Iraq's oil to the Mediterranean. Britain had to re-occupy Iraq again in 1941 and topple the government of Prime Minister Rashid Ali al-Gaylani when he staged a pro-Nazi coup in Iraq during the Second World War.

There was a culture of violence against Arab political leaders in the 1950s in the aftermath of the 1948 Palestinian war. King Abdullah of Jordan was assassinated in 1952, so as Egypt's Prime Minister Nukrashi, Hasan al-Banna the MB director of Egypt, and Prime Minister Riad al-Sulh of Lebanon. Iraq and Jordan formed the United Arab Kingdom (UAK) under the Hashemite dynasty in 1958, but it was very short union. General Abdul Karim Kassim carried out a military coup d'état in Iraq in the same year, and his men murdered King Faysal II, most of the Iraqi royal family, and all cabinet members of the UAK government. The cruelty of the coup leaders toward the Iraqi royal family regime suggests deep aversion against its pro-Britain policies.

After five years of Kassim rule, his regime was ousted in a coup led by leaders of the Arab Socialist Baath Party. In-fights and coups within the party led to the ascendance of Saddam Hussein to the presidency of Iraq in 1979. He was officially the fifth president of Iraq, but he had been holding power in Iraq as the leader of the Ba'ath Party in Iraq along with the head of state, Ahmad Hasan al-Bakr. Saddam was behind the economic and political decisions of al-Bakr regime. He directed the nationalization of Iraq's oil industry in 1972 and he was behind the decision to grant limited autonomy to Kurdish region in 1974.

Iraqi culture is built to a large extent on tribal traditions. When Britain conquered the Levant in 1917, its colonial office printed a brief guide to the history of Arab Territories that included this statement: "Beyond the immediate vicinity of the towns, which are few in number, Mesopotamia is a tribal country." We cannot understand Iraq's politics without understanding the importance of tribal traditions. Iraq's justice system has been tribal, and it continues to be even more tribal after the 2003 US invasion, where the tribe and clan elders pass and enforce arbitrary judgments based on set of tribal norms and customs to settle disputes. The tribal norms that existed before the building of the state, like offering women as commodities in settlements of disputes, are in direct conflict with Iraq's civil laws and its constitution today. The tribal laws today are set at the same level of the state institutions and the government stands helpless in regulating the tribal communities.

Cultural tribal values include allegiance to members of one's tribe or clan, avenging the blood of a tribe member, and demonstrating one's manly courage in fights. The majority of Iraqis are more loyal to the tribe than their nation-state. The Shi'a tribes feel they are closer to Iran, while the Sunni tribes feel closer to the Arab nations, the Kurds and Turkmens tribes feel they are different races from the rest of the Iraqis. The Chaldean, Syriac, Assyrian, and Armenian Christians feel they do not belong to their ancestral homeland any more. They are leaving the country, to join family and friends in the West, by the thousands. When the US invaded Iraq in 2003, Iraqi Christians community exceeded 1.4 million, then an orgy of sectarian violence was unleashed against them since then, and as of 2017 their numbers has fallen to an estimated 275,000.

The post-2003 insurgency in Iraq including the emergence of ISIS terror group was a tribal-sectarian uprising. It started as a Sunni's rebellion against the Shi'a tribes and Shi'a-dominated Iraqi regime. ISIS' mini state never was a viable entity, but its establishment and survival was in part because the Iraqi military was too hollowed out by the state's 2003 collapse and by the government's growing corruption. The Sunni and Shi'a identities were embedded in Iraq social and religious norms since the establishment of the nation-state. It was the long abused Shi'a struggling against the state in the pre-2003 period. The Shi'a was the majority acting and treated by the regime like a minority. After the US invasion of Iraq, the struggle became a bloody civil war between Iraqi Sunni and Shi'a. The violence will continue because avenging is a tribal creed in Iraq. The area that became known as Iraq was often the battle ground during the Ottoman rule that had languished in which neighboring states fought for dominance. This is because the dividing line between majority Sunni and majority Shi'a in the ME runs through the area that has become Iraq. Given Iraq's lack of an organic identity, its governments have frequently resorted to force to hold the country together. Iraq is likely to remain a sectarian war zone because Both Shi'a-Iran to the east and Wahhabi-Sunni Saudi Arabia to the south support militant groups engaged in violent acts.

Today, with ISIS defeated, Jihadists are not the only challenge that Iraq will face going forward. The Iraqi political landscape is more fragmented than it was in the past. The corrupt political class that has ruled the country since the fall of Saddam Hussein and the system of governance that supports the out-of-control sectarian elite threatens Iraq's long-term stability. It is a challenge for the government in Baghdad to prevent Iraq's division into the three main tribal areas, the Sunnis, the Shi'a and the Kurds.

Saddam's Iraq Wars:

In the same year when Saddam became officially the president of Iraq, there was a profound development in neighboring Iran. The Shah of Iran, Muhammad Reza Pahlavi was overthrown by a popular uprising and the pro-West monarchy was replaced with anti-West Islamic-Republic under Ayatollah Ruhollah Khomeini as the supreme leader. The Shah's regime was viewed by the alienated Iranians as egregiously corrupt and his security forces were committing serious human rights violations against dissidents. The Shah was a close ally of the US ever since he had been returned to the thrown in 1953 by a coup initially planned by the British. Once the Shah was dethroned, he became a liability to his allies and the subject of dispute between the US and the new Islamic-Iranian regime. Iranian students stormed the US embassy in Tehran, taking more than 60 American hostages. It was a way for the student revolutionaries to declare an end to the US interference in their country's affair. The US under President Carter abandoned the Shah and refused to give him asylum, or even medical treatment on a temporary basis, because his entry to the US would unleash repercussions against the US embassy employees being held hostages in Tehran. Only Anwar Al-Sadat of Egypt welcomed the Shah, who died shortly after his arrival in Cairo.

The Iranian revolution produced profound changes at a great speed with unpredictable Arab leadership in the region. Saddam Hussein and the Gulf States' leaders were afraid that the revolution might spread to their countries. Encouraged by the US, and with the Gulf States promise to provide financial support, Hussein ordered a surprise military attack on Iran in September 1980. Hussein's war on Iran was the spark that started a chain of bloody wars and events which have destabilized the ME.

The nation-state of Iraq was founded between World War I and II, as the British Empire was unravelling. It was designed as one of many weak states patched together of disparate and not necessarily compatible neighbors. Iraqi regimes have at times resorted to force to hold the country together. Further, in the 1970s, the CIA was arming and inciting the Iraqi Kurds to rebel, leading to internal wars.

Saddam Hussein raised the level of force to violence and brutality, especially in suppressing the Kurdish people's uprising during the 1988 Iraq-Iran war and the 1991 Shi'a rebellion after his military was expelled from Kuwait. Saddam was the initiator and the cause of four regional wars. His military invaded two countries the US led a war to liberate Kuwait and thirteen years later another US-led coalition invaded Iraq and overthrew him. Saddam was captured by the US military and handed to the Iraqis. He was tried and convicted by Iraqi court, and executed ironically in the headquarters of his former military intelligence service.

Under Saddam's watch, Iraq experienced an era of economic prosperity, then strife, wars, foreign invasions and communal violence. Iraq saw the best and the worst under his rule. Saddam turned into a ruthless dictator, but within the first few years of his reign, Iraq was on a road to economic, social and industrial progress that was envied by all ME countries. During that time, the unemployment, poverty, illiteracy and infant mortality rate were low. Iraqi standards of living, all levels of public educational system and health care were the best. Unfortunately, the days of Iraq's prosperity were short-lived when Saddam decided, with the support of the US and the Arab Gulf States, to invade neighboring countries.

First his armed forces crossed Iran's western border in 1980. Saddam started a war to overthrow the new Iranian regime before it gained strength and stabilized. Conflicts contributing to Saddam's decision to attack ranged from centuries-old religious schisms to Arab-versus-Persian ethnic disputes to Saddam's ambition to consolidate his power in the Arab world.

Saddam believed Iran was in turmoil and that his forces could achieve quick victory. The conflict turned into a war of attrition, with each side showing a marked disregard for the human cost. The Iraq-Iran war was one of the most barbaric in modern history. It lasted eight years and settled into stalemate with entrenched front where both nations engaged in air and missile attacks against military and oil installations. They even attacked each other's oil tankers in the Persian Gulf. The number of people killed on both sides exceeded one million, and Iraq used chemical weapons against the Iranian military and against its own citizens, the Iraqi-Kurd civilians for sympathizing with Iran.

By 1988, when the oil-exporting capacity of the two nations was severely reduced and their economies suffered badly, they accepted a United Nations-mediated cease-fire. After half a million Iraqi dead and more than $70 billion of wasted treasure, Iraq was a bankrupt country and Saddam could not overthrow Khomeini regime or redraw the border with Iran in his favor. Iraq's economic plight and the Gulf States reluctance to give him more financial aid, Saddam took the fateful decision to invade Kuwait in 1990. He ordered his army to cross the border, occupy and annex the state of Kuwait, a sovereign state and a member of the Arab League. The Western and regional powers which had come to his aid in fighting Iran united in opposing him.

The unprovoked action against the small oil-rich state was also a major threat to the international oil supplies that would impact the world wide economies and security. Saudi Arabia called on the US and other Western governments to intervene, and the UN Security Council demanded the immediate withdrawal of the Iraqi military from Kuwait. When Saddam defied the UN demands and even threatened Saudi Arabia, the US rushed its own troops to the region. The US foreign policy team forged an unprecedented international coalition consisting of the NATO allies and the Middle Eastern countries of Saudi Arabia, Syria, and Egypt to oppose Iraqi aggression. Even Russia condemned Iraq, its long-time client state, but it did not commit troops.

The US-led coalition unleashed its ground and air attacks to defeat the Iraqi occupation forces. After 42 days of relentless attacks, followed by "Operation Desert Storm," a 100-hour land war which expelled Iraqi forces from Kuwait, the US accomplished its mission and declared a ceasefire. The retreating Iraqi military torched Kuwait's oil wells as the last act of aggression against Kuwait. While the Iraqis were retreating, the Americans, Canadians, British and French attacked and destroyed a column of up to 2,000 trucks and other vehicles, blowing them to bits. It is not clear how many men were killed.

The crisis sparked by Iraq's invasion of Kuwait widened the gap between wealthy, oil-producing countries and their poor neighbors. The disparity added to regional instability even after the crisis was defused. High oil prices brought windfall profits to the Persian Gulf states, but others like Egypt, Jordan, Syria, Tunisia and Yemen became reeling under the economic losses resulting from the invasion and the UN imposed sanctions on Iraq. Because Jordan, Yemen and the PLO Chairman Yasser Arafat supported Saddam

Hussein's invasion, their national expatriates in the Gulf lost their jobs and were deported. These countries lost the income from remittances of their migrant workers who used to work in Iraq, Kuwait and Saudi Arabia and they lost trade with Iraq because of the sanctions. Saddam Hussein's invasion of Kuwait was the root cause of the US invasion of Iraq that was the trigger of the "Arab Spring." But he had undertaken the attack after consulting with the US ambassador.

The 1991 war is referred to by the media as "the First Gulf War." Besides the humiliation, Saddam's military adventures were too costly in terms of the human casualties and suffering and material loss to Iraq, Iran and Kuwait. Iraq also had to surrender some of its strategic border territory to Kuwait and Iran. Iraq was forced to recognize Kuwait's independence and accept the UN-demarcated borders that awarded a port and an oil field to Kuwait. And in August of 1990, when Iraq was involved in the invasion of Kuwait, Saddam Hussein accepted Iran's terms for the settlement of the 1980–1988 war with Iran. It included the withdrawal of Iraqi troops from any occupied Iranian territory and the division of sovereignty over the Shatt al-Arab waterway that had been exclusively Iraqi before the invasion of Iran.

Before the First Gulf war, the UN Security Council imposed sanctions against Iraq to compel it to withdraw from Kuwait, to pay reparations, and to eliminate its weapons of mass destruction. It included preventing the import of all products and commodities originating in Iraq as well as the transfer of funds to Iraq for these activities. It prevented the availability of funds or other financial or economic resources or to any commercial, industrial or public utility except for humanitarian purposes. After the end of the war, the UN Security Council took steps to implement the sanctions under Chapter VII and imposed more stringent economic sanctions to include linkage to removal of weapons of mass destruction. The effect of the sanctions on the civilian population was catastrophic.

The Invasion of Iraq—"The Second Gulf War"

In 2002, President George W. Bush accused Iraq of possessing and manufacturing weapons of mass destruction (WMD) to justify his administration decision to go to war. The accusation had been denied by UN inspectors who had spent a year searching for such weapons without success. Bush ordered the invasion of Iraq on March 19, 2003. The accusation was later proved erroneous by his own military inspectors after the invasion, the occupying and destruction of a sovereign state, and the human rights violation of its people. After proving the WMD claim was a lie, US adopted "the spread of Western democracy" as the new foreign policy theme, but after the US military left Iraq, the country has functioned as a sectarian state, a failed democracy.

Some elements within the Bush administration including Vice President Dick Cheney tried to link Saddam Hussein's Iraq to al-Qaeda in order to justify the invasion they had already decided on. But Saddam was as much bin Laden's enemy as America, if not more, since he was not a "true" or devout Muslim. He made a show of sometimes going to the mosque, but his regime was in fact a socialist dictatorship. UK Prime Minister Tony Blair claimed in 2003, when his 40,000 troopers joined the US led coalition to invade Iraq, that Iraq's invasion would deny jihadis an arena and prevent Saddam from using them as proxies in his standoff with the West. Twelve years later, the ex-Prime Minister Blair acknowledged that without the Iraqi war there would be no Islamic State (ISIS).

The simplest explanation for the US led invasion was to demonstrate the US military might against a visible enemy to deter others and to dispel any appearance of weakness following the 9/11 terrorist attack. The historian Daniel Lieberfeld, wrote in his article "the Iraq War and Conflict Theory" that the US invasion of Iraq was meant to "maintain uni-polarity hegemony, and to avoid post-9/11 momentum decline in US actions, by demonstrating US willingness to use force." Saddam Hussein's Iraq was a perfect country to be made an example since the animosity between the US and Saddam went back at least to the first Gulf War, more than one decade earlier.

The US led military invasion, "Operation Iraqi Freedom" and the ensuing occupation and insurgency, caused death and injuries to hundreds of thousands of Iraqis, leaving chaos and utter destruction that strengthened the power of grassroots extreme Islamists and trained more stateless terrorists. The human life, suffering and material cost to the US as a result of this war was high. When the US withdrew in December 2011, number of US military personnel killed in Iraq were 4,804 and 31,952 were wounded in action. There were hundreds of US veteran amputees, thousands suffer from brain injuries and mental illness, and many committed suicide. The estimated monetary war cost to the US was more than $1.7 trillion with additional $490 billion in benefit owed to war veterans, expenses that could grow to more than $4 trillion over the next four decades, according to the "Cost of War Project" by the Watson Institute of International Studies at Brown University that was published on the tenth anniversary of the US-led invasion of Iraq. The war according to the report had killed at least 134,000 Iraqi civilians and may have contributed to the deaths of as many as four times that number.

The 2003 US/UK invasion of Iraq that was utterly without credible pretext was the major crime of the twenty-first century and the biggest policy debacle of our generation. It is ironic that the invasion was led by the US, the country that advocated the UN Universal Declaration of Human Rights and adopted the Bill of Rights of the US Constitution. Iraq's invasion, the so called "Second Gulf War" and its protracted armed conflict led to the destruction and suffering in a country where the civilian society had been already devastated by years of American and British sanctions. The measures taken against Iraq after the 1990 first Gulf war and before the invasion had been regarded as "genocidal" even by the diplomats who administered the sanctions and some even resigned in protest for this reason.

The war consisted of two phases: the first was a conventionally fought war in March-April of 2003 in which US and British troops with small contingents from many other countries invaded Iraq and rapidly defeated its military. Iraqi troops simply chose not to resist the invading coalition forces. Saddam Hussein was captured, turned over to the Iraqi authorities to stand trial for various crimes against the Iraqi people. He was convicted and executed on December 30,2006. The second phase in which the US-led occupation forces fought a bloody and costly insurgency. Despite the defeat of Iraq's conventional military forces, the American invasion was the vital first step in a series of tragic events. A Sunni-insurgency against the occupying forces emerged resulting in thousands of coalition military, insurgent and civilian deaths.

Central to the Sunni grievances is the belief that the invasion destroyed a regional order, ousting a stalwart of Sunni rule, and inviting the rival Shi'a sect to take over. The sense of loss that was formed along the fault-lines of sectarianism was profound, with the Sunnis passionately believing that the US must have known exactly what they were doing. The insurgency against the occupying forces was carried out by a mix of Jihadis who believed the war had been preordained in prophecies and non-ideologues who were enraged by losing jobs, status and dignity. The invasion generated millions of refugees, largely destroyed the country, instigated a sectarian conflict and ironically gave al-Qaeda affiliates [ISIS], the perpetrators of the September 11 attack a foothold that is now tearing apart Iraq and the entire region.

President Barack Obama formally withdrew the US military in 2011 and decided not to put more American lives in harm's way in Iraq. The Iraqi regime sectarianized government institutions including the military and the security forces to the benefit of the Shi'a majority. ISIS exploited the ensuing rise in the sectarian tensions to gain local support of the Sunni population and inadvertently helped to lay the groundwork for it to conquer almost

40 percent of Iraq in 2014. The US military troops and air-force bombers returned to be involved in the sectarian conflict. President Obama ordered US military advisors to go back fighting alongside Iraqi forces near the front lines against ISIS in a war that he had declared its end, and then President Trump has doubled US deployments. Trump granted more latitude to the US commanders against the terrorist state than they had since Iraq's ground war more than two years before.

By the time President Trump ordered bombing ISIS, he was the fifth US president to order dropping bombs on Iraq since the first Gulf war of 1990. Finally, ISIS as a state has been defeated, but like al-Qaeda, its militants may keep terrorizing the region and elsewhere. Al-Qaeda terrorist organization was created when Russia invaded Afghanistan to shore up a communist regime, and ISIS terrorist organization was created when the US invaded Iraq based on faulty intelligence. President Obama had not learnt a lesson from Iraq's war. He led the charge, albeit from behind, into Libya in 2011 to overthrow another tyrant, only to find out the country falls into the hands of terrorists.

The 2003 war empowered ethnic and sectarian groups and allowed the full unfettered of previously suppressed tribal identities. It highlighted the fact that there were multiple and contradictory visions of what it means to be Iraqi or even to be part of the Arab world. The Iraqi Sunnis have lost out to the Shiites and the Kurds after fourteen years of the American invasion ended decades of Sunni dominance.

The war on ISIS including the 25,000 coalition airstrikes, especially in the city of El Mosul, caused death and injuries for thousands and displaced hundreds of thousands, mostly Sunni civilians. As their ruined towns wait rebuilding, they have not received help from a cash-stripped central government that is focused on fighting the militants and more recently, the Kurdish separatists. The Iraqi government has forsaken their own Sunnis and forged closer ties with the hard-line Shiite theocracy of Iran that wields big influence over the policies of Iraq's sectarian regime. With Iraq's government controlled by Shiites, and the Kurds governing their own autonomous area, the Sunnis who account for about a quarter of the total population became the neglected minority, victims of sectarianism and the tyranny of the majority.

Saddam Hussein was a ruthless dictator who oppressed Iraq for more than thirty years, used chemical weapon against his own people, and unleashed two regional wars against Iran and Kuwait. But that does not justify destroying a country and committing massacres of innocent civilians who might have been Saddam's victims themselves. It does not justify the crimes and abuses committed against Iraqi prisoners by the US military in Abu Ghraib jail. There were other means to get rid of Saddam who did not pose an imminent threat to US national interests in 2003 or that he would be the man to provide mass-casualty weapons to Osama bin Laden.

While there is no doubt that Saddam Hussein repressed his own people, the Iraq we see today is arguably worse than Saddam's Iraq. As bad as Saddam may have been, at least under his authoritarian regime, the country held together, ethnic tension was controlled, Al-Qaeda had not taken root, and people had a more stable security situation. The United States spent billions, with some estimates putting it at over 2 trillion on this war which has cost ordinary Iraqis severely. The British charity Oxfam, estimated that around "28 percent of Iraqi children are malnourished, and 70 percent lack clean drinking water" in 2018. This according to Oxfam is actually far worse than when hard sanctions crippled the regime's food distribution system. Instead of "creating democracy," as the Bush administration claimed, the US started a perpetual cycle of wars and created an utter mess that is near impossible to resolve.

Organizations like Freedom House do not view Iraq today as a functioning democracy, rather as a system that functions on corruption. Critics will claim that at least it is more democracy than under Saddam, which, while true, is by no means worth the human sacrifice. It is an astonishing fact about the US intellectual and moral culture that some informed and enlightened personnel associated with that war still call it, "the liberation of Iraq!" They attempt to put a moral façade over a war crime.

Iran has been the winner in President George W. Bush "war on terror." The attacks and regime change of the Iran's two bitter enemies, the fiercely Sunni Taliban government in Afghanistan from the east and the Saddam Hussein regime in Iraq from the west were of great benefit to Iran.

Since then, Iran has cultivated strong political, economic and sectarian ties with Iraqi-Shi'a and increased its power to promote its power cross-border Shi'a solidarity. In Iraq's 2010 elections, Iran-supported Shi'a political parties emerged victorious and they have been controlling power in Iraq. The Arab Spring in Syria brought an opportunity for Iran to project even more power across the ME. The rise of Sunni extremist groups including ISIS gave Iran a major role as the defender of Shi'a Muslims. Iran according to the Western news media sent military advisers, volunteers and arms to Bashar Al-Assad regime and to its traditional Lebanese ally, Hezbollah, and the Houthi militia groups in Yemen.

Since the 2003 invasion of Iraq and the toppling of Saddam Husain regime, the US has been acquiescing to Iran's influence and accepting Iranian dominance over the Iraqi government. The US effectively enabled Iranian's proxies to take over Iraq as the two countries share border and common sectarian interest because their populations are majority Shi'a-Islam. With the rise of ISIS threat, Iran's regional role was elevated even more by giving its proxies a military role in fighting the terrorist state, even while undermining the power of Iraq's Sunni minority. Iran and its Shi'a proxies have enormous influence over Iraq. Its Revolutionary Guards fight side by side with Iraq's Shi'a militias in the open and it has cemented its influence over the Iraqi military.

During the 1980–88 Iran–Iraq war, the US aided Saddam to weaken Iran and eliminate its future threat to the US interests in the region. The US 2003 war delivered Iraq to Iran and empowered it to challenge the US traditional Arab allies perhaps to keep them even more dependent on the US for their defense. Big powers do not have friends, they only have interests.

During the 1980-88 Iran–Iraq war, the US aided Saddam to weaken Iran and eliminate its future threat to the US interests in the region. It was offering intelligence and logistical support to Iraq and at one time it was also selling the Iranians weapons and spare-parts in what would become known as the Iran-Contra scandal. A member of President Reagan National Security Council, Lieutenant Colonel Oliver North, whose office was in the basement of the White House, was selling weapons through intermediaries to Iran, with the profits being channeled to support the Contra rebel groups in Nicaragua.

Iraqi Kurds

Iraqi Kurds belong to large ethnic tribes of about 25 million people that have always lived in the historic Kurdistan region, a large contiguous area in Southwest Asia. They trace their roots back to the biblical Medes of ancient Persia more than 2,500 years ago. Many of them lived, until recently, a nomadic lifestyle in the mountainous areas of Turkey, Iraq, Iran and Syria. They developed their own life style, customs and language, and their refuge has always been the mountains, the steep pastures and valleys.

Most Kurds are Muslims about 75% of them are Sunnis. Majority of Sunni Kurds follow the Shafi'i interpretation of the Islamic legal code while majority of the Turkish Muslims adhere to the Hanafi school of thought and most of the Arabs follow the Hanbali doctrine. More than 15% of the Kurds are Shiites living mostly in Iran. The rest are followers of several indigenous Kurdish faiths of great antiquity and originality. There are small communities of Kurdish Jews, Christians and Baha'is and followers of mystical practices including participation in Sufi orders. The most notable of these are the Yazidis who are small in number and whose belief and spirituality show influence from a mix of the religions of the nations that had ruled the region through history.

The Yazidis are a most peaceful community in the Middle East, but they are often charged with worshipping Lucifer or the devil by people who do not take the time to understand their faith. Yazidis are monotheists, believing in one God, and that the sun as the source of energy, and life is the emanation of God. When they pray they face the sun. They believe there is a group of seven archangels through which God delegates His authority; good and evil exist in the minds of human beings and it is up to the individual to choose; non-believers do not go to hell, according to Yazidis, and they believe in reincarnation.

Kurdistan was a province within the Ottoman Empire until the end of First World War. When the war triumphs, Britain and France, divided the newly conquered lands, the 1920 Treaty of Sevres recognized the rights of the Kurds to have a state, but the historic Kurdistan was divided among a number of new nation-states, namely Turkey, Iran, Iraq, Syria and Armenia. Each one of these states, especially Turkey which had the largest share of Kurdistan, refused to recognize an independent Kurdish state. The Kurds lost their traditional seasonal migrations and nomadic way of life. For decades, the Kurds of this area have been struggling for recognition as a nation with its own culture including the language. They have revolted against the Turks, Arabs and the Persians in trying to establish an autonomous or independent state but have always been defeated. Today, only Iraq officially recognizes a "Kurdish Autonomous Region" (KRG) in the north, Iran recognizes the Kurdish entity in the northeast region only by name, and Turkey continues its policy of not recognizing the Kurds even as a minority group.

The Turkish Kurds have been receiving harsh treatment at the hands of the Turkish government. Turkey tried to deprive them of their identity by designating them "Mountain Turks," outlawing their language and even forbidding them from wearing traditional Kurdish costumes in the cities. The government also encouraged the migration of Kurds to the cities to dilute the population in the uplands. This conflict still exists as the Turkish Kurdistan area has been depopulated, thousands of villages have been destroyed and a state of martial law has been implemented. In Iraq, Kurds had faced similar repression before earning their autonomy.

Iraq's recognition of the Kurds was granted after decades of abuse and human rights violations by the Iraqi governments that had been controlled by Arab nationalists since Prince Faysal Ibn Al-Hussein was given the throne by the British in 1920. The war against the Kurds for demanding autonomy was described by Western news media as systematic attempt to exterminate the Kurdish population. During the 1980s rule of the Ba'ath Party, Iraq's government military under Saddam Hussein committed massacres against the Kurds who were accused of supporting Iran in the 1980-88 Iran–Iraq war. Chemical bombardment of towns and villages took place in hundreds of communities across Kurdistan. Thousands of men, women and children were allegedly executed in a 1988 military operation named the Anfal, Arabic for spoils of war. The Kurds rebelled after the first Persian Gulf War that ended the Iraqi occupation of Kuwait, only to be crushed again by Saddam Hussein Iraqi troops thousands were killed and millions fled to Iran. The United States has helped the creation of the Kurdish Autonomous Region by relegating the region as a safe haven for the Kurds within Iraq and imposing a "no-fly" zone north of the 36th parallel.

There has been historic tribal intra-Kurdish competition for the Iraqi Kurds community leadership between the main political parties that goes back decades. The Kurdistan Democratic Party (KDP) founded by Mustafa Barazani in Erbil in 1946, and the Patriotic Union of Kurdistan (PUK) founded by Jalal Talabani clan in Suleimaniyah in 1975. The two parties have their own militias (peshmerga) which battled each other in periods of fight between the two factions. From 1994–98, the two Iraqi Kurd factions fought a bloody war for power over the control of northern Iraq. In September 1998, the two sides agreed to a power-sharing arrangement. They formed together the Democratic Patriotic Alliance of Kurdistan that acts as a political block within Iraq. The alliance contested the 2005 Iraqi parliamentary elections jointly and it is represented in the Iraqi parliament. Jalal Talabani was elected by the national parliament as the first post-US-occupation president of Iraq until he suffered a stroke in 2012 and passed away in 2017.

The pre-existing competition over the leadership of PUK movement over Suleimaniyah region between the Talabani clan and Kosrut Rasoul has been accelerated by the death of Jalal Talabani. The war against ISIS and the battle of the Iraqi national government to retake Kirkuk from the Kurds unified all the factions and competing tribes despite their political differences.

The men and women of peshmerga fighting force were an effective force in the war against ISIS especially the battle to retake the territory it occupied since 2014. After participating in the defeat of ISIS and liberating the ruined and depopulated city of Mosul, Iraqi Kurds held a referendum on September 25, 2017 to affirm their right to declare independence. The move was strongly opposed not only by the Iraqi government, but also by Iran and Turkey. The two countries fear a Kurdish state on their borders will encourage their own

Kurd population to rise up demanding similar states of their own. The vast majority of the Kurds voted for independence, and the leadership faced a decision about whether to declare outright independence from Baghdad. The three countries, Iraq, Iran and Turkey, took actions to force KRG to call off the plans for declaring independence. The Iraqi Supreme Court declared the referendum illegal, pending legal review. The Iraqi government and Iran stopped flights to Kurdistan, and the two governments held military exercises along the border with Kurdistan to demonstrate solidarity against the referendum. Understandably, Israel was the only country in the region supporting Kurdistan Independence.

The Iraqi Council of Representatives voted to authorize Iraqi Prime Minister Haider al-Abadi to use any means including the military to retake the disputed Kirkuk and its oil fields from the Kurds who claimed it was part of their autonomous region. The Iraqi prime minister and the leader of the Iranian-proxi Badr Organization demanded Kurdish forces relinquish control over Kirkuk and Iranian Revolutionary Guards Quds forces commander traveled to Iraq and delivered an ultimatum from Ali Khameni to the Kurds leadership. To avoid a regional crisis, Masoud Barazani, the Iraqi Kurdish leader decided to order the peshmerga to withdraw from Kirkuk and he gave up his position as the president of the Autonomous Region. He declared that he would not extend his presidential term after November 1, 2007. Barazani failed to achieve the independence that he and his father before him championed for nearly four decades due to the political and military realities facing Iraq and the region. Yet Barazani family has not given up power completely. Nechirvan Barazani is the Prime Minister of the KRG region and Masrour Barazani is the head of the security forces.

Turkey's Kurdistan Workers' Party (PKK), that has been waging a guerrilla insurgency in southeastern Turkey for years demanding independence, has been against the Iraqi-Kurds' decision to seek local self-government within a federal Iraq. The PKK wants any independent Kurdish state should be a homeland for all people of historic Kurdistan.

The Arab Spring in Iraq

The 2011 Arab Spring in Iraq led widespread anti-government demonstrations in the Sunni triangle and contributed to a civil war and the rise of ISIS. The protest was violently quashed and Prime Minister Maliki labeled the demonstrators as terrorists linked to al-Qaeda. Repressing the protest exacerbated the crisis of the Sunnis representation. The Sunni Iraqis, who were estranged from the state and the political process, rebelled against the center government. They were disillusioned by the Shi'a elite's monopoly over power and the impunity of the sectarian Shi'a militias. Sunni leadership was sidelined or exiled to Kurdistan region or abroad, and many were imprisoned. As a result, Sunni Iraqis lost all trust and hope in engaging with the political process.

Even when Sunni representatives are part of the government as stated by the constitution, their voice is overlooked by the executive, and they continue to face difficulty emerging as strong leaders with substantial constituency. Sunni leader Saleh al-Mutlag who was enticed to take the symbolic position of deputy prime minister complained about his lack of power, "I've never been allowed to participate in writing bylaws or in big decisions."

It was too difficult for the Iraqi Sunnis to adapt to the changing circumstances that went from rulers to being ruled and suppressed in post-2003 Iraq. The Shi'as were allowed to have their heavily armed militia, the Popular Mobilization Forces the Kurds had their state-sanctioned Peshmerga forces but the Sunnis were denied the right to have weapons. The Sunnis did not have a reliable political party that could defend their political and economic interests.

Iraqi Sunnis pursued a policy of disengagement from the central government and that led to political and security vacuums. Tribal leaders are influential in Iraqi society, but inter and intra Sunni tribal conflicts remain a problem prohibiting the emergence of a united confederation of tribes that can speak with a pan-tribal Sunni voice. Intra Sunni conflict and absence of strong institutions and political parties to represent them created a crisis of representation and that facilitated the emergence of Jihadi groups like al-Qaeda and ISIS. Some Iraqi Sunnis supported ISIS and more were indifferent.

Distrust of the Shi'a-dominated central government and fear of Iran's influence have kept Sunni Arabs from attempting to combat ISIS, even though their leaderships were staunchly against the group. After ISIS defeat, the tendency to link Sunnis with the Islamic State continues to be a major struggle for the Sunni community and will continue to prevent re-engagement with the central government. Members of the Sunni population affiliated with ISIS and the non grata Baathists continue to call for a boycott of the state and attack the government and government-sanctioned paramilitary. As long as the central government remains antagonistic, these groups will continue to exist.

In the 2018 national parliamentary elections, the first after ISIS defeat and the fourth since the 2003 US-led invasion, the Iraqi political landscape splintered by fragmented intra-sectarian factions, tribal and ethnic divisions. There was a democratic process, but it was marked by the identity politics which grouped people along sectarian and ethnicity lines rather than ideology. The Kurds were driven by the sense of ethno-nationalism and the secessionist movement the Shi'a had their central religious establishment driven by a sense of being oppressed for long time before gaining their political rights. The Sunnis had no powerful party, but they were told that the Iraqi Communist Party represented them.

Even among the Shi'a, there was little of the euphoria that characterized past elections in Iraq. People felt there was no change and most candidates mocked people with their corruption. More than 55% of the registered voters especially the young Iraqis stayed away from the polls because they had been disappointed by the politicians who "have made Iraq one if not the most corrupt countries in the world," according to Iraqi reporter Jane Arraf.

12. ALGERIA

Many generations of Algerians had been fighting and dying in continual rebellions and wars since the early 19th century, more than 120 years of which, the fighting was against the French colonialists. For seventeen years, they fought all-out war against the French when their armies invaded Algeria in 1830 then in 1871, they fought for decades against the Cremieux' extension of colonial authority and then they fought the bloodiest war in the 1954–1962 War of Independence. The Algerians never stopped harassing the French occupying troops till the last soldier had to leave after independence. And in 1991–2002, Algeria had its Islamist uprising against their own government. We do not have the number of Algerians who died fighting the wars against colonialism, but the War of Independence took the lives of more than one million Algerians and the cost of the Islamists' rebellion was close to 200,000 lives.

Algeria was part of the Ottoman Empire since 1671, but at the time when France invaded it in 1830, the country was enjoying full autonomy with weak central government. It was an Ottoman regency controlled by native Algerian governor 'dey' and supported mostly by some privileged tribes and people of mixed Turkish and Algerian ancestry. Local tribe-leaders, religious leaders and military people chose the dey that governed for life and ruled with high degree of autonomy from the Ottomans. The Algerians then paid allegiance to the Ottomans only symbolically in their Friday prayers by wishing the Sultan long life and recognizing him as the leader of Muslims. Sources of the Algerian local government's revenue included taxes on the agriculture produce, annual religious tributes paid by Muslims, and protection payments rendered by government armed sailors in the Mediterranean, regarded by international laws as pirates. When pirates from the North African countries seized American merchant ships and held the crews for ransom, the US under President Thomas Jefferson dispatched American warships that joined a Swedish flotilla in blockading Tripoli in the 1801-1805 'Barbary War' in which US military captured the Tripolitania city of Derna and gave American negotiators leverage in securing the return of hostages. Algeria was too big to be under full control by its weak central government. Its tribes and desert people lived under complete autonomy with their centuries' old unwritten traditional laws.

In the 19th and 20th centuries, France described its colonial adventures in Africa and Indochina as its duty to bring Western civilization to what it perceived as backward indigenous peoples but the potential for commerce and natural resources provided the true impetus for the conquest and colonization. France suppressed and enslaved the people of its colonies and exploited the resources of their countries. In the case of Algeria, the country represented untapped region for economic expansion. France planned to settle and annex the country. When the French troops landed in the coastal city of Oran, the second largest Algerian city in 1830, or when they tried to expand from the coast into the south in 1857, they massacred, looted and raped villages and desecrated mosques. Weeks after they captured the city of Algiers, the French declared the area that was the whole Mediterranean region as an integral part of France. Large influx of French and other European countries' citizens, mainly peasants and working class, settled in Algeria. The French colonialists eliminated the traditional political leadership and replaced it with French authority. They took possession and redistributed land owned by the tribes, religious foundations and farmers. The French changed Algeria's economy into a producer of cash crops (wine, olive, wheat, citrus fruits and tobacco) that was exported mainly to France. This caused food scarcities and forced many Algerians who had been uprooted from their land, wandering in the cities or colonialists' farming areas in search of work.

The French divided the areas under their control into three different administration systems. The settlers elected mayors and self-governing councils in Algiers and Oran areas where the European-settlers constituted majority of the population government was to be controlled by appointed French administrators in the areas with Muslim-Algerians majority and the remote territories populated only by indigenous Algerians were administered by French military commanders.

The Algerian tribesmen, who had fought many foreign invaders before, put up stiff resistance against the French invading armies. Tribes unified by their common Islamic religious sentiment tried to lay siege to the French military unit in the city of Oran. There were many stories of the bravery of ordinary people and tribal leaders who answered the call to defend their motherland. The director of a religious school in the town of Mascara led the harassment against the French troops. Abdel-Qadir al-Jaza'eri, an Algerian national legend, used Islam and the concept of nationality and independence to bring people together and get the support of local tribes to wage war against the French invaders. He established a state in the mountainous areas with Mascara as its capital and extended it to include parts of the oases in the Sahara region. Abdel-Qadir was an open-minded visionary who brought people of all religions including Christians and Jews to help in building a modern state. In 1837, the French tricked him by signing the Treaty of Tafna in which they recognize his control over two thirds of the country, mainly the interior if he recognized France's sovereignty in Oran and Algiers. He signed the Treaty and a year later, French troops marched through his territory, and Abdel-Qadir renewed the resistance. The French military grew larger in numbers and more brutal. They suppressed the native population's resistance using and practiced a scorched earth policy and Abdel-Qadir was defeated in 1847. His ultimate failure was due in considerable measure to the refusal of the Kabyles, Berber mountain tribes in the east, to join the common cause with the Arabs against the French. After the French overthrew their own constitutional monarchy in 1848, the new government of the Second Republic ended Algeria's status as a colony and declared the land they controlled an integral part of France. In 1870–71, the French Minister of Interior, Adolphe Crémieux, issued decrees that added more to the Algerians' long-standing grievances and triggered the most native insurrection since the time of Abdel-Qadir. Crémieux ordered the assimilation of all Algeria into France, and he granted the Algerian Jews French citizenship. And when France lost Alsace Lorraine to Germany in 1871, he made Algerian land available for the Alsatian and Lorrainer refugees to settle them.

The French citizens-settlers were able to elect deputies to the French parliament and the indigenous Algerians were made only French subjects with no political rights. The settlers had power and high incomes while the Algerian majority developed inferiority complex and suffered from subservience and poverty. These conditions created nationalist generation that would become major revolutionaries during the War of Independence. Religious leaders and Algerian intellectuals were calling for independence for decades, but when World War I broke out, it became a movement that was recognized by the French government in Paris. France promised to give the Algerians self-rule, but like all promises of the colonialists, the promise went unfulfilled. World War II inspired the Algerian nationalists to unite and support their demands for independence with military actions. They formed the National Liberation Front (FLN), began a guerrilla war against France and sought diplomatic recognition at the UN to establish a sovereign state. It was in 1954, when Jamal Abdel-Nassir of Egypt was leading Arab Nationalism movement. Egypt provided arms to the FLN, and its fighters engaged in serious fights first in the countryside, then in and around the city of Algiers. The French military actions of uprooting people from their homes and putting them in camps did not produce political or military success. Thousands of Algerians joined the FLN, and France's allies were alienated. US Senator John F. Kennedy complained that the war in Algeria became a Cold War liability and detriment to economic interdependence between France and those historically associated with France.

The French people elected Charles de Gaulle as prime minister in 1958 and president in 1959. De Gaulle believed that while the war against the FLN in Algeria was militarily winnable, it was not good politics. France's defeat in Vietnam had disillusioned de Gaulle concerning colonialism. In the summer of 1960, de Gaulle spoke of Algeria as being Algerian. In his New Year greeting to his fellow French he spoke again of Algeria as belonging to Algerians. In a referendum on Algerian self-determination, 75.2 % of the vote in France was in favor. In March it was announced that there would be talks between French government and representatives of "Algeria's Muslims." The talks dragged on into 1962, and finally a 98 page agreement was reached. The Europeans, it was agreed, would receive seats in Algeria's assemblies in proportion to their number. Around 800,000 of those in Algeria of European descent moved to Europe. On July 3 of 1962, Algeria became officially independent. It was the Algerian people deep religious faith that has prevented their social disintegration and preserved their own tradition which was challenged by the French culture.

The Arab Spring in Algeria

Algeria in 2011 was like other Arab countries plagued by corruption, restricted freedoms and deteriorating socioeconomic conditions. But amid the turmoil that visited the region, Algeria was the only Arab country practically untouched by the "Arab Spring." Algerian society was profoundly affected by the years of colonial rule, by the War of Independence, and by the subsequent post-independence regime policies that has undermined democracy. Algeria had its own Arab spring in 1991-4, a bad experience that left the vast majority of Algerians with fear of another uprising that would fail and cause more bloodshed and instability. The closest mass movement came to ousting an Arab regime was in 1991 following a coup negating an

Islamist electoral victory in Algeria. The conflict began when the Islamic Salvation Front (FIS) had appeared poised to win the national parliamentary elections in what was, up until then, the region's most promising democratic experiment and one of its earliest. The elections were cancelled after the first round and the military took control of the government with the approval of the Western policymakers who fear the Islamists in power.

Young Algerians revolted against the tyrannical practices of the National Liberation Front that had ruled the country with iron fist since the war of independence. They protested the single-party system, absence of presidential term limits, the mismanaged socialist economy and the human rights violations by the police and secret service. The uprising was suppressed with bloodshed and torture.

The regime of President Abdel-Aziz Bouteflika regime, a de facto dictatorship that has been in power since 1999, exploited such fear along with the use of the country's oil wealth to control the people and hide Algeria from world's view including the Arab Spring. Algeria's Islamists as the only organized opposition to the ruling regime seemed too exhausted to try again. They were still reeling from the military general's success in crushing their rebellion. The decade long civil war that followed the military coup saw extreme violence and brutality against civilians. It has been referred to as "the dirty war" that left more than 200,000 people dead, thousands of prisoners disappeared and more than a million displaced.

When their neighbors in Tunisia rebelled and forced their dictator Bin Ali to flee the country, Algerians hoped for change too. It happened that the "Arab Spring" came at the time when the Algerians were celebrating the fiftieth anniversary of their independence that had been thwarted by an authoritarian regime. There was unrest, some riots, protests and localized strikes by opposition groups, but they had little public support. The conjunction of discontent did not seem sufficient to threaten the Algerian regime that had always repressed unrest with blood. The protest was contained swiftly by well trained and well equipped police force and the government promise of deepening "the democratic process." The Algerians were afraid to renew the struggle for a true liberation and real democratic change. Fear of civil war by majority of Algerians was exacerbated by what was happening in Libya, Syria and Yemen. The European intervention in Libya even revived the painful memory of their anti-colonialist struggle.

The government used the cash from the oil and gas reserves to buy loyalty of the state employees through payoffs in the form of higher salaries and housing vouchers. In 2011, the government of Bouteflika lifted the state of emergency that had been in place since 1992 and promised to amend the constitution by revising the laws governing political parties, the media and women's participation in public life. The oligarchic coalition that monopolizes power in Algeria has a large base which makes it too difficult to dislodge. And failure of Algeria's 1988 democratic experiment divided democrats, damaged civil society and left a political vacuum. In the 2014 national elections, the aging and sick Bouteflika was re-elected with 82 % of the vote as Algerian president for a fourth term without even campaigning in public. The opposition calls Bouteflika "the living-dead president." They alleged that the regime is so corrupt that in July of 2017, Bouteflika sacked Prime Minister Abdel-Hameed Tebboune for cracking down on corrupt businessmen with vested interest in leaders of the regime.

13. QATAR

Qatar is a small peninsula, jutting out of the much larger Arabian Peninsula into the Persian Gulf that covers approximately 4,000 square miles between al-Bahrain to the northwest, Iran across the Gulf to the northeast and the United Arab Emirates and Saudi Arabia to the south. Until 1760s, Qatar was an abandoned extension of Arabia desert with little resources to sustain life until members of Al-Khalifa and Al-Thani clans of the Utub tribe migrated to it from central Arabia. Al-Thani called Qatar their permanent home living primarily in settlements near the coast on fishing, pearling and seagoing trade with neighboring countries. Their cousins, Al-Khalifa moved to Bahrain which they have been ruling ever since, but they did not give up their interests in Qatar. They wanted to rule both, Qatar and Bahrain. After years of conflict between the two clans, the British intervened in support of Al-Thani.

In 1867, Britain recognized Qatar as a separate entity from Bahrain and Muhammad Al-Thani as the representative of its people. He was the first Al-Thani leader to settle in Doha and draw other tribes to the area which he controlled. His son Qassim Al-Thani (1878–1913) is considered the founder of the Emirate of Qatar. Fifty years later, Abdullah Al-Thani signed an agreement with the British that established Qatar as a British protectorate and Al-Thani as the ruling family. The agreement provided Britain control over Qatar foreign relations and gave special rights for the British subjects in the country. Oil reserves were discovered in Qatar in 1939, but its exploitation started after World War II. Oil and natural gas became the main source of revenue that has funded the expansion and modernization of Qatar infrastructure.

Qatar received independence from Britain and adopted a constitution in 1971. It established the country as an "Emirate" that the ruler will always be chosen from Al-Thani clan and will be assisted by a council of ministers and a consultative council. Most of the cabinet ministers and high ranking officials have been members of the ruling family. Some high level appointments have been made outside of the royal family, but the consultative council never been elected. Its members have been appointed by the ruler. Qatar held elections for the "municipal council" for the first time in 1998 a number of women ran for office but none were elected. Voters approved a new constitution in 2003. It provided for a 45-member parliament with 30 members to be elected and the rest appointed by the emir. Qatar's population has been estimated at 2.5 million in 2017, but its indigenous Qatari's make up less than eighteen percent of the total population. The rest are non-citizen expatriate workers from other Arab countries, India, Nepal, Philippine, Bangladesh and Sri Lanka. Because the vast majority of the expatriates are males, women account for less than twenty-five percent of the population.

Al-Thani clan owns the State of Qatar with all its resources, but members of its ruling clan had their own occasional infighting over the control of this property. Khalifa Al-Thani usurped power from his cousin Ahmad Al-Thani in a palace coup in 1972, then Ahmad was ousted by his own son Hamad Al-Thani in another bloodless coup in 1995.

The increase in state income from oil and natural gas concessions strengthened regional and international Al-Thani clan position. It enabled Qatar with its small apolitical population to jump from a disenfranchised tribal society to a globally connected metropolis. Qatar's unelected emir with no domestic constraints has long been seen as the Arabian Peninsula's maverick. He allegedly rushed to patronize the forces of regime change in Libya and Syria in the Arab Spring. But Qatar most known establishment is the first Arab satellite news TV channel network, Al-Jazeera. It was launched in 1996 as independent TV channel employing correspondents all over the world and broadcasting to the Arab world.

Al-Jazeera often gives democracy advocates and dissenters a platform to criticize other Arab undemocratic regimes. Al-Thani clan has established an emirate regime like the rest of the Gulf States in which the supreme power is in the hands of its emir and his family. Their constitutional monarchy does not tolerate any political opposition. Al-Jazeera, which sold itself as the region's front of cutting-edge critical journalism, replaced its director, Waddah Khanfar, who was an ardent supporter of civil rights, with a member of the Emir's al-Thani clan. Al-Jazeera is rightly quick to report criticism in other Arab states, but its editors do not review Qatar own human rights violations. They gagged any mention of the Emir's prison sentence for human rights advocates including a Qatari poet and others who criticized him.

Earlier in 2015, Qatar joined the Saudi–led coalition against the Houthi rebels in Yemen. But in 2017, the Gulf Arab states and Egypt decided to severe diplomatic ties with the State of Qatar. Bahrain, the United Arab Emirates, Saudi Arabia and Egypt closed their airspace and sea-lanes to Qatar shipping. They claim that Qatar has been providing financial and moral support to groups considered extremists or even terrorists. They do not like Qatar's willingness to host members of Egypt's MB, Palestinian Hamas and Afghanistan's Taliban organizations. They accuse Qatar of meddling in the internal affairs of others.

14. KUWAIT

Kuwait is a 6,880 square miles Arab country on the north-west of Persian Gulf with 120 miles of coast it shares its borders with Iraq and Saudi Arabia, and a maritime border with Iran. Its history is part of the Arabian Peninsula's nomadic tribal history, periods of settlements, times of peace, invasions and conflicts, the ocean-pearl industry and the trade with India. Its indigenous people have been mostly from eastern Arabia, Iraqi and Bahrain tribes as well as Persians. The name of Kuwait which may mean "small settlement" was given to the area by the Ottoman Iraqi rulers when it was a district within the Iraqi Basra Province. That was before oil was discovered and there was no development, no electricity and even no roads. Life in Kuwait was difficult especially in summer when temperature exceeded 120 F and the sand storms blowing. The temperature in winter goes as low as 34 F. Only the tribe people who had been born and raised in the Arabian Desert could have survived Kuwait's environment then.

Kuwait area as well as Yemen, Oman and Bahrain were part of the pre-Islamic Persian Sassanid Empire. The region's self-sufficient desert tribal lifestyle shifted to the coastal harbor for its trading potential. The small town of Kazma (Kadhima) in the bay of Kuwait was established as a stop place for caravans coming from Persia and Mesopotamia (Iraq) en route to the Arabian Peninsula. It was the site of the Battle of Chains in AD 636 where the Muslim armies defeated the Sassanid, who lost southern Mesopotamia to the Arabs, and integrated it into their newly established Islamic State. Under the early Islamic period, Kuwait was part of Iraq. The town of Kadhima was used as a trade port and a resting place for pilgrims.

In the early decades of the 16th century, Kuwait was a Portuguese colony, an important one in the logistics of its global commercial empire. The

Portuguese built a small defensive settlement on Kuwait's shore as part of their trade support network. In the late 17th century, Kuwait rapidly became a commercial center for the transit of goods to and from India. It gained more importance for trade during the Persian siege of Basra in 1775–1779. Iraqi merchants, then, took refuge in Kuwait, established major boat-building facilities, and many maritime trading activities with India were diverted to Kuwait. It continued to take trade away from Basra after the Persians withdrawal well into the 1850s.

Kuwait's last known settlers when it was just an extension of Arabia and before it had a name of its own were Bani Khalid clans from Anaiza tribe that was roaming the deserts of Najd. They settled in Kuwait for a while in peace tending their camels next to its few oases and in 1613, Bani Khalid built a small fishing village in the area's bay for local consumption. This village grew up to become the present-day Kuwait City. Bani Khalid never cared to exploit other commercial resources of the more than hundred miles of the sea. In 1682, another clan from the same Anaiza tribe called Bani Utub migrated to this land to escape famine due to the drought in Najd. Then in 1766, Bani Khalid relocated to Zabarah in Qatar leaving Kuwait for their cousins, Bani Utub.

It was prosperous time for Bani Utub who became the sole proprietors of Kuwait. Nature was both cruel and generous for them. They had to endure the sand storms and burning heat of summer, but they discovered the commercial value of a natural resource of their sea, the pearls, a commodity in demand by the wealthy Europeans and Asians. The nomadic desert people abandoned their grazing ways for pearling, trade and shipbuilding. Collecting pearls from the ocean floor and trading it for goods including food, cloth, wood, spices, and coffee in neighboring countries and across the Gulf became a major source of their livelihood. They learnt how to dive and collect pearl and they learnt how to sail and trade. The Kuwaiti entrepreneurs made the transition from camel caravan drivers to savvy sea trader capitalists. New social and political arrangements suitable for a settled economy were created by a succession of ruling tribal leaders. There was a typical Arab tribal class hierarchy within the Utub tribe, and Al-Sabah family was at the top due to its members' trading and management skills. Al-Sabah controlled the sailing boats fleet and the harbor, the hub of Kuwait's pearl trading industry they became the most influential clan.

Kuwait's strategic location and the instability of the neighboring countries helped foster economic prosperity during the late 18th century. Kuwait had what was considered a large sea commercial fleet for such a small country. The successful pearling industry attracted many Arab and

Persians from neighboring countries. It was estimated that by 1800, Kuwait's sea trade exceeded 15 million Bombay rupees per year. When the artificial cultivation of pearls was introduced by the Japanese, the Kuwaiti product could not compete with the cheap pearl that flooded the international markets their economy collapsed, but not for too long.

Events in Portugal including the destruction of Lisbon in the 1755 earthquake, Napoleon's occupation of the country and the loss of its biggest colony, Brazil, left Portugal crippled and diminished its power to maintain its colonies including Kuwait. The Ottomans expanded the Iraqi Basra Province by annexing the territory of Kuwait as a district of Basra in 1756, Kuwait's merchants elected Sabah bin-Jaber as the first Emir of the area and Kuwait enjoyed a degree of semi-autonomy under the Ottomans.

Once the Ottomans showed weakness and could not defend their large empire and Britain was looking for colonies to chip away from the Ottoman Empire, Kuwait, too small and too weak to defend itself, was an easy target. The British colonialists established close relations with Al-Sabah family, and in 1899 Kuwait became a British colony where Britain provided protection in return for Kuwait allowing the British to control its foreign affairs. The agreement paid off in 1922 when Britain intervened on behalf of Kuwait against Iraq and Saudi Arabia claims to some parts of Kuwaiti border land. After World War I, the Saudis of Najd and their Wahhabi Ikhwan Bedouin tribes tried to fill the power vacuum left by the fall of the Ottomans. Clashes with Kuwait's local defenders at its borders through 1919–1920 were culminated by the Battle of Jahra west of Kuwait where thousands of armed Wahhabi tribesmen attacked and over-ran Kuwait's Red Fort before the British intervened. The British imposed and enforced the 'Ugair Protocol' which defined the international borders between Kuwait, Iraq and Najd.

In 1927, the US-British Kuwait Oil Company discovered large oil reserves in Kuwait and the exportation began in 1951. The landscape of this country changed by foreign oil companies busy surveying the desert, drilling holes and pumping the black commodity, oil tankers loading in the harbor and thousands of foreign workers building infrastructures everywhere. Oil would fuel the country's development into the present modern state. By the mid-1950s, Kuwait became the largest oil exporter in the ME. Its economic and social life has changed dramatically since then. The population became more urbanized and the number of rural people has dropped significantly. With its small population and the ninety billion barrels of oil reserves, per capita income became one of the highest in the world.

In 1961, Kuwait was the first of the Persian Gulf countries to gain independence from Britain and its government attained full control of the oil industry in 1976. The legitimacy of Kuwait's political system under Al-Sabah clan is based on consensus and mutual agreement with other local clans and tribes. History of Kuwait is different from Saudi Arabia where the Saudi family seized power by force. Al-Sabah clan of the Utub tribe was successful business people and sea and caravan traders while the Saudis were warriors on a mission to conquer lands and enforce Wahhabi version of Islam on its people.

Kuwait today is a sovereign Arab country, a hereditary monarchy (Sheikhdom), a conservative state with a Sunni-Muslim majority and large Shi'a minority. It is a US ally, a member of the UN, the GCC, the Arab League, the Organization of Islamic Cooperation (OIC), the Organization of Petroleum Exporting Countries (OPEC), and the World Trade Organization. It has modern civil state institutions described by legal observers as semi-democratic in nature. It passed a constitution in 1962 that established a monarchy headed by the hereditary Emir, a member of Al Sabah clan in 2009, women were given the right to vote and run for office. Naturalized citizens do not have the right to vote until they have been citizens for 30 years or if they were appointed or elected to any parliamentary, cabinet or municipal post. Still, any criticism of the royal family is not allowed.

Kuwait has a population of some four million, of whom more than two-third are foreign expatriate workers, one of the highest migration rates in the world due to the discovery of oil and the rise of living standards. Kuwait is located next to three more populous and militarily powerful neighbors of Iraq, Iran and Saudi Arabia. That is why it has been seeking protection by having alliances with Western powers. Kuwait's foreign policy today is founded on a long-standing alliance with the US. Seven months after Saddam Hussein invaded and annexed Kuwait to Iraq in 1990, the US intervened by leading a military coalition force and liberated the country. The Sabah royal family that had to flee for their lives to Saudi Arabia returned to Kuwait torn by a seven-month ordeal under the Iraqi occupation. The Emir's pre-invasion opulence was battered by the Iraqi occupation and the opposition became more aggressive in pressing for greater democracy and voting rights for women.

The government of Kuwait incorporates a constitution and hereditary monarchy. Its democratic institutions include an advice-and-consent autocracy political system. Kuwait's constitution establishes three separate branches of government, executive, legislative and judicial. The head of the state, the Emir, is chosen from the ruling Sabah clan and confirmed by the National Assembly. The Emir appoints a member of the royal family as the prime minister who is in charge with forming a cabinet of ministers that must be approved by the National Assembly. Up to fifteen individuals may be appointed by the government to the legislative body, the National Assembly, that consists of fifty members and the rest are elected by the eligible citizens to serve a term of four years. Up to 15 legislators may serve as both lawmakers and ministers. Candidates do not campaign as members of political parties, but they can form parliament blocks. The National Assembly of Kuwait is considered as one of the most independent in the Arab world. Besides drafting and approving bills, it has the power to override the Emir veto of bills with two-third vote and it can remove ministers from the cabinet. Like most Arab countries, there are two judiciary court systems in Kuwait, the civil law courts and Sharia law courts that deal mostly with family cases. The civil courts system includes low, appeal, and the constitutional.

15. United Arab Emirates

The United Arab Emirates (UAE) is a 1971 federation of seven small emirates on a total of 33,000 square miles: Abu Dhabi (the largest), Dubai, Sharjah, Umm al-Quwain, Fujairah, Ajman, and Ra's al-Khaimah. This group is located at the south-east end of the Arabian Peninsula on the Persian Gulf along part of the Gulf of Oman, between Saudi Arabia and Oman. In addition to a federal president and prime minister, each emirate has a separate ruler who oversees the local government. The Emirates are controlled or rather owned by tribal families, and the federation is governed by a supreme Council made up of the seven emirs, who appoint the prime minister and the cabinet.

The history of this sandy land that has grown from a quiet backwater to one of the World's important economic centers covers the Iranian Sassanid rule, early days of Islam when its tribes embraced the faith, the era of the Ottoman Empire, Portuguese, Dutch and British colonialism, the pearl trade and the oil and gas discovery. Its location between Europe and the Far East attracted European colonialists, particularly Portuguese, Dutch and British, and merchants from the two continents. It was also an important trading post for camel routes between the coast and the Arabian interior. The area was tied to Islam from the early days of the faith and the spread of Islam in Far East by armies of traders.

Nomadic groups whose tribal names are still carried by modern Emirates people managed to live in this land's harsh desert environment for centuries by establishing seasonal and semi-seasonal settlements. They subsisted, then, on hunting, animal husbandry, and agriculture. And when the Portuguese sought control of the coasts in the 18th century and created support centers in the area for their trade with Asia, Bedouin tribes settled on the coast, joined the seafaring people and engaged in the pearl trade business. The town of Abu Dhabi became an important commercial center.

The tribes of the Gulf area embraced Islam during the Prophet Muhammad lifetime. Nine years after the Prophet migrated to al-Madina and established the first Islamic state, the Gulf area's tribe leaders travelled to al-Madina, declared their conversion to Islam. They revolted against their Sassanid rulers, and declared their allegiance to the Islamic state. Following the death of the Prophet, some south of the Gulf Arab tribes that had given loyalty to the Prophet began to withdraw from the Islamic confederation and refused to pay zakat. This action was viewed by the new leadership in al-Madina as insurrection against the Islamic state and a rejection of the Islam faith. Muslim army sent by Caliph Abu-Bakr fought a bloody battle against the rebellious tribes, brought back the area into the Muslim fold and assured the unification of the Arabian Peninsula under the newly emerging Islamic Caliphate.

Muslim rulers and European colonialists encouraged the global trade. For centuries, the land Silk Road to China was busy with activity and Muslim Arab and Persian merchants from Yemen, Oman and the coastal emirates navigated the Indian Ocean and dominated the sea-borne trade with India, China, Indonesia, Sri Lanka, Java and Sumatra. They created their own prosperous trading-business colonies along the rim of the Indian Ocean and carried with them the Islamic culture. Arab merchants are accredited for introducing Islam into these countries without forcing their culture on the local population.

Arab traders of the south and south-east of the Peninsula controlled the two strategic centers on the trade route between Europe, Africa and Asia for centuries. They dominated the city of Aden in Yemen at the entrance to the red Sea and the city of Hormuz located on a dry and barren island at the entrance to the Persian Gulf. Arab sailors from Ras al-Khaimah travelled to faraway lands, including India and China. The powerful locally-based al-Qawasim clan who ruled Ras al Khaimah and Sharijah operated a fleet of commercial and some military ships and controlled the area that is now the United Arab Emirates, the Strait of Hormuz, islands in the Persian Gulf and lands on the opposite shores of the Gulf. This allowed them to dominate all trade and levy tolls on the merchandise that passed through the Strait of Hormuz until the Portuguese explorers broke the Arabs' hold on Asian trade routes.

The Portuguese were the first to build ships with deep hulls that remained stable in the oceans and they made long voyages in the high seas. The opening of the sea route to India by the Portuguese explorer Vasco da Gama

(1460-1524) had one of the early far-reaching repercussions on the civilized world commerce. When da Gama made his voyage around the Cape of Good Hope in 1498 and landed at the Indian port of Calicut, he revolutionized the commerce with Asia. Da Gama got significant help from Arab sailors familiar with the ocean routs to India. He enlisted Arab navigators to take him from East Africa across to his destination in India. At the time, the Arabs and the Persians held a monopoly of trade with India and other Eastern nations.

The Portuguese then embarked on an ambitious program of militant and mercantile activities that paved the way for colonizing the Gulf area. They established Portuguese hegemony over the area and the sea-borne trade from East Asia via the Gulf and the Red Sea routes. They used their ships to transport goods around Africa and extended their control to the local trade through the Arabian Sea. The Portuguese colonized coastal cities in Oman, building forts and customs houses on the coasts. Through these fortified settlements and backed by their naval patrol, the Portuguese enforced their monopoly of the commerce and forced local traders to buy safe passes and pay custom duties in the offices of Esta Da India in Oman and Hormuz. For more than a century, the Gulf area was regarded as a key of Portuguese Empire in Asia. The Portuguese influence on the region's coast was visible in the form of triangular fortresses with bastions and round towers built in the 16th century. Portuguese power declined in the face of indigenous uprisings and external competition from Britain. The British colonialists were the last Europeans to establish formal relations with the Arab tribes of the Emirates in the 19th century.

Before the rise of the Portuguese power in the Gulf, Iran was the dominant military power in the area and the Arab rulers of Hormuz who had effective control of the Gulf ports had to pay annual tribute to the Safavid shah of Iran. Things changed with the Portuguese arrival the sheikh of Hormuz had to pay tribute to the new landlords, the Portuguese and the Iranians were too weak to confront the Portuguese. Shah Abbas I of Iran (1587-1629) invited the British to challenge the Portuguese in the Gulf and receive half the revenue from the ports.

Like the Portuguese, Britain's interest in the Gulf area that began in the 17th century was driven by trade and commerce. Its powerful East India Company was the front for colonizing India and establishing a foothold on the land and in the water-ways to India. As the company's businesses became increasingly important for the British economy by the 1770s, the position of the company developed from one of economic domination to direct colonial rule protected by the British navy and standing army. Britain prevented other European powers from gaining a foothold in the Gulf, and in 1820, they called al-Qawasim clan of Ras al-Khaimah "pirates" for levying tolls on the trade passing the Strait of Hormuz. The British navy destroyed their entire commercial and military fleet and enforced a partial truce in 1820 and a permanent truce in 1853. For over one hundred and fifty years, the Gulf region including the Strait of Hormuz was under the British control.

The British called the Emirates area "The Trucial States" after signing binding agreements with each Emirate that they would not cede any territory except to the United Kingdom and to refrain from engagement with any foreign government without prior consent from the British. In return, the British would protect the coast from any aggression by sea and provide assistance against any attack by land. The agreement that was signed in 1892 transformed the Emirates area into a long term British protectorate. Ocean pearling was the source of income for the people of the Gulf in the 19th and the early 20th century until the commercial cultured pearl was invented.

16. The Arab Spring in the Gulf States

The Gulf monarchies include the seven sheikdoms of the UAE, plus Kuwait, Qatar, and Bahrain. They are very similar in governing systems and social makeup. None of the ruling families, with the exception of al-Jaber family of Kuwait, has to face an elected parliament or to deal with a free press that might criticize them. They have a free hand in the decision-making process with no accountability. In the absence of institutionalized policy procedure and domestic constraints, the decisions are as good as the leaders who make them. The legislative, the executive and to some extent the judicial power are placed in the hands of the royal families. Vast majority of their populations are expatriates with no political rights and subject to deportation if they deemed in violation of their work-contract conditions. Public opinion is a minimum constraint and the US effectively ensured the external security of the states by having military bases in the region.

There were no demonstrations in the squares of the UAE and Qatar cities demanding the kind of political change occurring elsewhere during the Arab Spring, but there were individual activists calling for democratic reform. That did not prevent their governments from intensifying their crackdown on freedom of association, assembly and freedom of expression, according to "Front Line Defenders Organization." Human rights advocates and members of their families in the UAE were subjected to prolonged arbitrary detention, torture, judicial harassment, unfair trials, physical and digital surveillance and dismissal from work. Laws with vague legal provisions have been used against human rights advocates. By 2012, there were fifty political prisoners in UAE jails, mostly bloggers, writers, poets and lawyers according to Human Rights Watch.

In August 2014, the UAE issued a new Counter-Terrorism Law providing the government power to prosecute critics and dissidents and human rights activists as terrorists. Article 176 provides for up to five years imprisonment for "whoever publicly insults the state president, its flag or national emblem." These are examples of cases where peaceful critics received harsh sentences by anti-terrorism courts: Ahmad Mansoor was jailed with four others in 2011 for initiating a petition calling for democratic reforms. They were accused of publicly insulting the UAE leadership and sentenced to three years imprisonment. In 2014, human rights defender Osam Al-Najjar was sentenced to three years in prison for posting tweets considered harmful to the state's institutions by the government. Dr. Nasser bin-Ghaith was sentenced in 2017 to ten years in prison for tweeting about human rights violations and politicizing of the judiciary.

In Bahrain, Shi'a protesters have been regularly taking to the streets since the start of the Arab Spring. They have been demanding equality, freedom, and social and economic justice. They have long felt discriminated against in access to employment, housing and social services. The demonstrators have been met with a campaign of brutal repression by the ruling Sunni-regime. Saudi Arabia sent military forces to help the authorities quell the demonstrations in 2011. Its forces have been stationed in Bahrain and continue to police the streets of the capital, Manama.

The Gulf States owe their existence as sovereign countries to the British who kept them out of annexation by Saudi Arabia, Iraq and Iran. Britain made them protectorates and bequeathed them their borders and their independence to guard the approaches to India in the last century. The Gulf monarchies are important to the world economy they produce over twenty percent of the world's oil and possess thirty percent of its oil reserves. In the 1990 "Operation Desert Shield" military campaign against Iraq, the US demonstrated its commitment to protect the Gulf States from their more powerful neighbors' aggression and safeguard its regional oil interests. Marc Humbert of the Associated Press reported that New York governor Mario Cuomo told the Rochester Chamber of Commerce in 1990 while the US was preparing to evict Saddam military from Kuwait: "Now you're on the edge of war because of oil. Be honest—who cares about the Kuwaiti royalty...You're there for oil. You know it and I know it."

The common reliance on the US as the guarantor of security and maintaining strategic stability is a major factor that unites the Gulf State. These countries are strategic allies with the US. Qatar has al-Udeid Airbase, a permanent home for about 10,000 American military personnel and over 100 US-led anti-ISIS operational coalition aircrafts. The US Fifth Fleet which patrols the Persian Gulf, the Red Sea and parts of the Indian Ocean area is headquartered in Bahrain, and US established Camp Arifjan in Kuwait. They know that while the US spokes-persons talk about democracy in rhetoric especially during the Arab Spring, Washington prefers the stability of their authoritarian rule more than the risky outcomes of democratic experiments.

This frees each monarch to pursue whatever local and regional policy he chooses as long it is within the confine of the security relationship with the US. The Gulf States were not affected by the Arab Spring, not because they were monarchies, but because they enjoy having the material resources to buy off most of the internal decedents and acquire outside support. These small states and Saudi Arabia are united in their collective assault on their citizens' right to free speech, and they have been playing a big role in the region as the ME's de facto financial house. They throw their citizens in jail for criticizing other Gulf nations and they try to shape the future of Egypt, Iraq, Syria, Libya, Yemen and even Lebanon during and after the Arab Spring. They formed the Saudi–led coalition against the Houthi rebels in Yemen, and they are working with the US that has been engineering a regional solution to the Palestinian–Israeli issue, "the Deal of the Century."

Arab Spring in Kuwait

What took place in Kuwait during the "Arab Spring" has been distinct from the ME wider regional upheaval. Abundant oil revenue provided the Kuwaiti people with high standards of living. They are coddled by generous cradle-to-grave welfare system that provides free education, guaranteed job, subsidized housing, electricity and food. Life of the Kuwaiti nationals was too good to revolt like the ones that toppled the governments in Egypt and Tunisia. To achieve stability, the Emirate leadership took into consideration the needs of most Kuwait society that has divisions across tribal, as well as sectarian lines.

The Kuwaitis who protested were not against the ruling system and the Emir. "They just want to make corrections to the laws and the constitution that brings Kuwait forward," according to Musallam al-Barrak, a member of Kuwait's National Assembly. Some opposition activists made more demands, including elected prime minister, fully independent courts, and financial disclosures for government officials and members of parliament. Like all foreign workers in the Gulf States, the expatriates in Kuwait were happy as long as they had jobs and pay-checks.

During the 2011 "Arab Spring," there was political protest against the Prime Minister, Nasser Al-Sabah, a nephew of the Emir. The protesters declared that their anger was targeted at the ineffective Prime Minister and his corrupt administration, not the Emir, Sabah Al-Ahmad Al-Sabah. Protesters stormed the National Assembly demanding the resignation of the Prime Minister, accusing him of alleged payment of bribes to the pro-government members of parliament. The Prime Minister was replaced by the Emir, and the Parliament was dissolved pending early elections in February 2012 that resulted in the Islamists opposition making big gains. Four months later, the Constitutional Court ruled the election had been invalid on technicality and reinstated the previous parliament. Members of the opposition boycotted the sessions, forcing the Emir to dissolve the Parliament again in October 2012. The Emir changed the electoral laws by decree which the opposition claimed it favored the pro-government candidates, and he called for elections in December of the same year. The opposition boycotted the elections and lost their legal fight against the Emir decree. The government was accused of restricting freedom of expression when journalists and politicians were charged with offending the royal family. But Kuwait stands out from the other Gulf States and most Arab countries for having the most open political system and most critical and outspoken media than others in the ME according to a 2013 Freedom House report. Case in point: in the 2016 parliamentary elections, the opposition candidates secured close to 50 percent of the seats. But things are not perfect.

The "Bidoons" are a stateless minority group of people that has been neglected and even mistreated by excluding them from the social and economic rights enjoyed by Kuwaiti citizens. While Kuwaiti citizens enjoy a range of benefits by virtue of being citizens, Bidoon people live in slum-like neighborhoods on the outskirts of Kuwait City while their children recruits account for 40% of the Kuwaiti army. Their numbers exceed 100,000, a significant percentage of the country's small population. Most of the Bidoons are the descendants of nomads who failed to register as Kuwaitis when the country declared independence in 1961. During the Arab Spring and when human rights organizations raised the issue of this minority, a law was passed in 2013 to grant citizenship to only 4,000 of Bidoons after extensive screening.

In its foreign policy in the region, Kuwait leadership has become the grown-up in the childish but serious post-Arab-Spring Gulf States' dispute. The Emir of Kuwait Sheikh Sabah al-Ahmed al-Sabah has been mediating between the State of Qatar and the four Arab countries of Saudi Arabia, Bahrain, the United Arab Emirates and Egypt who severed their diplomatic and trade relation with the tiny State of Qatar. They accused Doha of supporting extremists and funding terrorism. Kuwait has not yet achieved a breakthrough to resolve the Gulf crisis despite the international support for the negotiation.

The Arab Spring in Saudi Arabia

During the Arab Spring, only the Shi'a minority in the eastern province of the country took to the streets in big numbers demanding reforms. The rest of Saudi Arabia did not experience the kind of popular protests that have occurred elsewhere. But human rights activists, women and students drew encouragement from the Shiites' struggle and increased their criticism of the royal family corruption and lack of freedom and civil rights. Some Sunni activists used social media to call for a "Day of Rage" to be held in March 2011. The Saudi government dispatched security personnel across the country and reaffirmed the ban on protests. Anyone who defied the ban faced immediate arrest, prosecution and imprisonment on charges of "inciting people against the authorities." Khalid al-Johani, a teacher, was one of those arrested in 2011. He was imprisoned for one year because he called for greater rights and democracy during an interview by BBC television station. Saudi author Turki al-Hamad was arrested and imprisoned in 2012 for criticizing the government on his social media site, Twitter.

Human rights organizations and independent groups are not permitted to operate legally in the country. The government enacted an anti-terrorism law in 2014 to target human rights advocates and government critics. They receive harsh sentences by the anti-terrorism court. Some are commonly sentenced to flogging of hundreds of lashes. Saudi authorities detained a women's rights defender and a blogger Lujain al-Hathloul at her home in Riyadh in 2014 amid an ongoing crackdown on human rights advocates. Issa al-Nukhaifi was sentenced to a six year prison term and a six year ban on social media by the Criminal Court of Saudi Arabia in 2016 for "inciting public opinion" in relation to twitter he posted criticizing the war on Yemen. Essam Koshak, a prominent human rights defender, was sentenced to a four year prison term and a four year travel ban in 2018 for criticizing the corruption and lack of freedom of expression in Saudi Arabia. Human Rights Watch said that Saudi authorities arrested more than dozen women's rights activists in July 2018 including Samar Badawi and Nassima al-Sadah. They had campaigned for the women right to drive and to end the Kingdom's male guardianship system, which requires women to obtain the consent of a male relative for major decisions.

The Arab Spring in Saudi Arabia took roots mostly in the eastern province of Qatif, home to millions of Shi'a Muslims who have long believed they were treated as second-class citizens. Shi'a-Saudis and some young Sunni-Saudis, fed up with the injustice of so many princes ripping off their country, demonstrated against the regime. The security forces alleged opened fire against the Eastern province Shi'a-Saudis demonstrators. They have long rebelled against discrimination and political exclusion. Scores have reportedly been shot dead the government claimed the troops fired only when confronted by armed people. Hundreds have been arrested, tried and convicted in criminal courts that were set up for terrorism cases and for "disobeying the ruler" crimes. The Saudi Interior Ministry announced it would crush the protest with an iron fist and accused Iran of fanning the flames. A popular Shiite cleric, Nemer al-Nemer was arrested and executed in 2016. He was a leader behind Arab Spring inspired Shiite protests in Saudi Arabia. Even after the crackdown, Shi'a activists, reform and women rights advocates, and relatives of security detainees continued to demonstrate sporadically.

Activists including teen-agers have allegedly received long prison terms for their peaceful participation in 2011 and 2012 protests. These are examples quoted by human rights organizations: Dawood al-Marhoon age 17, was arrested for participating in anti-government protest. At his trial, the prosecution requested death by crucifixion while refusing to have a defense lawyer. Another 17 year old boy, Raif Badawi was sentenced to 1000 lashes and 10 years in prison for using his blog to criticize Saudi Arabia's clerics. In October 2014, three lawyers, Abdulrahman al-Subaihi, Bander al-Nogaithan and Abdulrahman al-Rumaih, were sentenced to up to eight years in prison for using Twitter to criticize the ministry of justice.

Workers in Saudi Arabia have few legal rights, and they are not permitted to organize and do not have the right to strike. To deal with its middle class population discontent and potential problems to the regime, the Saudi government reached to its huge reserves. It sought to discourage more dissent by providing economic benefits worth around $127 billion to the citizens, including hiring 300,000 new state workers and raising salaries. To ease some of the tension that has been growing over women rights who are not allowed driving or travel unaccompanied, King Abdullah announced that Saudi women were to be given the right to vote and run in future municipal elections. The 2011 municipal elections were the second ever. They are the only public polls in Saudi Arabia to fill half the seats in local councils the other half are appointed by the government. King Abdullah died in January 2015 at the age of 91 and his half-brother, 79 year old Salman succeeded him.

The big news from Saudi Arabia under King Salman has been the 2015 change in its royal succession, the ruling system and its institutions. When the founder of modern Saudi Arabia King Abdul-Aziz died in 1953, his family decided to respect his will that succession would be from brother-to-brother not from-brother-to son. His son Saud succeeded him, followed by his brothers/half-brothers Faysal, Khalid, Fahd, Abdullah and Salman. Over the last sixty-five years, the House of Saud has faced and survived several challenges and crises including the forced abdication of King Saud in 1964, the assassination of King Faysal in 1975, and the illness of King Fahd in 2001-2005. The Saudi royal family survived many external challenges including the demise of monarchy in Egypt, Yemen, Iraq, and Libya, President Nasser Arab nationalism revolutionary threat, the fall of the Shah and Iran's Islamic revolution, the Soviet invasion of Afghanistan, the Iraqi occupation of Kuwait, the September 11, 2001 attack by Saudi citizens, the threat of Al-Qaeda, the US assault on Iraq, and the threat of ISIS.

The House of Saud sprawling clan that exceeds 30,000 members continues to rule as an absolute monarchy controlling the country's human and natural resources by remaining united, and the big decision making follows consensus among the senior royal clan members. The survival of the monarchy can be attributed mostly to the economy that had been fueled by enormous revenues from oil exports which turned the once underdeveloped country into a modern state with large middle class and vast development projects.

Saudi Arabia has an oil-based economy and strong government control over major economic activities. With about 17% of the world's proven petroleum reserves that is produced cheaply, it has been the largest exporter of the crude oil, and it has been playing a leading role in the Organization of Petroleum Exporting Countries (OPEC). The petroleum sector accounts for 90% of the country's exports and roughly 88% of the government budget revenue. Oil has allowed the Saudi people make the smooth transition from mostly poor nomads engaged in subsistent economy to mostly middle class with per capita income among the highest in the non-Western world. But wealth has been unevenly spread and the Kingdom is notoriously corrupt. With the rapidly increasing demand in emerging economies such as China and India, price of crude oil saw unprecedented rise after 2008 worldwide recession going from $25 per barrel to a record high of almost $125 by 2014. Saudi Arabia was one of the biggest beneficiaries of the oil boom. Unemployment became low, the agriculture sector received generous subsidies, and six million foreign workers came to do the menial and high technical jobs.

The government provides free education and health care as well as a variety of welfare programs, but much of the welfare spending comes from the Islamic system of the requirement that individuals and businesses must donate 2.5% of their wealth to charity. Despite this effort, there is poverty especially among families headed by women. Women who find themselves without a man's income struggle because the Kingdom's strict religious culture makes it hard for women to find jobs. But image-conscious Saudi government denied the existence of poverty and the subject was avoided by the state-run media until 2002 when then Crown Prince Abdullah visited a Riyadh slum and promised that "the government would meet its obligation toward its own people."

Spurred by the high oil prices, the US and Canada increased their effort to produce more oil including the use of "fracking" and extracting oil from shale and "oil sand." The oil supplies exceeded the demand world-wide, causing the drop in its price by more than 50%. In the wake of falling oil prices, the Saudi government could not continue to operate the country as a welfare state. The Kingdom incurred a budget deficit estimated at more than 13% of GDP, which was financed by drawing down on reserves and making big changes in the economic model. A value-added tax was introduced for the first time and subsidies on petroleum products and utilities are reduced. Crown Prince, Muhammad Bin Salman (MBS) announced the country intends to list shares of its state-owned petroleum company, and expand the role of the private sector in health care, education and tourism. He has been promoting the kingdom's economic plan to wean itself off independence on oil.

King Salman decided to change the brother-to-brother succession system, that had sustained stability and smooth transition from one regime to the next since 1953. He denied his half-brother Muqrin the position of crown prince and gave it to his nephew Muhammad bin Nayef. Then in a June 2017 surprise move, he removed his fifty-seven year old nephew from being the crown prince and elevated his thirty-one year old son from his third wife, Muhammad Bin Salman, as the next in the succession. The move has sparked speculation that the eighty-one year old King Salman may be considering abdication at some future date.

MBS had been the most powerful person in the Kingdom since he was appointed by his father as the defense minister in 2015. He determined to confront Iran in the war-ravaged Yemen. Alarmed by the rise of the Houthis, a group he believed to be backed militarily by Iran, Bin Salman led a coalition with seven Arab states declared war on the Houthis and began an air campaign against the Houthis aimed at restoring the internationally recognized Yemen government. When he became the Crown Prince, Bin Salman had already earned the reputation of being a hawk in matters of national security. The new royal heir represents a significant generational power shift in a country that had accustomed to the rule of old men. Policymaking authority has been concentrated in Bin Salman to a degree unprecedented in Saudi modern history, and he is not even the king yet.

The Crown Prince acknowledged that his country had been "not normal" for the past 30 years, blaming rigid Islamic doctrines that had governed society in reaction to the 1979 Khomeini Iranian revolution. He vowed in rhetoric to return the country to "moderate Islam" and asked for global support to transform the hard-line kingdom into an open society that empowers citizens. He said: "After the Iranian revolution, people wanted to copy this model in different countries, one of them is Saudi Arabia. We did not know how to deal with it. And the problem spread all over the world. Now is the time to get rid of it." He promised fast and revolutionary change in a country where, historically, nothing moves fast and even "revolutionary" has been a dirty word.

Bin Salman has the potential to transform Saudi Arabia into a less rigid society to appease the kingdom's restless youth, the children of the country's middle class, well before his father passes from the scene. The Crown Prince can ease some of the social restrictions on the codes of public behavior imposed by the religious establishment and he can champion economic reforms by diversifying the economy and reducing dependence on oil revenue. But despite his rhetoric, he will be judged only on liberal democracy reforms, eliminating corruption, and establishing equal rights and obligation under the law. He has taken away from the Wahhabi religious police the power of arresting people for breaking the clergy's standards of moral conduct on social behavior he has lifted the ban on women driving cars and the ban on movie theaters. The decision comes after decades of the ban, which was justified using Islam as a pretext. Following the lifting of the driving ban, women were allowed to participate in Saudi Arabia's National Day celebration for the first time and watch public sports events. Up until now, such sports and entertainment venues have been men-only areas. The new laws increased women's rights including the right to vote and to run for office in municipal elections that had been granted by King Abdullah in 2011.

Although such novelties are presented as major social revolutions by Saudi standards and are welcome by Saudi youth, they are hardly as groundbreaking or revolutionary. Even after these improvements, Saudi Arabia continues to be one of the most gender unequal countries in the Middle East. Saudi legal system is based on Sharia laws that do not provide equality for men and women. There are many basic civil rights women are still unable to have by law without permission from the men in their lives. These include applying for passport, travelling abroad, getting married, opening a bank account and starting certain businesses. MBS call for a "moderate" Islam is actually apolitical version under a revamped authoritarian monarchy for he says nothing about democratic institutions, free speech, representation and consent. The social liberalizing of Saudi society was a personal gift from an authoritarian ruler, not an opening for democratic institutions and laws that guarantee civil rights and free speech for all citizens.

At the same time of lifting the ban on female drivers, the Saudi authorities detained women who campaigned for the right to get behind the wheel. Activists Louiain al-Hathloul, Iman al-Nafjan, Aziza al-Yousef and Aisha al-Mane were arrested along with four male supporters without a warrant. They were accused of "destabilizing the kingdom, breach its social structure and mar the national consistency." Scores of Saudi human rights activists including the prominent human rights activist Fahad al-Fahad have been serving years in prison on charges related solely to their peaceful call for reform. Saudi Arabia is seeking the death penalty in counter-terror court for five Shi'a civil rights advocates including a woman, Israa al-Ghomgham, simply for participating in peaceful protest, according to Amnesty International's Middle East Director of Campaigns. Salman al-Awda, an advocate of human rights within Sharia laws, is facing the death penalty for alleged ties with the MB and public support for imprisoned dissidents and inflaming society against the rulers.

Forming political parties in Saudi Arabia is a crime and the country continues to oppose the idea of free elections and parliamentary democracy even after the Crown Prince social reforms. The survival of the Saudi dynasty at the head of an absolute monarchy is based on the alliance between the fanatic Wahhabi clerics and the Royal Family. The Crown Prince cannot cut the cord and make the transition to an open form of Islam within democratic system of government that may limit the power and privileges that he and members of the royal clan currently have. Wahhabi clerics, who have been subservient to the royal family and their independence has been eroded, issue religious addicts sanctioning every government political decision, military action in Yemen including the massacres of civilians, and measures against dissidents. The Crown Prince social reforms that are just nibbling on the edges are tarnished by his ruthless crackdown on freedom of expression.

While Bin Salman bills himself as a reformer promising to modernize Saudi Arabia in his "Vision2030" plan, the number of activist and dissident detainees that are locked away has apparently increased dramatically since his elevation. ME director at Human Rights Watch has said, "It seems that MBS's 'Vision2030' plan better describes the length of detention without charge than an inspirational time horizon for reforms." MBS told Jeffery Goldberg, "there is a different standard of freedom of speech in Saudi Arabia," suggesting that freedom is limited on topics of Wahhabi-Islam (not Shi'a or other Sunni-Islam), national security and the praise of the Royal Family.

Saudi Arabia under Bin Salman continues to be a tyrannical monarchy it does not have separation of powers, checks and balances and independent system of justice. The clergy still calls the Saudi-Shi'a minority "heretical snakes" and the school textbooks still advocate jihad (violence) against infidels (non-Muslims). MBS supported the campaign by Bahrain's monarchy to crush its peaceful Arab Spring uprising because the Saudis do not want a constitutional monarchy in a neighboring country. And Bin Salman provided billions of dollars to shore up President el-Sisi of Egypt his counter-Arab Spring-revolution.

After the political upheavals of the "Arab Spring" and the elevation of Muhammad Bin Salman to head the Defense Ministry, Saudi Arabia, the United Arab Emirates, Bahrain and Qatar declared war against the Yemeni Houthis, who were accused of being backed by Iran. Saudi Arabia that shares a long border with Yemen resents the expansion of Iran's influence at its southern border. The war in Yemen that was launched to restore Yemen legitimate government and put Iran in check has failed to do either. It has killed thousands of innocent non-combatant Yemeni people, starved millions and cost the Saudi economy billions of dollars, and there is no sign of progress. Iran had already military presence and political influence in Iraq and Syria.

Saudi Arabia leadership believes that the US under President Obama wanted a nuclear deal so badly, even if it fails to put a complete lid on its nuclear option, that it had tacitly approved Iran's activities in the Middle East, not only in Iraq, but also in Syria, Lebanon and Yemen. That is why Saudi Arabia views President Trump, who has a hostile stance toward Iran, as a crucial ally in his effort to cement a US-Sunni-Muslim alliance in the Persian Gulf against Tehran.

Saudi Arabia has escalated its anti-Iran rhetoric, thanks in part to Trump's message of seemingly unconditional support. President Trump 2017 trip to Saudi Arabia yielded a renewed commitment by Arab and Muslim leaders to combat "extremism" and accused Iran of supporting terrorism. This in effect was a Saudi declaration of alliance with Iran's traditional enemies in the region, the US and Israel. The Israeli media reported many Saudi officials' secret visits to Tel Aviv to discuss policies toward Iran as both countries view it as threat.

President Trump son-in-law and a senior advisor, Jared Kushner made many visits to Saudi Arabia and met with the Crown Prince with whom he had established a close personal relationship. The closeness between the two countries and the US administration's rhetoric regarding Iran suggests that the US would back up the Saudis if their confrontation with Iran gets serious. Saudi Arabia is already engaged in the proxy war with Iran in Yemen in one of the Saudi air attacks on the Houthis, the Iranian embassy in Sana'a was the target the Saudis forced the Lebanese Prime Minister, Saed al-Hariri, to resign in protest against Iran's interference in Lebanon the Saudis have been financing some Syrian rebels fighting against the pro-Iran Syrian regime and they had executed the dissenter Saudi-Shi'a cleric Sheikh Nimr al-Nimr.

In early 2017, the Saudi-led coalition of the Gulf States and Egypt abruptly expelled one of its members, Qatar, from the coalition, cut off diplomatic relations and imposed trade and travel ban with it. They ordered their citizens out of Qatar and gave Qatari visitors and residents two weeks to leave their countries. Qatar was accused of backing Islamist rebels in Syria and Libya, aligning itself with the Egyptian MB against Egypt's military regime and financing the Palestinian Islamist Hamas in Gaza. But the real reason for the diplomatic crisis is the journalist activities of Qatar government owned and funded Al-Jazeera news network. It often gives democracy advocates, including Saudi dissenters, a platform to criticize Saudi Arabia and other Arab regimes. Silencing Al-Jazeera is one of the conditions that the Gulf States put forth to normalize relations with Qatar. The Qataris have succeeded in resisting Saudi attempts to isolate them they strengthened their ties with Turkey, Iran, Russia and the US.

In November of 2017, three developments took place in Saudi Arabia under MBS that had serious implications in the region. First, Prime Minister of Lebanon, Saad Al-Hariri announced that he was resigning his post in protest against foreign intervention in Lebanon's domestic affairs. He announced his resignation on a Saudi-owned television channel from the Saudi capital, and the foreign intervention that he denounced was that of Iran. Al-Hariri actually was forced by the Saudi authorities to resign while in Saudi Arabia and prevented him from leaving the country. The strange resignation and the restriction about his movement was clearly a move produced and executed by the Saudis as an escalation of the confrontation with Iran. It should be noted here that Al-Hariri has dual citizenship, Lebanese and Saudi. His family owes its prominence to its large construction firm in Saudi Arabia. Al-Hariri had presided as a prime minister over a Lebanese government that included ministers from Hezbollah, allegedly a proxy organization for Iran and a declared terrorist group by the US and Saudi Arabia. Saudi officials made it clear they sought to confront Iran and its allies across the Arab world.

Lebanese President Michel Aoun, an ally of Hezbollah, declared that he would not accept Hariri's resignation until he returns to the country, suggesting that Al-Hariri's decision had been imposed by the Saudis. He asked "Why was Hariri not allowed to return to Lebanon to announce the resignation from here?" The answer is that Saudi Arabia wants its man in Lebanon to confront Hezbollah, but Al-Hariri or any Lebanese prime minister, for that matter, cannot alienate Hezbollah and have a functioning government. Muhammad Bin Salman and his advisors did not know that Lebanon is a parliamentary consensus democracy established on strictly confessional basis that accommodates its many religions and sects to preserve unity. Saudi money can influence who should lead the Lebanese-Sunnis, but it cannot disenfranchise the Lebanese-Shi'a faction from the government. Lebanon is not a monarchy or a dictatorship, and without Hezbollah's participation in the political institutions, there will be no government. Al-Hariri, who knew all that, had to choose between angering Saudi Arabia, to whom he beholds his family's prominence and his position as a prime minister, or resign. He chose the right thing but from the wrong venue.

Second, The Saudis claim that the Houthi rebels or their allies fired at least one ballistic missile from Yemen towards the Saudi capital, Riyadh. This action supports the suspicion that Iran is directly involved in the war in Yemen or through its proxies, and the war is expanding and far from over. The Lebanese Hezbollah, a non-government organization, is known to have Iranian ballistic missiles. It fired hundreds of them against Israel in 2006 war when Israel invaded Southern Lebanon. The Crown Prince and the Saudi ruling circle recognize that their country's worst nightmare will be materialized if the allies of Iran control Yemen to its south. And if that is not enough challenge, Iran already dominates Iraq in the north and its influence is entrenched in Syria and Lebanon.

Third and most serious was a coup within Saudi clan by the King and his Crown Prince to consolidate the young prince power over the Kingdom. Saudi Arabia issued a royal decree ordering the arrest of several Saudi princes, influential businessmen billionaires, journalists and notable figures, as well as the sacking of senior government officials. The most powerful figure to be arrested was Prince Mi'teb bin Abdullah, the son of the late King Abdullah, the head of the Saudi National Guard and a former candidate for the throne. Muhammad Bin Salman has made some very powerful enemies in the process, and with his father's support he has taken care to arrest anyone who might threaten his drive to preeminence. The arrested figures were reportedly being held in Riyadh's Ritz Carlton hotel. Most of those arrested have been freed after paying sizable restitutions. The wave of arrests cemented Bin Salman control over the kingdom's security institutions and threatened to bring down some of its powerful businessmen. He was quoted saying that because of the endemic corruption, his anti-corruption putsch was an example of the shock therapy the kingdom needed. He added that the kingdom could not meet budget target without halting this looting.

The massive arrests held in Riyadh's Ritz Carlton hotel were followed by the announcement of "anti-corruption" campaign that was intended to win public approval especially among the Saudi youth. The crown prince said the arrests are part of a fight against corruption while he and his life style exemplify the corruption in Saudi Arabia. He is one of those morally and politically corrupt rulers and for whom austerity and necessary sacrifices, and belt-tightening measures apply to others but never to him. Bin Salman net worth exceeds three billion dollars even when he never held a productive job. He allegedly bought a 54,000 square foot palace near Versailles in 2015 for $300 million. In less than two years, he bought for himself two luxury yachts for $620 million while forcing the Saudi people to tighten their belts.

The young Bin Salman purchased in 2015 one of the biggest and most expensive yachts in the world from a Russian billionaire after spotting it while on vacation in southern France for a staggering $500 million. He had bought another yacht for $120 million in 2014 when he was a minister and the special advisor to his father. US government intelligence sources confirmed that the Crown Prince was the buyer of a $450 million Leonardo da Vinci painting of Jesus Christ. While indulging with lavish luxury purchases, Bin Salman was pushing for implementing economic reforms that include drastic austerity measures, budget and employees salary cuts, following the drop in oil prices.

Despite the Crown Prince lofty rhetoric on reform, there are scores of activists and political dissidents languishing in his prisons on spurious charges, victims of a ruthless tyrant ruler not a reformer. There is wide-ranging crackdown on activists, journalists and writers who have been jailed with hardly any public explanation. Bin Salman has been overseeing the old intolerant Saudi approach to free expression and the treatment of human rights advocates. On his watch, two human rights activists, Muhammad al-Otaibi and Abdullah al-Attawi were sentenced in March 2017 to fourteen and seven years in prison, respectively, for briefly founding a human rights organization, publishing and disseminating information to the news media five years ago. They were punished even after they heeded the government's demands to close the organization. The sentence was imposed by the Specialized Criminal Court which is used to try dissidents and critics of the government. How to explain the punishment of a severe lashing to a blogger Rai Badawi, who has been jailed since 2012 following his online appeal for a more liberal and secular society? His sentence was 10 years in prison and 1,000 lashes simply for speaking out.

Saudi Arabia under Bin Salman remains a dungeon for those who want to practice free speech. The UN has concluded in a 2018 report that under Bin Salman, Saudi Arabia is systematically using anti-terror laws to justify torture, suppress all dissent and imprison human rights defenders. The report states that "A culture of impunity prevails for public officials who are guilty of acts of torture and other ill-treatment. Peaceful avenues for redress of grievances are foreclosed by the use of repressive measures to silence civil society." Sydney-based Saudi activist Manal al-Sharif described Saudi Arabia after the rise of Bin Salman: "We in Saudi Arabia are back to square one. We continue to live in a police state if you speak up you go to jail. And then there would be a defamation campaign against you, character assassination. We are seeing the same pattern again now." In August of 2018, Saudi Arabia expelled Canada's ambassador, called its own envoy in Ottawa, and froze new trade deals with Canada because the Canadian Foreign Affairs Minister called on the Saudis to release arrested civil-rights activists.

Jamal Khashoggi went missing on Oct 2nd, 2018 after entering the Saudi consulate in Istanbul to obtain paperwork to get married. He was a Saudi journalist and a critic of Saudi Arabia's regime, living in self-imposed exile in the US, and he wrote columns on the Middle East for the Washington Post. He was calling for political reforms in his country, but not for the government overthrow. Turkish officials have said, they had proof that Khashoggi was murdered and his body was dismembered inside the consulate. This act of shocking barbarism has strengthened the sense that Bin Salman, the de facto ruler of Saudi Arabia, is a rogue and ruthless dictator rather than a reformer.

Eighteen days after Khashoggi's disappearance and weeks of denial and a range of contradicting explanations for his disappearance, the Saudis came up with a story that nobody believed to absolve the crown prince from the heinous crime. The Saudis admitted that Khashoggi was a victim of premeditated murder, but they blamed only military officers and other security officials who have no family connections to the royal family, for his death. Some of those implicated in the killing are close to the Crown Prince. This narrative is one of many Saudi accounts that have changed several times they initially dismissed reports that Khashoggi had gone missing inside the consulate as "false" and when Turkish authorities reported that he had been killed there, the Saudis called the accusation "baseless."

The Saudis will never seriously investigate a plot that might implicate the kingdom's top leadership. No one believes the incredible Saudi accounts of the murder, including leading members of US Congress who call for full disclosure of accountability. The CIA believes bin Salman ordered the killing, according to Washington Post. Most America's allies don't trust the Saudi-friendly Trump administration to get to the truth if it implicates the Crown Prince. The US under President Trump cares for making deals with the Saudis, and that does not include human rights. Saudi Arabia is a deep-pocketed customer for US arms manufacturers and the US administration finds it too difficult to abandon the man they promoted to his current position, and implicate him in killing the Saudi journalist. The US had invested much of its ME foreign policy in the Crown Prince. It is a major partner in his war on Yemen, and Saudi Arabia has become central to the US's aggression projection toward Iran. Bin Salman has been also central to the promotion of President Trump's son-in-law Jared Kushner's "solution" to the Palestinian–Israeli conflict. The US will not be able to rescue the man they created and viewed by the rest of the world behind the horrific crime. Big powers do not have friends, they only have interests, and Saudi Arabia is not short on royalties ready to cooperate with the US.

The Crown Prince is a reckless architect of disasters and a threat to the stability and peace in the region. The war on Yemen that he launched in 2015 when he was minister of defense has been the worst thing that could have happened to the people of Yemen. Human rights organizations reported war-crimes committed by the Saudi-led coalition war that has decimated the Arab world's poorest nation. The catastrophic war is mostly overlooked by the Americans whose military has been providing the Saudis with intelligence, bombs and airplanes refueling, leading to accusation of complicity in possible war crimes. More than three years into the "Operation Decisive Storm" bombing campaign against the alleged Iranian-aligned Houthi rebels in Yemen has left more than 10,000 civilians dead. The coalition continues to commit serious violations of international law in Yemen.

The Saudis barred foreign journalists from northern Yemen, scene of the biggest airstrikes atrocities. Saudi pilots drop their bombs with disregard for the targets, leading to excessive civilian casualties. In August of 2018, the Saudi coalition air-force dropped a guided 500-pound bomb on a Yemeni school bus killing fifty-four mostly school children. The international Red

Cross medical team reported that it received the bodies of 29 children, all under 15 year old, and was treating 48 injured people, including 30 children. Save the Children Organization complained in a statement, "We have seen a worrying rise in these incidents and no action has been taken to hold the perpetrators to account."

In November of 2016, Bin Salman imposed a draconian blockade on Yemen ports. The Yemeni people ran out of food and medicine and started dying en masse from hunger and disease provided they were not killed by the indiscriminate air strikes. According to the UN humanitarian relief agency, three quarters of Yemen's 22 million populations were in need for food and medicine to survive. They include 1.8 million children under the age of 5 who were "acutely malnourished." The Yemeni civilian population is paying heavy price for Bin Salman effort to become more assertive on challenging Iran and its proxies.

Just allowing women to drive cars and watch sports, while at the same time dissidents, journalists, bloggers, businessmen, women's rights and human rights advocates remain in his jails, does not make the authoritarian prince a reformer or an Arab Springer. Saudi Arabia officials have failed to rebut the accusations that Bin Salman was complicit in the grisly killing of Khashoggi. Many strongly believe the Prince is a murderous despot who makes dissidents disappear in acid baths. The firestorm over this atrocity will not pass as it did after other Saudi actions like the kidnapping of Lebanon's prime minister and the killing of the children in Yemen.

Even President Trump, whose regional strategy appears to be constructed around Israel and the Saudi prince started removing his support for the latter. He referred the matter to the Congress to decide the US response to the crime. The murder of the Saudi journalist, the restrictions on freedom of expression, the ill-treatment of detainees, and the atrocities committed by his military in Yemen suggests that the Crown Prince regime is driven by paranoia and ruthlessness. It must have deep contempt for human rights and no respect for the sanctity of human life and the rule of law. The Arab Spring was a grassroots chain of rebellions against precisely the type of despotic regimes Bin Salman represents.

Even so, US-Saudi relations will remain as solid as ever because Saudi Arabia is too valuable an ally to lose. The aftermath of September 11, 2001, attacks on the World Trade Center that killed 2996 and injured more than 6,000 Americans, supports this view. All the news reported that 15 hijackers were Saudi citizens, and some US sources found a link between Saudi officials and the hijackers. US congress over-rode President Obama's veto and passed a legislation allowing relatives of the 9/11 victims to sue Saudi Arabia. Yet, the warm and long-standing relationship between the two countries was not affected. Oil matters more, and the US has dominated the region by maintaining numerous military bases on the territory of such "friends."

17. THE PALESTINIANS

The Palestinians' case covers stages that were triggered by several major events over more than a century and in each stage the Palestinians were the losers. These include the launching of the World Zionist Movement in 1897, the 1917 Balfour Declaration, the failure of the Palestinians 1936 rebellion and the abeyance of their national movement, the military victory of Israel over Arab states in the 1948 war, often referred to by the Palestinians as "Nakba" (catastrophe), the 1967 war "Naksa" (setback) that led to the occupation of the West Bank, Gaza Strip and East Jerusalem, and the 1993 Oslo Accords plunder. The Palestinians were victims of all the players in the ME, the British colonialists, the Zionist movement, the Arab states and mostly their own leadership.

The international Zionist movement, the secular Jewish nationalist movement that called for establishing a Jewish homeland in Palestine was launched by an Austrian-Jewish journalist, Theodor Herzl in 1897 First Zionist Congress. Twenty years later, the British colonialists decided to solve Europe's anti-Semitism problem by adopting Zionism and enforcing it on the expense of the indigenous Arab-Palestinians. "Balfour Declaration" was a political decision to serve the British colonialists own interests. To help gain Jewish support in the US and especially in Russia where the anti-Jewish government had just been overthrown, Britain's Foreign Secretary Arthur Balfour wrote a letter dated November 2, 1917 to Lord Lionel Rothschild, a prominent Zionist and a friend of the Jewish chemist and the future president of Israel, Chaim Weizmann. The one sentence letter stated that: "His Majesty's Government view with favor the establishment in Palestine of a national home for the Jewish people, and will use their best endeavors to facilitate the establishment of this object, it being clearly understood that nothing shall be done which may prejudice the civil and religious rights of existing non-Jewish communities in Palestine, or the rights and political status enjoyed by Jews in any other country."

In his book, 'Christian Zionist Heroes', Jerry Klinger wrote: "Theodor Herzel is revered as the founding father of the Jewish State. Yet, Herzl would have remained an obscure Austrian columnist with only an idea if a British minister, [Arthur Balfour], had not opened the doors of opportunity and guided him through it. ...The foundation and training of a Jewish self-defense army would never have happened if British officers were not willing to rescue their careers and their lives doing what they believed were the right thing to do."

The declaration by the colonial power did not refer to the non-Jewish communities as Arabs nor promised to guarantee their political rights. Chaim Weizmann argued in front of the Palestinian Royal Commission on November 25, 1936 that the Balfour declaration was regarded as the Magna Carta of the Jewish People and it "was in a sense comparable with another declaration made thousands of years before, when Cyrus allowed a remnant of the Jews to return from Babylon and rebuild the Temple." For Weizmann, the acceptance of Balfour Declaration had been the basis of any agreement he signed and any speech he delivered. The Palestinians were too weak to stand-up to the British and they were betrayed by Prince Faysal, the only recognized Arab leader involved in the politics of the ME.

Chaim Weizmann as the representative of the Zionist movement and Prince Faysal as the representative of his father, Sharif Hussein Ibn-Ali and a key figure in the revolt against the Ottomans, signed an agreement that formalized promises of mutual cooperation over Jewish immigration to Palestine. Article III of the Weizmann-Faysal agreement states: "In the establishment of the Constitution and administration of Palestine all such measures shall be adopted as will afford the fullest guarantees for carrying into effect the British Government's Declaration of the 2nd of November, 1917 [the Balfour Declaration]. Moreover, all necessary measures shall be taken to encourage and stimulate immigration of Jews into Palestine on a large scale, and as quickly as possible to settle Jewish immigrants upon the land." Bellow the signed agreement, Faysal added a hand written statement that he would be bound to comply with the agreement only if an Arab state were established. Faysal was crowned by the British as a king in Iraq and his brother Abdullah was installed Emir of Tans-Jordan.

Although the Palestinians considered themselves part of the Arab world, they had to espouse a nationalism of their own since their problem with the British was not addressed by the other Arabs. East of the Mediterranean,

Trans-Jordan and Iraq were under the leadership of the Hashemite who were close allies of the British Syria and Lebanon were under the French mandate. A dramatic change in the demographic balance took place in Palestine due to massive Jewish immigration under the British Mandate. There was a surge of Russian, Polish, Hungarian and Austrian, German and French Jewish settlers. As this vast European immigration and colonial enterprise was taking hold, the Jewish community was unified, purposeful and effective. The Palestinian nationalism intensified, and there was six-month local strike followed by the 1936 armed rebellion against the British.

The uprising started by peasants and workers from poor city neighborhoods, but once Haj Amin al-Husseini stepped in and brought it under his control, the revolt became identified with him personally. That led the traditional competing Nashashibi clan and its supporters to oppose the uprising. The Palestinians were divided between two groups controlled by the two Jerusalem influential families, the Husseini and Nashashibi. With no democratic institutions, Palestinians' will was in the hands of clan leaders and foreign Arab royalties allied with the British. The Husseinis established pan-Islamic "Palestine Arab Party," and their tribal enemy, the Nashashibi clan established the "National Defense Party," allied themselves with Trans-Jordan Emir Abdullah, opposed the uprising, and took moderate stand toward the British. The Palestinian clans had achieved prominence during the Ottoman era in the 19th and early 20th centuries and maintained their leadership under the British Mandate.

The bloody 3-year revolt exposed the failure of the Palestinians traditional leadership to overcome their personal and tribal feuds and face the real challenge. When the revolt was crushed, there had been significant human and economic losses among the Palestinians and no concessions from the British. The last two rebel leaders, Izzat Darwazi and Yusuf Abu Durr, crossed the borders into Syria and Trans-Jordan. The French administration in Syria arrested Darwazi and the Trans-Jordanians arrested Abu Durra and handed him back to the British authorities in Palestine, where he was tried and executed in 1940. The Palestinian's economy was devastated and more than 5000 Palestinians killed or executed by the British, 14,000 wounded, 5,679 detained, many leaders were exiled, and the Arab Higher Committee was proscribed. It was estimated that 10% of the adult Palestinian population were killed, wounded or exiled and the hope of independence was dashed.

When the Palestinians were uprising to bring about total clamp down on Jews being allowed into Palestine, the Jewish settlers were working towards building infrastructure, their economy thrived, their military capability improved, and Jewish immigrants continued to arrive in large numbers.

The Yishuv built modern port in Tel Aviv where only Jewish workers were engaged in loading and unloading ships.

By the end of the British Mandate, and when the UN passed the resolution to partition the country into two states, the Palestinian society was fragmented and political leaders were fighting each other in exile. They had no institutions that would run and defend their newly created state, whereas the Jewish community had been laying the foundations of their own state. While the Palestinian leaders were feuding with each other, the Yishuv were building their state institutions. They had their own elected political assembly, community councils, military and civilian organizations.

On November 29, 1947, the UN General Assembly passed Resolution 181 voting 33 to 13 with 10 abstentions to partition Palestine into two states, one for the Jews, and the other for the Palestinian Arabs. Jerusalem, as a holy city, was to become an international enclave under UN trusteeship. David Ben-Gurion accepted the partition plan on behalf of the Zionist settlers, even though they had always dreamed of controlling all of Palestine including Jerusalem. The Palestinian Arabs and the surrounding Arab states rejected the partition proposal. They felt this arrangement was favorable to the Jews who were implant foisted upon them and unfair to the Arab indigent population.

The Arab-Israeli War of 1948 broke out when civil war erupted between disorganized Palestinian Arab bands and poorly-armed volunteers of the Arab Liberation Army against the well-trained under joint-command Jewish Yishuv's armed groups. Military contingents from Egypt, Syria, Lebanon, Trans-Jordan and Iraq invaded the former Palestinian mandate immediately following the announcement of the State of Israel independence. The goal of the Arabs was to block the Partition Resolution and prevent the establishment of the Jewish State.

The Jewish fighters of the fledging State of Israel numbered more than the Arab military invaders combined. In the course of the 1948 war, Jewish fighters defeated the Arab states military by holding on all the areas assigned to them by the UN and seizing parts of the land designated to the Palestinians' state as well. The Jewish forces fought with the strategic goal of permanently ridding any area they conquered from the Arabs to insure the viability of the Jewish character in the areas under their control. During the ensuing war, 750,000 Palestinian Arabs became refugees and only about 65,000 city-dwellers and about an equal number of Bedouins remained within Israel.

Israel and the bordering Arab states signed separate armistice agreements. The left-over areas designated for the Palestinians were taken over by Jordan and Egypt. Jordan annexed the West Bank and East Jerusalem while Egypt assumed control over Gaza Strip. These armistice lines held until 1967. For the Arabs, the 1948 defeat at the hands of the newly established Israeli State was a seismic political shock that led to years of upheaval. For the Palestinians, it has been commemorated as "al-Nakba" or "the Catastrophe" and as expected, it has been celebrated by the Israelis as their War of Independence. Al-Nakba describes the pain due to the injustice inflicted upon the indigenous Palestinians when so many of them were uprooted from their homes during the 1947–48 war and were never allowed back.

In the 1947–48 war, Arab armies were not uniformly coordinated in strategy nor unified in their respective political ends, and their civilian leaders were engaged in inter-Arab political rivalries. The main objective of King Abdullah of Trans-Jordan, the commander in chief of the Arab forces in the war, was to annex those sectors allocated to the Arabs in the UN partition resolution. He was reportedly involved in secret negotiations with Israel and the blessing of Great Britain to divide Palestine between his kingdom and the Jewish state.

Trans-Jordan had no natural resources and its population was no more than 8% that of Egypt, but it was the only Arab country to claim some success in the 1948 war by keeping "East Jerusalem" that included the walled city with the holy sites under its control while Israel kept "West Jerusalem." Jerusalem, which was designated as an International enclave by the UN resolution was the only area the Jordanian military contested. Trans-Jordan, under King Abdullah leadership managed to save the eastern mountainous part of Palestine by declaring privately to the Jewish leadership emissaries on May 2, 1947 that its forces would not attack the UN designated Jewish state.

The Arabs' military were defeated this cast doubts on the legitimacy of their civilian governments and set the stage for military take-over in Egypt, Iraq, Syria, Libya and Yemen. In the aftermath of the 1948 war and after the signing of permanent armistice between Israel and the belligerent Arab states, Arab regimes were divided among themselves on the Palestinian issue and the Palestinians lost control of their destiny.

The Arab-Israeli war, the so called "Six-Day War," took place on June 5-10, 1967. Israel was preparing for this war once the 1964 Arab League summit made two decisions that Israel considered them as existential threat: diverting the Jordan River water in Syria and Lebanon and creating the militant PLO organization. Israel was also alarmed when Egypt purchased large amount of Russian attack armaments including tanks, fighter and bomber air-crafts. Israel was looking for an excuse to start the war and Nasser gave it to them.

When Egypt expelled the UN Emergency Force (UNEF) from supposedly demilitarized Sinai since 1956 war, mobilized its military in Sinai, and closed the Straits of Tiran in the Gulf of Aqaba to the Israeli shipping, Israel considered Egypt's action as a declaration of war and staged a sudden preemptive air assault. In few hours, Israel destroyed more than 90% of Egypt's, Syrian and Jordanian air forces on the tarmac. The three Arab countries armies were left vulnerable to the Israeli air and ground attack. Within three days, the Israeli military achieved an overwhelming victory on the ground, capturing the Gaza Strip, Egypt's Sinai Peninsula up to the east bank of the Suez Canal, the West Bank, East Jerusalem and the Syrian Golan Heights.

Arab's defeat was a self-fulfilled prophecy of "Israel threat" that had been the basis for justifying the establishment of the Arab authoritarian regimes. The Arab states lost on the battle field and in the world public opinion, but the big losers were the Palestinians. All historic Palestine became completely under Israel's control and the status of the newly conquered territories has become a major point of contention in the Arab-Israeli conflict. Many major events took place since then, including the 1973 war, Egypt-Israel peace treaty, the Oslo agreements, the Jordanian-Israeli peace treaty, the Palestinian Intifadas, the rise of Hamas, the two dueling governments in the West Bank and Gaza territories, and the "Arab Spring."

Currently, the Palestinians live as sizable groups under four distinct types of political arrangement. They are the Arab citizens of Israel, residents of the area under the control of the PA, citizens of Jordan, and refugees residing in Jordan and other Arab countries. Each group faces different circumstances and different problems, but they all have a national cause rooted in their aspirations for self-determination and liberation. Those living in the West Bank and Jerusalem are oppressed by the occupation forces, land confiscation, settlements building, restrictions on movement and worship. Israel annexed East Jerusalem and large area of the West Bank there are more than 130 Jewish-only settlements, Jewish-only roads, and more than 500,000 settlers in the West Bank. People in Gaza are trying to survive while living in poverty under siege.

The Palestinians in the Diaspora struggle to keep alive their right of return and to have their civil rights acknowledged in the countries where they live. The Arab-Palestinian citizens of Israel are fighting against racial discrimination as a minority and some of them are refugees denied the right of return to their own homes and properties located in the neighborhood where they are living in Israel. Because they are dispersed and weak, the Palestinians are highly influenced by the Arab world political climate.

The Palestinians in the occupied lands today are divided into two political parties, the Islamist Hamas and the secular Fatah. Relations between the two rivals are tense and at times erupted into deadly conflict. The two competing groups act like two hostile tribes reconciliation between them is not happening because of their strategic disagreements while their people are either in refugee camps in neighboring countries or under occupation. Hamas group was formed in 1987 as a militant "resistance" organization against Israel it won the 2006 general elections but was not allowed by Israel and Fatah organization to govern. Hamas took over Gaza Strip from Fatah in a bloody fight and established a separate government, and prompted the land and sea blockade of the Strip by Israel and Egypt. The secular Fatah leadership clings with all its meager power that it extracts from running the Palestinian Authority (PA), a self-governing body that was established in 1994 under the Oslo agreements.

The PA manages the daily life of the Palestinian population in the West Bank under the Israeli occupation. The PA security and intelligence personnel coordinate with the military occupation regime in tracking Islamic militants and other Palestinian activists deemed by Israel as threat to the occupation. According to the Oslo agreements that established the Palestinian Authority, the PA forces were required to facilitate Israeli raids into Palestinian towns and villages, those whom the PA purports to protect. This cooperation puts the PA, the putative vehicle toward independence in a position of servitude for the Israeli occupation and it contradicts the PA leadership's rhetoric. It leads to question the legitimacy of the Palestinians' leadership.

Decades before the "Arab Spring" uprisings, the Palestinians in the West Bank and Gaza had their own uprisings against the Israeli occupation, the first Intifada of 1987 that lasted until 1993, when the Oslo Accords, the secretly negotiated agreement between the PLO leadership and Israel aborted it and created the Palestinian Authority (PA). The PLO was rescued from exile in Tunisia by the Israelis and induced to enter into a demeaning dialogue with Israel in Oslo. It turned out that Edward Said was right when he called the agreement, "an instrument of Palestinian surrender, a Palestinian Versailles." The Oslo Accords led to many disasters for the Palestinians, which we are still witnessing today. It set aside international legality and compromised the freedom, sovereignty, and equality, the fundamental national rights of the Palestinian people. It created the Palestinian Authority (PA) in 1994, a self-governing body with limited powers over the daily life of Palestinian people in small, disconnected, "autonomous" areas that totals 18% of the West Bank designated by Oslo agreements as "A" areas, without sovereignty over the land, the borders, the skies or the natural resources. Israel annexed

Jerusalem and built Jews-only settlements and roads everywhere including the already over-crowded Gaza.

There was a second uprising (intifada) in 2000 when Israel's Prime Minister Ariel Sharon made a highly provocative visit to the holy Muslim site in Jerusalem, Al-Aqsa Mosque, referred to by the Jews as "Temple Mount." Unlike the first Intifada, the Palestinians used guns and suicide bombs and Israel launched a series of sweeping military offensives and administrative orders to punish the Palestinians. Israel carried out a large scale military operation with incursion into the city of Ramallah placing the PA President, Yasser Arafat, under siege in his compound in 2002 until he was transferred to a French hospital shortly before his death in 2004. Thousands died and wounded on both sides during the five years of violence. By the end of the second Intifada, Israel was forced to withdraw from Gaza Strip its eight thousand settlers were removed out of the Strip and resettled in the West Bank. The occupation of Gaza was replaced with a very tight siege transforming the Strip into a big jail for 1.7 million people, mostly refugees.

With the US encouragement, Israel allowed the Palestinians in the occupied lands to hold elections for a legislative council in 2006. The Islamic Hamas won an overwhelming victory defeating the secular Fatah faction and ending forty years of political domination of Arafat party. Even in Ramallah, the Fatah stronghold, Hamas won every parliamentary seat except the one reserved for a Christian. Hamas' showing was far stronger than any one predicted because Fatah and the PA leadership were widely viewed by the Palestinians as incredibly corrupt and ineffective at performing the basic duties of a government. Hamas was the face of change for a people frustrated with the ineffectual ruling party, Fattah. The results stunned Israeli, the US and the European officials who stated that they would not work with a PA that included Hamas, which they considered a terrorist organization. The European Union spokesman acknowledged that the Palestinians voted "democratically and peacefully, but the results may confront us with a new situation." Hamas was not allowed to govern, and it seized Gaza a year later after a bloody confrontation with PA forces loyal to Fatah thus leaving only the West Bank under Abbas, and the Palestinians had to live in two dueling governments in two territories.

The Oslo Accords failed to proscribe or limit settlement expansion even while peace talks were in progress. It provided Israel with the cover to pursue with impunity its illegal and aggressive colonial project on the West Bank while claiming they were engaged in rounds of negotiations called "the peace process." At the end of 1993 there were 115,000 Israeli settlers in the occupied territories. Today the number exceeds 400,000 and there are an additional 300,000 Jews living in settlements in East Jerusalem. Thousands more settlement homes are planned or under construction.

After decades of signing the Oslo agreements and the creation of the PA, the West Bank and Jerusalem are under occupation, Gaza is under siege, hundreds of Jewish-only settlements have been built, checkpoints and walls have been constructed by the Israelis, and many kinds of permits that a Palestinian needs to enter Israel or to pray in Jerusalem. The Palestinian activists continue to stage daily and weekly protests and confrontations with the occupation military and settlers in the West Bank and Jerusalem. And more recently there was a wave of knife and vehicular assaults against Israelis allegedly committed by Palestinians.

The creation of the PA has institutionalized the fragmentation of the occupied lands into A,B,C areas, and established different jurisdiction status for each of Jerusalem and Gaza Strip. The PA leadership ignored to address the rights of the Palestinian refugees who had been victims of the historic injustice inflicted on them prior to 1967.

The Arab Spring in the Palestinian Authority

On the eve of the "Arab Spring," while Arab people across the ME were uprising demanding democratic reforms, the occupied West Bank under the PA had yet to see a movement for such reform on the level of the rest of the Arab World. The political system they live under is deeply divided with Fatah faction dominant in the West Bank cities while Hamas controls the interior of Gaza and elections are long overdue. The Palestinians lacked a unified legitimate national leadership and democratic institutions endorsed by the majority of the Palestinian people. Since its establishment, the PA that is dominated by Fatah party and controlled by few aging elites has absorbed the institutions of the Palestine Liberation Organization (PLO) including the Palestinian National Council (PNC). The PNC was designated as the legislative body of the PLO that serves as the parliament for all Palestinians inside and outside the Palestinian territory. It is supposed to represent and unite all segments of the Palestinian society in the national struggle for liberation.

The PLO that is recognized internationally as the representative of the Palestinians became subservient to the PA which is under occupation and Israel can impose a destructive blockade on its territory, comparable to the siege on Gaza. By weakening the PLO, the Palestinians lost the effectiveness of the only institution that is supposed to negotiate on their behalf and link them together across borders and ideologies. The PNC ceased being a parliament and became a political rubber stamp that validates all decisions by Arafat and Abbas after him. They were leaders of Fatah, the PLO, the Palestinian Authority and the security forces. Arafat used the PNC to ratify his own political agenda that he mistakenly thought suitable for the Palestinians, but Abbas has been even worse. His agenda is entirely personal, divisive, elitist and corrupt, and it comes at a time when Palestinians' unity is critical in the face of possible collapse of the entire Palestinian national project.

There is no parliamentary check against Abbas' authority because the PA legislature has not met in a full session in twelve years since 2006. The Palestinian Authority has been transformed into an authoritarian bureaucratic entity holding the rights of the people hostage to the salaries of its employees. The PA security forces coordinate with the Israeli occupation military in preventing any effective resistance it has ceded Gaza to Hamas and completely ignored the Palestinians in the Diaspora, thus causing the split in the national movement it failed to end Israel's occupation, and the number of settlers in the West Bank more than quadruple since the signing of Oslo Agreement and the establishment of the PA. The relationship between the PA leadership and Hamas is so bad that when Israel assaulted Gaza in 2008 and caused death and destruction, the PA authorities did not even protest. The two rival factions have signed reconciliation agreements several times to end the decade long territorial and ideological split that has undermined their effort to free the occupied lands. The last agreement that focused on who should control the contested Gaza Strip was signed in Cairo in 2017 but the chances of success are questionable.

The people under the PA hung on shakily in fragments of the West Bank, too dependent on Israel and the West for survival to defy the status quo in any effective form but that of public opinion and individual actions. The people in Gaza suffered the most under stifling siege and more poverty. While the Arabs were busy with their 2010-13 uprisings and domestic affairs, attention had focused on the new conflicts in the Arab world and the momentum for addressing the Palestinian issue by the regional and international states faded.

The success of the Arab Spring to develop democratic institutions could have become a source of strength for the Palestinians who need the support of free Arab nations and demand similar reforms for themselves. The failure of the Arab Spring has negatively impacted the Palestinians whether under occupation in the West Bank and Jerusalem, besieged in Gaza or in the refugee camps in Syria and Lebanon. There is only pessimism and even the usual pro-Palestinian rhetoric by Arab people is missing when connecting the Arab Spring with the Palestinian question. The Palestinians' division has been deepened, tension between Egypt and Gaza has grown restrictions on people of Gaza entry to Egypt, their only access to the world Palestinian refugees in Syria have been killed thousands were forced to leave the camps that are completely destroyed and some have been forced to seek safety in Europe. Only more pain, suffering and Diaspora. The Arab Spring brought more malaise, more tightened blockade, severe poverty and more hatred toward them.

On December 6, 2017, the US President Donald Trump decided to recognize the city of Jerusalem as the capital of Israel and the US would relocate its embassy from Tel Aviv to Jerusalem. He fulfilled a promise he had repeatedly made during his campaigning. The US never was an honest broker in dealing with the Palestinian issue and the majority of the Palestinian people know that their leadership was making big mistake in trusting Washington. US Congress passed the 'Jerusalem Embassy Act' in 1995 that gave the White House till 1999 to carry out the dictate or face reduction in State Department budget for overseas embassies. All US presidents since then had signed six-month waivers. The US Congress and President Donald Trump lay to rest the myth that the US was serious about achieving a lasting peace between Israel and the Palestinians.

This move will serve to further delegitimize the aging and quite politically weak Palestinian Authority leadership for trusting the US to decide their people's fate. For six decades, the international community, including the US before the latest move, had not recognized Israel's jurisdiction over Jerusalem, and the Palestinians see East Jerusalem as the capital of their future state. When President Trump recognized Jerusalem as the capital of Israel, he made an already impossible mission more so. Under the 1947 UN Partition Plan, Jerusalem was designated as an internationally administered city because of its importance to the religions of Judaism, Christianity, and Islam.

In the wake of the US decision, the Israeli ruling Likud Party's central committee was encouraged to unanimously endorse a resolution calling for annexation of West Bank settlements. The central committee is an advisory body but the vote confirms that the Israelis do not care for the international norms and resolutions as long as the US supports them. Majority of the international community considers Israel's West Bank settlements, built on the West Bank and Jerusalem that were captured in the 1967 Mideast war, illegal.

Israel passed a new Jewish Nation State Law in July 2018 that officially defines Israel as the national homeland of the Jewish people. It asserts that "the realization of the right to national self-determination in Israel is unique to the Jewish people." It establishes Hebrew as the only official language of Israel. And the law considers the Jewish settlements as a national value and mandates that the state "will labor to encourage and promote its establishment and development." The law is a statement that establishes the constitutionality of the three historic Zionist principles: free return of the Jews to Palestine, free settlement everywhere, and the revival of Hebrew as the language of the state. It defines Israel as the country for Jews only, not for all its citizens. Arab parties said in a statement that Israel had "passed a law of Jewish supremacy and told us that we always will be second class citizens."

President Trump threatened to withhold future aid payments over what he called the Palestinian's unwillingness to talk peace with Israel. The Oslo accords have many faults, chief of which was the finance of the PA that Trump revealed by his threat. The PA was created with no attention to economic security. It is completely financed by the allies and supporters of Israel, rather than being economically self-sufficient. The PA allowed Israel to capture thousands of the daily Palestinian labor force who get permits to cross the check-points and work in the construction and agriculture. Vast majority of the Palestinians under the PA are non-productive bureaucracy including un-necessary big security forces living on the foreign handouts. Oslo created a consuming society susceptible to black-mail.

The Palestinians believe that their leaders have been dealing with the devious and duplicitous Israeli leaders since the Madrid Conference of 1991 and the signing of Oslo Accord agreements of 1993. They negotiated with Yetzhak Shamir 1988–92, Yetzhak Rabin 1992–95, Shimon Peres 1995–6, Benjamin Netanyahu 1996–9, Ehud Barak 1999–2001, Ariel Sharon 2003–6, Ehud Olmert 2006–9, and Benjamin Netanyahu 2009– incumbent.

The Israeli leaders had been pretending they were negotiating over who gets what of the occupied land while continuing to gobble it up by building ever-expanding Jewish-only settlements which effectively deny the land to the Palestinians. These settlements are illegal under international law as they directly infringe the Fourth Geneva Convention of 1949. Yet, as of this writing, plans for building still more illegal settlements have been announced. Yetzhak Shamir bragged that Israel would be willing to negotiate for the sake of negotiations for twenty years. Prime Minister Benjamin Netanyahu paid lip service to the idea of accepting a demilitarized state for the Palestinians in a 2009 speech, but when he was running for election in 2015, he solemnly pledged that there would be no such a state on his watch. And with no regional real backers, the Palestinians had to contend with their leadership increasingly shaky legitimacy and empty rhetoric.

President Trump administration is working on a "two state peace proposal draft for a comprehensive solution to the Palestinian–Israeli conflict." According to US Ambassador to the UN, the draft "won't be loved by either side, and it won't be hated by either side." It had been described by the Trump administration's rhetoric as "the deal of the century," although there is no evidence to suggest that such a plan, if one existed, would lead to a successful breakthrough. Trump's decision to recognize Jerusalem as Israel's eternal capital should make the Palestinians, who are not engaged in the process, wary of the American plans that would favor Israel. What is certain in Trump's plan is requiring the Palestinians to drop the refugees' right of return to homes in Palestine from which they had been exiled over the years.

The latest Palestinians' protest has been the 2018 "Gaza Return March" by the refugees in Gaza where thousands demonstrated inside the Strip along the buffer zone near the separation fence. The demonstrations were peaceful and the marchers kept well back from Israel's barrier fence, according to eye witness reporters. Israel's military snipers positioned on the barrier shot and killed and wounded scores of the protesters. By October, more than 260 Palestinians protesting for their right to return have been killed by Israeli snipers near the fence with Israel.

The Israeli violent response to the peaceful protest suggests that Israel is threatened by the slogans of the demonstrators' "Return march" to their pre-1948 homes. This is even more threatening since many of the refugees in Gaza live within a few miles of their former villages. According to Professor Norman Finkelstein, the expulsion of the Palestinians was the result of a long-standing Zionist desire to create a Jewish majority irrespective of the rights of the indigenous Arabs, and that when war came their organized planning to remove them was well developed.

On the subject of the "Two-State Solution' the gaps between the Palestinians and the Israelis on all the core issues are too wide to be bridged. They include borders, settlements, refugees, security and Jerusalem. Since 1967, Israeli conquering regime, Labor, Likud, religious and seculars have created a situation where it is impossible to have a two-state solution that produces a sovereign Palestinian state. The only "two state solution" under these conditions will be a Palestinian entity, no different from the existing PA under the same leadership they have now, perhaps with its capital in a small town outside the Old City of Jerusalem.

The Palestinians in the occupied West Bank, Gaza and Jerusalem should not respond with violence. They should stay where they are. Drop the demand for the "Two State Solution," and call peacefully for the bi-national "One-State Solution" that provides equal civil and political rights with the Jews, even knowing it is not a solution at all because it will never happen. The Israelis who build Jews-only settlements and Jews-only roads and demand recognizing the country as "a Jewish State" would never allow a one-state divided 50-50 between Jews and Palestinians with equal rights. The demographic trends would soon lead to a Palestinian majority even without the refugees' right of return. The two peoples have nothing in common. They have been fighting each other for more than a century they have opposing political ideologies and religious beliefs and they have different languages and different life-styles.

Israel's strategy of creeping annexation and its ideology to fulfill "the prophecy" of establishing greater-Israel over historical-Palestine have succeeded in killing the Two-State option and the growing talk of a single state. The Israelis vision of such a solution would be a dystopian-state where the Palestinians will be second class citizens in a Jewish state. The Palestinians' strength then lies in the power of their moral claim to challenge any instituted hierarchy between Jewish and Palestinian citizens that preserves Jewish supremacy within the "One State." The Palestinians will demand equal civil and political rights with the Jews. Israel, then, will have difficulty dismissing the parallels with South Africa's apartheid even if they try, let alone the Rome Statute's definition of apartheid as a crime in which a minority rules over the majority.

18. Israel and the West

After Britain and France won World War I, they divided the Arab countries to the east of the Mediterranean. Britain issued the "Balfour Declaration" that designated Palestine as a homeland for worldwide Jews. Since Israel was created in 1948, it has become the West's main political and military constituent in the Middle East.

In its first foreign policy decisions after its establishment, Israel placed itself on the side of France in Algeria's war of independence, at a time when France was increasingly seen as an outdated neocolonial power. In 1956, after repeatedly asking the British to remove their military from the area, President Nasser of Egypt nationalized the Suez Canal, which was owned by a British–French partnership. Israel joined the colonialist Britain and France in declaring war on Egypt. This provoked world-wide condemnation and forced even the US to call for restraint to avoid confrontation with the Soviet Union. But France provided Israel with the first military nuclear reactor in the ME, with enriched uranium and the means to produce plutonium and build hundreds of atomic bombs, to ensure its military superiority in the region.

The strategic and foreign policy position of the US were quite clear since the administration of Woodrow Wilson supported the British "Balfour Declaration." Wilson endorsed the idea of a "Jewish commonwealth in Palestine" widely publicized by a group of American Zionists. President Truman was the first leader to recognize the State of Israel, ten minutes after the Provisional Government of Israel proclaimed a new State of Israel on May 14, 1948.

The Soviet Union, too, gave Israel immediate recognition in the United Nations, and Moscow authorized Czechoslovakia to sell weapons to the new State of Israel which enabled it to survive. Unlike the Soviets, who were looking for strategic relationships, some Americans, influenced by their religious belief and their own history, saw the birth of Israel as a new Exodus and a return to the Promised Land. Explaining his decision to recognize the State of Israel, President Truman said: "I believe it has a glorious future before it, not just another sovereign nation, but as an embodiment of the great ideals of our civilization." The spread of the Soviets' influence, the rise of Arab nationalism and the rejection of Baghdad Pact by the Arab states encouraged the US to look even more favorably on Israel as a reliable ally in a largely hostile region.

Of course, others did see the strategic angle. According to the American historian Noam Chomsky, a 1958 US National Security Council memorandum noted that a "logical corollary" of opposition to radical Arab nationalism "would be to support Israel as the only strong pro-West power left in the Near East." President Reagan was quoted saying in 1981 that "with a combat experienced military, Israel is a force in the Middle East that actually is a benefit to us. If there were not Israel with that force, we'd have to supply that with our own."

Relations between the US and Israel became reversed after the 1967 War. Instead of Israel serving the US interests, the US has been serving the Israeli government, even if they sometimes harm the US's own interests. With the failure of Nasser-led Arab nationalism and the emergence of Israel as the super-power in the ME, the perceived Soviet Union threat to the West's interests diminished. Egypt under Sadat switched alliance from the Soviets to the US and signed a peace agreement with Israel in 1978. US policies on the Palestinian issue have been indistinguishable from the Israeli settlers' perspective. US administrations have integrated the extreme Israeli positions into its policy for the region.

President Richard Nixon was the "anti-Semitic who saved Israel," according to Jerry Klinger, the president of the Jewish American Society for Historic Preservation. The Nixon Watergate Tapes suggested that President Nixon hated the Jewish influence in the media and Hollywood, and private talk such as that captured on the tapes \earned him the reputation of being anti-Semitic. But Nixon actually was the opposite of an operational anti-Semite in his public appointments and his presidential decisions. He made Israel the largest single recipient of US foreign aid when he initiated the policy of virtually limitless US weapons sales to Israel. He appointed a number of American Jews to the highest positions in his administration including Henry Kissinger, Arthur Burns, Herbert Stein, William Safire, Larry Silberman, Amold Weber, and Richard Nathan. Nixon ordered airlifting war supplies including Phantom aircrafts and hundreds of tanks and tons of ammunition to replace Israel's military hardware lost in the first three days of the 1973 Arab-Israeli war (Yom Kippur war) directly at the front line. US Secretary of State Henry Kissinger, under Presidents Richard Nixon and Gerald Ford, concluded the separate Egyptian–Israeli peace treaty that made it easier for Israel to deal with the Palestinians on its own terms. It left the powerless Palestinians to fend for themselves against Israel and its allies in the West.

President Barack Obama allowed Israeli extremists to dictate the US foreign policy in the Middle East. Despite Obama's personal antipathy towards the Israeli Prime Minister Benjamin Netanyahu, his record over his eight years in office makes him one of the most pro-Israeli American presidents since Harry S Truman. Obama gave Israel considerably more money and arms than any of his predecessors. He fully lived up to America's formal commitment to preserve Israel's "qualitative military edge" by supplying Israel with ever more sophisticated weapons systems. His parting gift to Israel was a staggering military aid package of $38 billion over the next 10 years. This represents an increase from the current $3.1 to $3.8bn per annum. It is also the largest military aid package from one country to another in the annals of human history. This generous aid was made even though Netanyahu never missed an opportunity to attack Obama's policies in public. Netanyahu intervened in the 2012 presidential elections by backing the Republican candidate and he spoke against Obama while having the privilege of addressing a special session of both Houses of Congress. And Obama's successor, President Donald Trump, gave Israel the prize Israel has been seeking since 1967. He was the first to recognize the disputed Jerusalem as the capital of Israel.

Israel has been viewed by US liberals as enlightened colonialist a segment of the American people support Israel based on the biblical ties that, they are taught, connect Christians with Jews and others feel sympathy with Jews who were victims of the Holocaust crimes. And there is the US Jewish community and the Jewish Lobby. To be fair, there is a sizable American-Jewish minority that does not support Israel's policy toward the Palestinians.

The Americans confer on the establishment of Israel in Palestine a special status but when the mythology is over-looked, the Palestinian–Israeli conflict is not more unusual than any other violent conflict over the possession of land. It is just another case of settler colonization, similar to what happened in Algeria, South Africa, New Zealand, Australia, and North America. The conflict began because one powerful and internationally-connected group of people forcibly settled the land of a different, vulnerable people who did not have friends in high places.

While Palestinian leaders and the Arab ruling class share much of the blame for the Palestinians' tragedy, Israel has violated the rule of law, justice and equality towards the indigenous Palestinians. Israel's "Law of Return" allows any Jew in the world to acquire automatic Israeli citizenship and residency, but the "Citizenship and Entry into Israel Law" denies any Palestinian in Israel and the West Bank the right to unite even with his/her refugee spouse and live in Israel or in the PA territory. The Palestinians are in a regrettable position of belonging to the un-chosen tribe according to "the Godly narrative."

The US government supports Prime Minister Netanyahu, who presides over the most right-wing, pro-settler, and overly racist coalition government in Israel's history. Several ministers, led by the ultra-nationalist "Jewish Home Party," advocate outright annexation of the Palestinian West Bank area based on "Biblical scripture." The Cabinet majority is pushing for a new law that would "legalize" the illegal Jewish settlements on the West Bank including those built on private Palestinian land. If this law is passed by the Knesset, it will translate the ongoing practice of the ethnic cleansing of Palestine into official state policy. According to international lawyers, the settlements violate the fourth Geneva Convention, which prohibits the transfer of population into occupied territories.

The international Zionist movement was started by an atheist Austrian-Jewish journalist, Theodor Herzl, in 1897, as a secular Jewish nationalist project. He wrote essays and organized meetings that spurred Jewish emigration from Europe to Palestine, where less than 20,000 Jews had been living among close to 900,000 Arabs. Jewish religious movements played a minor role in Zionism during the pre-state period some religious groups even rejected Zionism altogether. But Israel has officially reconciled colonial Zionism and Jewish religion by naming the country a Biblical name and creating powerful religious government institutions headed by religious parties: the Ministry of Religious Affairs, the Chief Rabbinate, Chief Rabbinical Council and local religious councils. The Israeli government established the "Native Civilian Program" course for non-Jewish IDF soldiers and National Service Volunteers to convert. Zionism became more comfortable mixing religion and politics. The Zionist-right currently enjoys commanding positions in the government and popular opinion. It turned into a religious movement to re-establish the tribal Jewish culture which, according to them, was practiced there millennia ago.

Jews had lived and thrived in the Arab countries for thousands of years. When the Sephardic Jews were kicked out of Spain in 1492, the Arabs in Morocco opened their doors to them.

Once Israel occupied the West Bank, the government renamed the West Bank "Judea and Samaria" after tribes that allegedly lived in the region a thousand years before Christ. Religious parties with extreme anti-indigenous-Palestinians views have commanded significant number of seats in the Knesset and they have formed coalitions such as the "United Religious Front" and the "Torah Religious Front." They claim the land was received by the Jewish tribes from "God" and they are commanded to take it by dint of the "Covenant of the Treaty that God made with Abraham" two thousand years ago.

To set the record straight, this land was given to the European Jews by the British colonialists in the 1917 "Balfour Declaration" when the Jews in Palestine did not exceed six percent of the total population. The British Empire decided to solve Europe's anti-Semitism problem at the expense of the passive Arab Palestinians. Between 1917 and 1948, hundreds of thousands of Jews resettled from Europe to what was then British mandate Palestine and the 1948 war uprooted 750,000 indigenous Palestinians.

Zionists such as Prime Minister Golda Meir and Professor Efraim Karsh argued that there was no such thing as "Palestinian identity," a rhetoric frequently adopted by the Zionists who claim, in real colonialist fashion, that they did the world a favor by "civilizing and cultivating the land." This is land that was taken from the Arab Palestinians methodically and systematically. The Arab Palestinians failed to establish their own state institutions after the costly failure of their 1936 rebellion against the British Mandate and Jewish immigration.

Under the British Mandate, hundreds of thousands of European Jews resettled in Palestine and in 1948, their numbers exceeded 650,000. The Yishuv (as the Jewish community was known before Israel was declared on May 14, 1948), established their own state institutions including the military which was a combination of Jewish militias of the Haganah, right-wing Irgun and Tzvei Le'umi. Their highly motivated men and women fought and defeated the military of neighboring Arab states which had crossed the borders to block the Partition Resolution and prevent the establishment of the Jewish State.

When the state of Israel came into existence in 1948, some Palestinians were fortunate enough to remain in Palestine many of them became refugees in their own land. Roughly half of the Palestinian population at the time was cast out of the land of their fathers and grandfathers, left to roam the earth and settle in refugee camps in different countries and across different continents.

Arabs see Zionism as an ideology of racism, explicitly passing laws to welcome any Jew from anywhere in the world and become Israeli citizen, a right denied to the indigenous Palestinian refugees who were uprooted from their homes while their land was appropriated by the state.

The Arab Spring and Israel:

Due to its "imperial paranoia," Israel must have seen the 2011 Arab Spring and the volatility of the region as a potential threat. There is the potential to link the struggle for Palestinian liberation and the struggle against those Arab regimes that betrayed it. The Israelis fear both the rise of political Islam and the possibility of democratization in Arab countries. The crumbling of the existing regimes must be viewed by the Israelis as a threat to regional stability, despite their sometimes hostile rhetoric. This fear is not solely because of the specter that they might find themselves living among democratic nations. It was also because of the implications of a democracy that proceeded from the bottom up.

Israel fears that once those Arab regimes that are headed by autocrats and despots were replaced by extremist Islamic governments, the peace treaties with Egypt and Jordan would be undermined or even revoked. President Muhammad Morsi of Egypt, a Muslim Brotherhood Islamist, didn't tear up the peace treaty with Israel. He brokered a deal between Israel and Hamas instead, but Israel will continue to be suspicious of the Islamists.

If the Israeli leaders are confident of their democracy, they should welcome the creation of free democratic neighbors in the Middle East because "democracies do not go to war with each other." Israeli leaders like David Ben-Gurion suggested that he preferred dealing with a democratic Arab world headed by "decent people at the helm." But democratic Arabs are viewed by most Israelis today more as threat to their colonial project. Arab public opinion in Egypt and Jordan, the only two countries that signed peace agreements with Israel, has been against normalization as long as the Palestinian issue is not resolved according to international laws. Their anti-Israeli attitude would be translated into official foreign policy if they exercised their right to vote in fair elections under democratic regimes.

Given the deep resentment of Israeli policies among Arab nationalists and Islamist activists, even limited freedom and liberalization will increase the opposition to Israel's policies unless its government does indeed return the land for peace and acknowledges the Palestinians' right of national self-determination. More Arab democratic regimes, therefore, are likely to be less accommodating regarding the status quo in the Palestinian–Israeli conflict than authoritarian regimes. The autocratic regime of Saudi Arabia under Crown Prince Bin Salman has been good news for Israel. Its firm anti-Iranian position, anti-Muslim Brotherhood, anti-Hezbollah, and his positive response to the vaunted US "deal of the century" to end the Israeli-Palestinian conflict, makes him an important partner with Israel. The Crown Prince has been more aggressive than anyone else in trying to pressure the Palestinians to accept Kushner's ME peace plan.

The suspicion of MBS involvement in Khashoggi's assassination, his war on Yemen, and his clamp on dissenters, has certainly weakened him as a statesman. He has lost his international clout and reduced his role as a major player in the politics of the ME. That is bad news for Israel because it threatens to undo a constructed regional strategy built around the Saudi crown prince to legitimize Israel before embarking on open cooperation with it. Some US supporters of Israel say: "We should move past this [the Khashoggi saga], if only for the sake of Israel."

Tzvia Greenfield, a prominent Israeli member of human rights organization B'tselem and a former member of the Knesset, called for Israel to "treat the suspect [Bin Salman] with kid gloves....For 50 years we [the Israelis] have prayed for a key Arab leader who agrees to sign a significant pact with Israel. Such a leader has finally arrived and calls to depose him are destructive."

In 2004 survey, residents of Israel were asked using questions designed to draw specific answers to ten basic questions about the Palestinian–Israeli conflict. The most significant finding was about 76% endorsed the two-state concept solution. In another similar survey conducted in 2017 on the principle of the two-state solution among Israeli Jews, only 46% said they back a two-state solution. These findings suggest that by the pass of time, the Israelis' support to the establishment of an independent Palestinian state has dropped. So, what do the Israelis want?

The Israelis today purportedly would like their country to have three achievements, Jewish-democracy-with-the Jordan River as its eastern border, but Israel can be only any two of them. If they choose the expansion to the River and democracy, then they have to absorb millions of Palestinians in Israel which ceases to be Jewish. If they remain Jewish and expansive, Israel will continue to deny the Palestinians full civil rights, Israel then will no longer be democratic, but an apartheid state. The only practical choice is to have a genuine sovereign Palestinian state next to Israel.

The US that has shielded Israel from critical UN resolutions can play an important role in all of this by acting as an honest broker and helping Israel make the right choices. The US cannot be both a fair arbiter between the Israelis and the Palestinians and continues to side with the extreme ideologue Israelis and ignore the plight of the Palestinians. The US can support Israel but not necessarily its government policies. To be consistent in its application of its values, the US should urge Israel to resolve the Palestinian issue by not becoming a perpetual occupier and losing its claim to democracy.

19. The Legacy of the Arab Spring

The Arab Spring was an overdue historic moment, as the first step for many countries in the Middle East on the road to democracy. It was no different from what Western democracy went through before making the transition, which is a long process, a generational struggle, not a solitary event. The massive popular uprisings calling for political freedom, economic and social justice have struck at the heart of the Arab republic-regimes. It has unseated long-standing leaders, and significantly shaken the royalist dynasties. The Arab Spring represented a rejection of the secular, socialist, pan-Arabism, nationalist, military regimes that had come to power in the last century and had developed into corrupt, crony governments ruling by pervasive security apparatus. Arab Spring demonstrators held their elites responsible for their economic and political problems and rejected the claim that their failures were caused by colonialism or the Zionists.

Much is unresolved, much is worrisome, and there are lessons to be learnt by the activists and the regimes. Authoritarianism often inhibits learning because it gives regimes power to repress dissent, not available to democracies, but Egypt's MB certainly learnt their lesson. They won the election with a narrow margin, but their leadership treated the victory as a popular mandate and as a result, they squandered an opportunity to promote democratic transition. The MB leaders were driven by ideological zeal rather than realistic assessment of Egypt's politics. The Islamist ideology was tested and found wanting. They alienated their Christian constituents and did not realize that they had to placate the powerful old state institutions represented by the military, police, judiciary and the media and win over crucial elites and other political actors to stay in power. The Islamist parties have learnt that just adherence to the faith precepts is not what the public wants. This is even more decisive in Egypt, a country with large non-Islamic communities.

After living under corrupt authoritarian regimes for decades, demands for full citizenship and the recognition of individual political rights were the unifying theme across the Arab World. The increasingly wretched economic situation in most of the Arab countries fueled these frustrations. The uprisings have shown the power and the limitation of mass protests in the absence of strong civil societies.

Some analysts argue that the Arab Spring was a reactionary movement led primarily by conservative Islamists against secular regimes. They base such conclusion on the fact that Islamic parties won the free elections in Egypt, Morocco and Tunisia in the aftermath of the Arab Spring uprisings. But main stream Islamists did not play role in the uprising although their activists did eventually join the protests and embraced the Arab Spring. The Islamists won the elections because they had been the only opposition groups that had long established organized parties. Arab rulers had ensured no opposition party or civil society institution was strong enough to challenge them.

The demonstrators failed in challenging the myth that "democracy couldn't hold in the ME." To their disappointment, they discovered that democracies are more difficult to create than they thought. The masses found out that immediate transition from authoritarian regimes to democracy proved to be elusive. There were no organized parties or civil society institutions strong enough to challenge the weapons of authoritarianism that included ideology, repression, payoffs and crony capitalists' solidarity. The Gulf States including Saudi Arabia, with the exception of Kuwait, criminalize the formation of political parties. But Arab Spring of 2011 was only the first step in the long road to democracy.

Years after the Arab Spring, little remains of the hope that the Arab people from the Arabian Gulf to the Atlantic saw in their uprising. Instead, the Arab Spring has given way to political and sectarian violence and to economic stagnation in many countries. Millions of refugees, ruined cities and one-third of the Arab League states looking completely different from the way they did a decade ago. The three civil wars in Libya, Syria and Yemen, the military coup in Egypt and the sectarian regime in Iraq have spawned horrendous human cost. They destabilized the region, created radical jihadists and political violence throughout the region, and Syria became a source of refugees swamping the ME and Europe. The bloody civil wars have resulted in the deaths of hundreds of thousands and more than seven million refugees. Yemen, even more than Syria became a bitter proxy battle-ground between Saudi Arabia and Iran.

The Arab Spring in Iraq led to a rebellion in the Sunni triangle that contributed to the emergence of the terrorist state of ISIS over 40% of Iraq and parts of Syria and the establishment of franchises in many countries. It took two years of international air-campaign and the complete destruction of many towns including the City of Mosel to defeat. The Arab Spring failure and the political chaos that created the jihadist groups led to widespread economic stagnation throughout the ME non-oil states. The attack on tourists has impacted the tourism industry in Egypt, Jordan, Lebanon and Tunisia, resulting in high rates of unemployment.

King Salman decision to change the brother-to-brother succession system was inspired by the Arab Spring. He wants to have a young face on the Saudi throne, not necessarily to make the transition to democracy, but it was a defensive move for al-Saud family rule survival. Salman realized that his country's traditional society seemed frozen in time under aging leadership and strict conservative Wahhabi control while the rest of the world including young Saudi generation were going through social modernization. Crown Prince Muhammad Bin Salman implemented some social reforms to appease the Saudi youth. Allowing women to drive and to vote in municipal elections were big steps toward social and political reform in Saudi Arabia standards, even though women all over the world have been driving since the car was invented and the Saudi Arabian municipal councils have little or no real power in the Kingdom's overall policy making.

The power of a country in the Arab ME is measured by the size of its bank-account, not by the size of its population. Qatar with its 2.7 million people is more influential locally and internationally than Egypt with its ninety-nine million populations. The authoritarian Saudi regime has been the leading power behind the counter-Arab-Spring-revolutions. It is the main supporter of the violent repressive Egyptian regime of President el-Sisi who claims that the Arab Spring protesters of Egypt were traitors paid by foreign powers to sabotage the country. Saudi Arabia and the Gulf States supported Jihadist groups in Syria and Iraq they destroyed Yemen, and weakened the internationally recognized government in Libya by financing its warlord Khalifa Haftar who has been engaged in "the second Libyan civil war."

Failure of the Arab Spring was an invitation for foreign intervention to further their economic and strategic interests. French-led UN Security Council Resolution to create no-fly zone over Libya in 2011 was the tool to topple Gaddafi's regime, not to protect civilian population. French-led NATO military intervention was driven by opposition to Gaddafi's policies in Africa, his anti-West rhetoric, and France desire to have greater share of

Libya's oil production. The active involvement of Russia in Syria's civil war in support of the Syrian regime was an opportunity to establish a client-state and to have a strategic naval base in the Mediterranean, something Russia has always sought to have. The conflicts boosted Russia's arms sale in the region significantly and that helped it to make up for its economic crisis which was caused by the drop of oil prices.

The US defense industry was the biggest beneficiary of the Arab Spring failure. In his maiden trip abroad after winning the election, President Trump was acting as an arms-salesman in Saudi Arabia. He sealed hundreds of billions of dollars for military hardware deals with the Saudis, solidified the decades-long alliance with the regime and established personal friendly relationship with influential members of the royal family.

The Gulf States including Saudi Arabia have been able to suppress the protesters and for the moment contain demands for political change in most of their cities by using the carrot and stick approach. They have withstood the tidal wave of the popular uprising because they have the resources that enabled them to buy off, or rather weaken the internal dissent, and acquire outside support. At the same time Bahrain and Saudi Arabia have been able to repress their Shi'a-Muslim protesters and contain demands for political change.

Rents may provide for provisional, but not sustainable stability for the authoritarian regimes. They can buy loyalty with their renter money they can enforce hereditary rights, but they cannot buy legitimacy. The Saudis claim they earned "divine legitimacy" by being the Custodians of the Islamic two holy places and enforcing the Wahhabi-Islamic doctrine. Ability of the ruling families in the oil-rich countries to monopolize the political decision-making by relying on coercion and expediency is an acknowledgement of their vulnerability. Their royal families cannot tolerate any criticism because they must believe their regimes are more mortal than many observers are ready to admit.

After the popular uprisings of the Arab Spring, a quasi-alliance has come about between the Gulf Arab monarchies and Israel due to mutual concern about the Iranian expansion in many Arab countries. Once Iran became a regional power, the Arab regimes rushed towards Israel for self-preservation and as a way of pandering to the US. Israel and Saudi Arabia are viewed as a linchpin in their efforts to check the region's ambitions of Iran.

The counter-revolutionary action that defeated the Arab Spring forces is just a phase of a long-term process that ripens the revolution. Old social, economic and political structures that underpinned the 2011 Arab Spring are still in place or even worsened, and the crisis of the ME government's legitimacy has not been resolved. The Arab Spring that overthrew three dictators taught us that ME stable regimes which seem unshakable and invincible may be weaker than anyone thinks. The brutal execution of the Saudi journalist Khashoggi just for advocating reforms in his country suggests that authoritarian Arab regimes are terrified of a second Arab Spring and that the corrupt autocratic princes of Saudi Arabia have the capacity and the will to be ever more ruthless. The repression they use against their people to snuff out dissent makes future unrest more likely.

INDEX

Printed in the United States
by Baker & Taylor Publisher Services

Printed in the United States
By Bookmasters